PENGUIN BOOKS

SACHIN TENDULKAR

ESPNcricinfo has been the No. 1 cricket website in the world since it first went online in 1993. With a monthly average of over 20 million readers worldwide, it is also among the largest single-sport websites in the world.

The site pioneered live ball-by-ball updates and it continues to be the leader in the field, integrating into its live coverage various elements from its searchable data feed to give fans a truly rich live-match experience. This is backed up by text- and video-based match analysis content, providing a comprehensive coverage menu.

The site runs its own global news operation, and its news and match coverage are supplemented by text and video content that includes opinion pieces, features, interviews and blogs.

ESPNcricinfo maintains the game's widest and most authoritative database, with details of about 65,000 international and domestic players, officials and administrators, over 45,000 matches and more than 2500 grounds.

The strength of its journalism has given the site the status of cricket's pre-eminent global voice—one that is followed by fans, players and administrators alike.

ESPNcricinfo's previous book titles are *Sealed with a Six: The Story of the 2011 World Cup*; *Timeless Steel*, an anthology on Rahul Dravid; and *Talking Cricket*, a collection of interviews with the legends of the game.

SACHIN TENDULKAR

The Man Cricket Loved Back

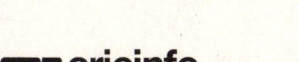

PENGUIN BOOKS

An imprint of Penguin Random House

PENGUIN BOOKS

USA | Canada | UK | Ireland | Australia
New Zealand | India | South Africa | China | Singapore

Penguin Books is part of the Penguin Random House group of companies
whose addresses can be found at global.penguinrandomhouse.com

Published by Penguin Random House India Pvt. Ltd
4th Floor, Capital Tower 1, MG Road,
Gurugram 122 002, Haryana, India

First published in Viking by Penguin Books India 2014
Published in Penguin Books 2015

The views and opinions expressed in this book are the authors' own and the
facts are as reported by them which have been verified to the extent possible,
and the publishers are not in any way liable for the same.

ISBN 9780143424017

Typeset in Minion Pro by R. Ajith Kumar, New Delhi
Printed at Replika Press Pvt. Ltd, India

www.penguin.co.in

This is a legitimate digitally printed version of the book and therefore might not
have certain extra finishing on the cover.

CONTENTS

THE IMPORTANCE OF HEROES

SAMBIT BAL

On a sweltering mid-April night in Chennai in 2010, when heat and humidity conspired to turn the human body into a dripping mess, I watched a desperately dehydrating Sachin Tendulkar hit a ball in the air to bring a moment of delicious ambivalence to the ground.

Before going further, background and context are necessary. I had travelled to Chennai that day to conduct my version of the Tebbit Test. For those unfamiliar with the term, it refers to the controversial proposition by Norman Tebbit, the British Conservative politician, that immigrants of South Asian and Caribbean origin needed to prove their loyalty to the UK by supporting the England cricket team. My loyalty test was far less pernicious. I wanted to explore whether the IPL's idea of city-based franchises had grown enough for Indian fans to support another team over Sachin Tendulkar.

I chose Chennai because, by all accounts, the local fans had got behind Chennai Super Kings (CSK) with great fervour. To make up for the lack of a local cricketer as their team's icon player, they chose

Mahendra Singh Dhoni as their adopted son of the soil, and unlike many other venues, where fans turned up to partake of the merriment and cheered every big hit irrespective of the uniform, spectators at the M Chidambaram stadium had been raucously partisan. It is said that Doug Bollinger, the Australian quick bowler who had a couple of good seasons with CSK, was startled to find his name being chanted. It was a first for him.

But Chennai also enjoyed a special bond with Indian cricket's favourite son. Tendulkar averaged close to 90 in Tests here, his highest among Indian grounds, and many of his memorable Test hundreds, including a heroically tragic 136 against Pakistan in 1999 and a series-turning 155 against Australia, came here. His last hundred at this venue was a last-innings effort, which he brought off with a boundary that also sealed an improbable chase against England. Like the rest of India, Chennai has loved Tendulkar as its own, but on this day that bond was going to be tested against the tide of provincial pride.

Or perhaps not. The Super Kings players got their due. Dhoni received a grand ovation to the crease. They cheered when Mike Hussey's image flashed on the giant screen, and they got behind Bollinger when he ran in to bowl. But through the day, the loudest cheers were reserved for Tendulkar. They cheered him when he strolled out before the toss, they cheered even louder when he was being interviewed on the square, they cheered when he stopped a ball, and they cheered his boundaries with nearly the same enthusiasm as they did those by their own.

But Mumbai Indians had now fallen behind the game. Tendulkar had got the chase off to the perfect start, hitting crisp, risk-free boundaries in the first six overs, but he had to retire ill in the ninth over, which sparked a sensational collapse that forced him to return five overs later with his team six wickets down and the asking rate nearly 13 runs an over, and the rhythm of his innings punctured.

And so we rewind to the opening paragraph. The crowd rose

to its feet, as it does for almost every stroke in the IPL, and as the ball swirled in the air it became possible in those few moments to palpably sense the dilemma the crowd had been struggling with all evening. The Chennai fan wanted the ball to land in the hands of a fielder, but the Tendulkar fan in him willed the ball to soar beyond the ropes. There was a cheer when Murali Vijay pouched the catch at long-on, but it was tinged with lament, and grew louder, more intense and more joyful as Tendulkar made his way out. They were simply cheering him now.

I had my answer.

⬦

Heroes are central to the sporting experience. Simon Barnes wrote in *A Book of Heroes* that the provision of heroes was the basic point of sport, and that if it didn't provide heroes, sport wouldn't command our imagination. I think it is a far more universal truth. Heroes are a necessity of life. We need them to project our hopes and aspirations on, and the virtues and values we hold as ideal.

You could argue that Tendulkar was the hero India needed. The country was broke, corruption was rife, Amitabh Bachchan, the grand star of India's escapist films, was sulking, and Sunil Gavaskar had retired. Tendulkar was 16 when he made his Test debut, and he wiped off a bloody nose after being hit to hit the next ball for four. A country was captivated, and would remain so for 24 years.

To most Indians who signed up for Tendulkar, Gandhi was an idea, a symbol, a picture on currency notes. About Jawaharlal Nehru's socialism there were doubts. About the current crop of politicians there was despair and contempt. It was only film heroes and cricketers who captured the imagination. But South India didn't care about Hindi films, and in cricket too, Indians' loyalties were tested between the West and the North. Gavaskar's fans were forever antagonistic towards Bishan Singh Bedi, and later they were often forced to take sides between him and Kapil Dev.

But with Tendulkar the boundaries melted. From the moment he first wore the national colours, he belonged to all of India, and to every Indian. That a boy stood tall among the best men was heady, but there was a bigger story. Old-timers got misty-eyed about CK Nayudu, but Nayudu's legend was built on one spectacular 116-minute assault on a touring MCC side that yielded 153 runs and featured 11 sixes. Otherwise, the school of Indian batsmanship revolved around passive resistance, an art passed down the ages from Vijay Merchant to Gavaskar. They were heroic without doubt, but for years the Indian fan had longed for a batsman who could quell attacks with a punishing bat. Salim Durani built a reputation by hitting sixes, and Kapil had been India's most consistently aggressive cricketer – but he was an allrounder who earned his place with his bowling.

Tendulkar inherited some of the priceless virtues of the Bombay school – the balance, the compactness and the appetite for big runs – but the man he really wanted to bat like was Viv Richards, not Gavaskar. His first Test hundred, like many of Gavaskar's, was a match-saving effort, but the mould and the tempo were Tendulkar's own. Manoj Prabhakar, who batted with him for the best part of that innings, speaks of trying to rein in Tendulkar in the early parts and giving up quickly upon realising that the young man had his own special way. Eighteen months later, Tendulkar played the innings that established his greatness: a dazzling, counter-attacking 114 in Perth, on the paciest, bounciest pitch in the world. It was only the second time he was batting at No. 4, the position he would make his own for the rest of his career. India had never seen anything like that from one of its own, and from that point onwards the country could never have enough of Tendulkar.

It was the '90s that made Tendulkar. It was the decade of great bowlers. Pakistan had Wasim Akram and Waqar Younis, South

Africa's pace battery was led by Allan Donald, West Indies had Curtly Ambrose and Courtney Walsh for the best part, Glenn McGrath and Shane Warne arrived soon for Australia. And it was against these bowlers that Tendulkar averaged 58. With a qualification of a minimum of 2000 runs, only three other batsmen averaged over 50 in this period, and Tendulkar's closest rival, Brian Lara, averaged 7 fewer. For perspective, the corresponding figure of batsmen averaging over 50 in the following decade was 19.

It was an age when Indians sought validation and acceptance from the outside. How the West saw the country mattered a great deal. That was an era when Indian newspapers faithfully reproduced words of praise or criticism from English and Australian papers as if they didn't think their own voices carried enough heft. India accepted its heroes without qualification only after they were certified as worthy by the higher powers.

Many Indian cricketers had received global acclaim before him. Bedi's beautiful left-arm spin was hailed as the finest of his times, Gavaskar was easily the best opening batsman in the world for over ten years, and Kapil found a place alongside the great allrounders of his era. But Tendulkar was unique in one way.

He wasn't the best No. 4, or the best middle-order batsman, or the best young player. He was, in his pomp, quite simply the best batsman in the world. Shane Warne said so. Steve Waugh said so. As did Viv Richards. And Don Bradman said he saw himself in Tendulkar. This was a whole new experience for the Indian fan. Their team was still losing, but their boy had trumped the world. For that, the country remained forever grateful, and even when Tendulkar's form dipped and he was no longer the best batsman in the world, or even in the Indian team, late in his career, affection for him and faith in him never dimmed. His goodwill account was inexhaustible.

And as the opening up of the economy unleashed the entrepreneurial spirit of millions of Indians, Tendulkar became a singular icon of success and strength for a confident and increasingly assertive nation. His celebrity was nourished and amplified by the television boom, and he was greedily embraced by Indian marketers, who needed a shining light to spread the gospel of consumerism.

It also appealed to his countrymen that he didn't let stardom interfere with his innate decency. His lack of activism in cricket matters was sometimes held against him, but he could never be accused of lowering the dignity of the game. The late Peter Roebuck found it remarkable that a player of such uncommon gifts and high profile had so few inner demons to conquer, but to those who have known Tendulkar, it came as no surprise: despite all the riches and fame, he held on to his middle-class values. Among his contemporaries, Warne and Brian Lara had more charisma, and were considered to possess greater talismanic abilities, but who would you rather give your daughter to in marriage? Tendulkar was the perfect hero for Indian sensibilities.

That he "carried the aspirations of a nation" became a somewhat facetious and lazy expression. The truth is that in no other public figure have Indians made such a deep and abiding emotional investment.

No cricketer in the history of the game has sustained excellence in so many varied conditions and through so many changes in the game for such a long a time, and it is improbable that anyone will. But it can be ventured with a greater degree of certainty that no cricketer will be as deified and as adored as Sachin Tendulkar has been.

Which brings us to the final part of the Tendulkar story.

A day before Tendulkar's final day in cricket, I was asked by a television channel if there had been a grander farewell for a sportsperson. I offered the standard answer: few sports could beat the combined scale of size and emotion afforded by cricket's fan base, and no other sportsperson has been adored so obsessively for so long by so many people.

But being in attendance for his final day in cricket brought home the more profound part of the truth. Perhaps no sportsman, certainly no cricketer, has loved his sport so obsessively, so absolutely, and for so long as Sachin Tendulkar has done. There were thousands of moist eyes and heavy hearts around the ground, and millions more around the world, but no loss was greater than that of Tendulkar himself.

When great sportsmen leave the stage, more so ones as well loved as Tendulkar, they take part of us with them. But for him, he was leaving his very essence behind. Fans spoke of the emptiness that followed his departure, but can it be greater than the one in Tendulkar's heart? Can we even comprehend it?

Anjali, his wife, came closest. Cricket can do without Tendulkar, she said, but can Tendulkar do without cricket?

Tendulkar's final performance in the India colours will count among his finest: the 74 runs he scored in his final innings will be as special to his fans as many of his hundreds are, but it was his farewell speech that moved millions to tears. It wasn't profound or insightful, it didn't contain a vision for cricket, or even dazzling oratory. It was merely a thanksgiving.

But it was lifted by its stirring earnestness, the poignancy of the moment, and most of all by its intimacy. In thanking everyone from his father to his fans, Tendulkar revealed more of himself than he ever did in the past.

He spoke for nearly 20 minutes but he didn't need a written speech because the words came from within; and the words were moving because they carried emotions fans could relate to. For a naturally shy person, this was a virtuoso performance. But in the truest sense, this was no *performance*. "It is getting difficult," he said at the beginning, "but I will manage." And then he was in the zone. The speech contained his signature qualities: humility, grace, simplicity and composure.

Lara, Tendulkar's great rival, left with these words, delivered with a flourish: "Did I entertain you?" he asked the fans in Bridgetown after West Indies had bowed out of their home World Cup with a loss to England. The crowd roared back its approval.

Tendulkar's final words were a heartfelt thank you. "Sachin, Sachin will reverberate in my ears till I stop breathing," he said. The crowd wept.

As photographers crowded him after the speech, standing high in the Garware Pavilion I pictured in my mind the perfect finish. Tendulkar breaking free of the throng that surrounded him and taking a lap of the ground all by himself. Just him on his beloved turf, and nothing between him and his fans. A purer finale was hard to imagine.

But of course he was never going to be left alone. Photographers, reporters, administrators, policemen, hangers-on surrounded him as he began his final lap, and then he was obligatorily hoisted on their shoulders by his team-mates. Still, it was a quite a finish.

I have been fortunate to have experienced first-hand some big moments in cricket in the last 15 years. I watched the Wankhede throb all day and then explode when MS Dhoni's thundering six won India the 2011 World Cup. But that emotion was triumphalist and somewhat feral. Journalism trains you to soak up the atmosphere on such occasions, but it inures you from being affected by it.

This was different. The intimacy, the deeply personal nature of the occasion, melted your defence. Resistance would have been futile and artificial. You were glad to be there, and to surrender to the moment.

India is given to exaggeration, and the way everyone was cashing in on Tendulkar's final series had begun to grate, but there was no artifice here. Cricket became incidental on that day, and it didn't matter any more that the feebleness of the West Indians had reduced the contest to a mockery. It became what it was meant to be: it was now between Tendulkar and his fans.

It was pointed out that none of India's recently retired greats received the send-offs they deserved, but to begrudge Tendulkar his farewell on that count would be missing the plot. His story is unique. You could argue that it is an outcome of circumstances, but it is hard to imagine any cricketer having the kind of connection with his fans that he did. It wasn't the sort of craze fans find themselves possessed by for rock stars and film stars. It was love, true and deep, a sense he was theirs, and a gratefulness for the joy he brought them.

At the press conference the following day, Tendulkar spoke about not having yet reconciled to the idea of not playing cricket again. He didn't know, he said, why it hadn't sunk in. *"Kahin na kahin toh main khel loonga."* In cold words, it translates to "Somewhere, somehow, I will find a way to play." But the translation doesn't come close to capturing the longing and poignancy of that statement. Spoken with a wistful smile, the words offered a glimpse of the hole in his life.

After saying goodbye to the crowd, he went – and mercifully he was allowed to go alone – to bid farewell to the "22 yards that had been my life". And it was while he was talking to the wicket, he said casually at the press conference next day, that he began to feel really emotional.

Talking to the wicket? It was impossible in that bedlam that passed for a press conference – you could only get a word in if you shouted down 15 others – to venture a follow-up, but you got it.

Here was a man who spoke of cricket in his sleep, who regarded his bats as his fellow travellers, who saw every cricket ground as his temple, and he was now speaking of talking to the pitch. They conferred godhood on him to glow in his glory, but the truth is that he was the biggest worshipper the game could ever find, and in that lay the foundation of Tendulkar's greatness.

There is a photograph (*see second insert of pictures*) of Tendulkar

I have come to love. It is from a training session during the 2012 IPL. He still retains his cherubic look, but the face looks lived-in here; the hair is flowing longer than usual, the eyes are shut, fists clenched around an imaginary bat, and he is rehearsing a shot. His team-mates are a blur behind him, and he seems oblivious to them. He looks more a Sufi saint in a trance than a cricketer: it's a picture of utter submission to his craft.

How could cricket not love him back?

Sambit Bal is the editor-in-chief of ESPNcricinfo

THE VIRTUES OF BEING LITTLE

GIDEON HAIGH

The Little Master: the nickname gives equal weight to both qualities, mastery *and* littleness. But while the mastery makes sense, the littleness does not so much. Tendulkar stands 165cm tall, the mean height of the Indian male. By rights, then, he should be the Average Master. Or maybe the Average Master Blaster. There is something interesting at work in that abiding Tendulkar alias. What might it be?

Like all really sticky and popular nicknames, its origins and authors are unclear – it seems to have affixed as naturally as "The Greatest" to Ali or "The Stilt" to Wilt Chamberlain. The original "Master" was Sir Jack Hobbs, capable to leaping from the pages of *Wisden* to the denouement of *Slumdog Millionaire*. And the original Little Master was, of course, Sunil Gavaskar – google "Little Master", in fact, and it is still Gavaskar's smiling features that beam out at you from the right-hand side of the screen. It was Gavaskar who famously handed on his pads to his anointed successor, in the way that WG Grace is

11

said to have handed on a bat to Victor Trumper, like a kind of relay baton of batting, or Olympic torch of excellence; the epithet seems to have been transferred the same way.

Gavaskar notwithstanding, there's no doubt that on 99 out of a hundred occasions when the words "little" and "master" are coupled worldwide every day, they refer to Tendulkar, and that they trip readily off the tongue, subtly in tension. Because, as we all know, mastery is usually to be equated with dominance, an overshadowing or overpowering by figures of "stature" to whom we "look up". Tendulkar is "little" in an age that at least nods to an idea of "heightism" – that there is such a thing as discrimination against the, er, vertically challenged.

The concept has its basis in a famous experiment 30 years ago by two American psychologists, Leslie Martel and Henry Biller, who asked several hundred university students to rate the qualities of men of varying heights, on 17 different criteria. Knowing nothing else about them, the students ranked the short men, those between 157cm and 165cm, lowest – they were deemed less mature, secure, positive, confident, capable, successful and even masculine than taller peers. Cross-cultural studies by the anthropologist Thomas Gregor, moreover, have found the attitude pervasive, neither western nor eastern. "In no case," he says, "have I found a preference for shorter men."

There is even a Twitter account, Exposing Heightism, which captures and collates evidently heightist tweets – more profuse and vehement than might be imagined. On an average day, it turns up such examples as: "Why are short guys even a thing?", "Why does God make short men?", "Men under 5'7 are females", "Any man shorter than 5"9 should join the circus!!!!", "Short men are not men they're children. GROW UP you childish assholes", "Short men aint useless. They can be used as TV stands or can be useful in the toilet to hold tissues." No cricket lovers here, evidently.

Because for Tendulkar, "littleness" has always been a virtue, an addition to his specialness, an enhancement of his exemplary nature. Why? In sport, of course, the little have their day, and the race is not always to the swift or the battle to the strong. While there *are* games in which standing tall, bulking large or reaching wide are advantageous, just as many exist where such attributes either mean not much or are a mixed blessing: what the tall tennis player may gain in power on serve or net coverage, for example, they might lose in access to low volleys or handling returns at the body. And cricket, of course, prides itself on encompassing perhaps the widest variety of body types, shapes and sizes: it has featured batsmen from Gundappa Viswanath (163cm) to Tony Greig (200cm), fast bowlers from Harold Larwood (170cm) to Mohammad Irfan (216cm), slow bowlers from Rangana Herath (168cm) to Suliemann Benn (201cm).

Plus, there's Bradman. Cricket's most historically exalted figure stood 170cm, and rather relished the cutting of rivals down to size. When he met Babe Ruth in 1932, he is reported to have looked him appreciatively in the eye, and opined in solidarity that "us little fellows could hit them harder than the big ones". In his time, others referred to Bradman, in endearment and tribute, as "the little chap" and "the little fellow". In later life, Douglas Jardine is said to have mused that his team's Bodyline victory was far closer than it looked: "We almost didn't do it, you know. The little fellow was bloody good." For Tendulkar, then, there have always been big little shoes to fill, as it were.

But this goes a little deeper I think. As observed, Tendulkar's is merely the average male height in India. His "littleness" was first observed in contrast to the physically larger figures of foreign opponents. The first time I saw the teen Tendulkar, in England in 1990, he did indeed look tiny, relative to the likes of Devon Malcolm and Gus Fraser, hurling themselves down at him from their great heights, not to mention Graham Gooch, whose bat looked wider still and wider than the Empire itself. Into the bargain, Tendulkar appeared impossibly young and fresh-faced, as though in need of a chaperone as much as a batting partner. The impression lasted, of course, for as long as it took for Tendulkar to play a few deliveries, making obvious his precocious certainty. When he batted his team to safety at Old Trafford, he looked a mature batsman and old soul indeed. But I suspect that Tendulkar came to be "little" partly because India was seen, and rather saw itself, that way – weak, meek, faintly embattled, vaguely outmatched, generally vulnerable.

And his being "little" has remained as an artefact of Indian cricket before its great commercial expansion and geopolitical ascendancy – today's "Indian moment", so to speak, which has all the hallmarks of a long hegemony. "Little Master" somehow expressed India's culture of victory against the odds, against the grain, against the big boys, and has gone on expressing it long after India became the biggest of all boys itself. With him, then, might go not only among the mightiest of cricketers, but a way of looking at the world – the transition from a time in which India succeeded *in spite of* to an era in which it succeeds *because*.

Gideon Haigh *is the author of* The Summer Game, The Cricket War *and other books*

THE VIEW FROM THE OTHER END

RAHUL DRAVID

My batting partnership with Sachin Tendulkar didn't get off to an auspicious start at the international level. It was only the second time we were batting together when we played Pakistan in an ODI in Singapore in 1996. He hit to midwicket and called me through for a single. I can't remember if I was slow in taking off or if there wasn't a single in it: Mushtaq Ahmed, by a long way not the quickest of the Pakistan fielders, ran me out. It wasn't a sign of times to come, though. Only three of our 143 partnerships in Test cricket would end as run-outs.

Not that that run-out is the abiding memory I carry from my early days of batting with Tendulkar. What I remember is the time I moved to No. 3: he would come out to join me in the middle, ask me what the pitch was doing, how the bowlers were bowling. It was a bit intimidating for a relative newcomer like me. By that time Tendulkar was already the best batsman in the world, and here I was, seven years his junior in international cricket, in awe of this man who was younger and smaller but playing these incredible shots. And he expected me to help him make up his mind as to how to go about the innings. What do you tell him?

This feeling of awe went away on my second or third tour, and Tendulkar did have a part to play in it. One of the good things about batting with him was that he never tried to impose his game on you. I was a pretty dour batsman to start off with, and I can imagine at times it might have frustrated him to be denied the strike for a long period. However, he never let it show.

This was a batsman you wanted to impress. He told me it would be great if I could get 250 runs in three Tests on my first South Africa trip. When I exceeded that number, I felt really pleased with myself. You wanted his general approval, but when we were out there in the middle it wasn't long before we were batting as equals.

Of course, you are never equals when it comes to batting with Tendulkar, especially in India. In my initial days at No. 3, if I was the second wicket to fall, I would hear loud cheers soon after I got out. Did I score that many runs? No, it was Tendulkar coming out to bat. And not just the crowd – if you were at the pitch in a third-wicket partnership with Tendulkar, you could see the intensity rise. Bowlers wanted his wicket. Captains knew they needed to get him early. Fielders would become more alert, bowlers would grow a leg, general chirping – not sledging, they had already tried and failed by the time I arrived on the scene – would increase, the ball would be thrown around more. And of course the crowd would be louder.

This heightened intensity around Tendulkar allowed me to go under the radar a bit and sort my game out, especially early in my innings. In a way, I preferred it that way, with all the attention on this man, and you quietly accumulating a few runs. Quite a few other batsmen have benefited from this phenomenon. Most of it was because the bowlers knew they needed to get Tendulkar out early. As conspicuous as the rise in intensity was when he walked in, the drop in morale on the field was as evident when he got off to a start, when he got past that early unsure period. If he did get out, you could actually feel people leaving the stands, if only for a break. Until then, nobody moved.

Tendulkar didn't like talking much when he batted. Well, except maybe with Virender Sehwag, but that's down to Sehwag's personality more than Tendulkar's. "Keep going" was the usual phrase we used when we batted together. If the going wasn't that good, "hang in there" would come in handy. When playing against Pakistan, we used to speak in Marathi because the Pakistan players could understand English and Hindi. There wasn't a lot of talking, though. He understood my game and respected it, and I his.

Because we began to understand each other's game so well, each of us could tell when the other was losing concentration. That was a significant part of our partnerships – when we could almost look at the other guy and tell he was loosening up a bit. All we needed at such times was for the other guy to come up and say, "Just tighten up a bit." Or even a certain look from him could convey to me I was becoming complacent. A recent example of it was in Perth, in 2007-08, when we added 139 for the third wicket.

It had been a bitter tour, and to come back well in Perth after the ugly scenes and a disappointing defeat in Sydney was important. That Test was probably more than just about techniques. I worked hard there, but there were times when I was a little desperate, almost too eager, to score. That is when he came up to me and said, "The partnership is more important. Don't worry about hitting the ball; the longer you bat, the better the timing will become. That's more important than looking good." He must have seen something in the way I was playing: after he got out, when on 93, I tried to drag a gentle Andrew Symonds delivery from well wide of off and ended up edging it to cover. He must have seen I was out of character in that innings.

I could tell when it was the same with him. One sure indicator that he was in good touch was when he played that flick to the leg side. Cricket is a game where you naturally have more fielders on the off side, and especially in limited-overs cricket, bowlers like to bowl tight lines, just short of length. Most of us wait for a loose delivery for release, but Tendulkar had this accurate shortish delivery sorted. He would be on his toes, on top of the bounce, and would often beat midwicket to the fielder's right. Sometimes he even beat square leg to his right with that flick, not to the full ball but the ones pitched short of a length. That made you marvel from the other end, and it rattled the bowlers a bit.

You could tell Tendulkar was not in touch when he didn't move fully forward while playing the front-foot defensive. It happened rarely during his career, but when he was uncertain he would be caught on the crease. The only other time you could tell he was not at his best was when he premeditated his shots. And I could see when that happened. If he saw the ball doing crazy things as he waited for his turn to bat, there were times he would go in with a pre-decided way to bat.

At The Oval in 2011, he must have seen Graeme Swann get a few to jump, which is probably why he went out and tried to sweep Swann off his rhythm. That sweep proved to be his downfall: he gloved one up on 23. I was unbeaten at stumps on day three of the Test, and I noticed a shrug of Tendulkar's shoulder, seemingly saying, "I should have trusted my defence more."

The other side of this premeditation was that he could correct it before you realised it. In the middle of a tour, in the middle of a Test, in the middle of an innings, in the middle of a session, in the middle of an over, he could change his game, the width or the direction of his stance, the spot he tapped his bat on when he took stance. And he could do it without anxiety. From the other end, you looked on and thought about how it took you painstaking net sessions to make adjustments to your game.

In the second innings in that Oval match, when the pitch had deteriorated more, Tendulkar played just the one sweep shot in close to four hours for his 91. You could get him out in a particular way, but you couldn't keep doing it for long, because he would go over dismissals in his mind and work his game out.

A lot of his game depended on what made him feel comfortable. I have asked him about the impromptu changes he often made to his game, and he would always say, "I feel comfortable this way." Still, at times he would be quite set about how he wanted to play a certain bowler. It's about mental strength, in a way, where he backs himself to do a certain thing against a certain bowler. When Ray Price bowled in the rough, people wanted Tendulkar to take him on, but he backed himself to block him out. Against Dale Steyn in Cape Town in 2011, he backed himself to defend and defend, no matter how long it took. For an hour he was stuck at one end, defending and leaving, sometimes getting beaten, but he didn't play a single get-out-of-jail shot.

That session reminded me of a partnership with Tendulkar that I quite cherish. Against Australia in Mumbai in 2001, we were up against a rampant bowling attack: Glenn McGrath, Jason Gillespie, Damien Fleming and Shane Warne. This was an Australian team on a roll and we were just coming out of the whole match-fixing saga. We had fallen behind by 173 in the first innings, had lost two early wickets in the second, the nightwatchman, Nayan Mongia, had retired hurt, and McGrath and Gillespie were bowling really well on the third morning.

For about an hour there, we didn't take a single. The few runs that came during that hour came in boundaries. Tendulkar took McGrath and I faced Gillespie for one hour. It was high intensity. The bowling was good, the fielders were alert, they were in our ears – Michael Slater would later have a go at each of us because I didn't walk for a disputed catch – but we enjoyed that period immensely. Tendulkar says those are the kind of sessions you never forget in your life, but that partnership of 96 – Tendulkar scored 65 of those – is not remembered as fondly as other partnerships of ours, because we collapsed after that to give Australia a target of just 47.

However, we would go on and make it one better two Tests later. We had won the Kolkata Test after Mumbai to level the series, but it was important we proved it wasn't a fluke. We lost the toss on a turner in Chennai, and the only way we were going to win was by taking a first-innings lead there. Tendulkar's game was *on* during that Test. He hadn't made a big contribution in the series until then, and those were the days when it was almost impossible to go through a three-match series without a Tendulkar century. The inevitability of that hundred was amazing, and we added 169 for the fifth wicket, which in the context of the match and the series was significant, because we ended up struggling while chasing 155. I remember that partnership fondly because of its fluency and assuredness.

Over such a long period of time, scoring 6920 Test runs in the company of each other, we have gone through the routine stuff over and over again. He didn't mind telling me if he didn't fancy a certain bowler, leading up to stumps on any given day. I never hesitated to tell him I would rather not face a certain bowler, so he would be ready for a tapped single. Sometimes we just needed to look at each other and we knew a bunt for one was around the corner.

And what a runner Tendulkar was. That run-out at the start of my career couldn't have been less indicative of the way we batted together. He didn't do a lot of fitness work or run a lot, but put pads on him and place him on those 22 yards and you had possibly the best runner of our times. His judgement of the single was impeccable. He knew the value of the single in keeping the strike rate going in ODIs, or to get off strike in Tests. Apart from judging runs perfectly, he ran his partner's runs as hard as he did his. There was never panic in our calling; a lot of it was done through the eyes, or the routine "Yes, no, wait."

Ours was a well-rounded partnership. We didn't do things that were visibly out of the ordinary. There weren't many high-fives, there weren't many talkative periods.

One of the times I remember I felt different playing with him was in Bristol in 1999. His father had just passed away; he had come back from India after the funeral and wanted to play immediately. We added an unbeaten 237 in less than 30 overs that day. There was a sense of quiet around him. You could almost sense he was batting for something more than himself.

That salute to his father, looking towards the sky upon reaching a century, has become a Tendulkar ritual ever since. Other than that, it is difficult to remember any rituals to do with his game; he was not the superstitious kind.

I do remember, though, that he hated it when somebody said "good luck" as he went out to bat, or if anybody greeted him in the middle with those words or others to that effect. He made it a point to tell me that it might be quite natural to wish a batsman luck as he goes out to bat, but he didn't want to hear it. Clearly, he didn't need much luck.

Rahul Dravid played 391 of his 509 international matches with Sachin Tendulkar.
He spoke to Sidharth Monga, assistant editor at ESPNcricinfo

A ROOM IN BULAWAYO

TELFORD VICE

The man from the BBC was quite certain what he wanted.

"All we need, old boy," he crackled down the line from London, pipe, slippers, smoking jacket, hot potato and all, "is for you to get Sachin Tendulkar on the telephone so that we can interview the little fellow." How about I prove instead that JFK is alive and well and sharing a hash pipe with Confucius and Van Gogh in Morocco? That would be far easier.

It was September 1998 in Bulawayo. I was on my second Test tour as a cricket writer. By then, Tendulkar had played 61 Tests and 198 one-day internationals. He was 25, and no longer the cherubic messiah who had strolled on to the world stage like the rest of us might wander on to a misty beach. In the nine years since he had made his debut, he had grown into a man. And not just any man. He was Sa-chin, Sa-chin.

I was simply me. Get him on the phone? Are you mad?

I didn't say that to the man from the BBC. I said, "Shouldn't be a problem."

As a breed, team managers are blazered bumptiousness in old man's trousers and sensible shoes. They exist in some strange place where things are important because they say they are. The manager of the Indian team that toured Zimbabwe in 1998-99 had a master's degree in bumptiousness.

"You want what?" he growled through his moustache, arching an eyebrow at me in recognition of my existence.

"An interview with Tendulkar, sir," I replied, as respectfully as I could manage.

Instantly his eyebrow un-arched and he lowered his moustache, along with the rest of his face, back to his newspaper, flicked his fingers at me as if he was dismissing an insect from his presence, and said, "Mmm . . . Delhi."

Of course, he meant I needed permission from the BCCI. Which was based, as it is now, in Mumbai. They're a tricky bunch, managers.

"We need to talk to the BCCI," I told the man from the BBC.

He didn't blink: "BCCI, eh? Jolly good. Roger that. Wilco."

Two days later, he was back on the line: "Sorted, old thing. BCCI are happy campers."

Back I went to the manager, who was where I had left him three days before, still reading the same page of the same newspaper.

"BCCI say it's fine for us to interview Tendulkar, sir," I said, trying hard to mask any hint of triumph.

His eyebrow was cleared for take-off. The bristles of his moustache were pointed straight at me.

"Delhi says it's fine?"

It was more of an involuntary gulp than a question.

"Yes, sir."

He held up a single, important finger. "Wait."

Then he slapped his paper on to the arm of his chair and got on the phone to the BCCI in Mumbai: "Hello? Delhi?"

The BCCI, bless them, told him that, yes, a man from the BBC had called. And, yes, they had given their permission for Tendulkar to be interviewed.

With slow, deliberate gentleness, the manager, now ashen-faced, put down the receiver. His eyes were fixed on far pavilions as he said, "Seven o'clock tonight. Squash court."

The Bulawayo Holiday Inn is deficient of much that touring cricket teams take for granted – sometimes eggs, other times water both hot and cold – but it used to have a well-maintained squash court. At 6.55 that evening I made my way there to find a crowd of around 100 staring through the glass back wall at Tendulkar, racquet in hand, swatting a ball about with a team-mate whose name has long since escaped my memory.

I found a spot on the bleachers and waited, but not for long, before Tendulkar spotted me and said loud enough for all to hear, "BBC?"

I nodded.

"One moment, please," he said, holding up an index finger and tilting his head to the side.

I nodded again and smiled.

Tendulkar returned his attention to the game for a minute or two. Then he shook hands with his opponent, opened the glass door, stepped off the court, grabbed a towel, walked towards me, and asked, "Where are we going to do this?"

Which is when things might have become awkward.

"Excellent, what," the man from the BBC had chortled when I told him that I should be able to have Tendulkar on the phone by 7.05pm that night. "We'll call you in your hotel room at that time. Tally-ho."

Why the arrangement was not to call Tendulkar in his room, or the manager in his room with Tendulkar at his elbow I will never know. But who was I to question a man from the BBC?

"Umm, the call will be to my room. We need to go there," I told Tendulkar, and waited for him to laugh in my face and return to his game of squash.

His surprise was obvious.

"Your room? Is that all right with you?"

I managed another nod.

"Fine. Let's go."

With that, we started walking, side by side, the 200 or so metres from the squash court to my room on the ground floor. We were not alone: the people who had been watching Tendulkar play squash were not going to have the object of their adoration plucked from their midst so easily.

They buzzed around us like bees as we made our way. For those few moments, I was given an inkling of what it was like to be Tendulkar. He was the nucleus of a giant atom, generating the energy to simultaneously keep the chattering crowd moving as well as to keep it a respectable distance from him. This seemed a tenuous arrangement that would implode any moment now, swamping us in frenzy. I glanced at Tendulkar's face for reassurance. It was a picture of calm. This – 102 people squashed into a hotel corridor in polite pursuit of him – was how he lived much of his life.

Which is not to say he was immune to the effects of constant scrutiny. A few evenings previously, I happened to be at the same restaurant where Tendulkar and a few of his team-mates were headed. The sound of the door of an expensive car closing caught my attention – there are not many flash cars in Zimbabwe – and I looked up to see Tendulkar standing on the pavement opposite and glancing around furtively for signs of a mob. Having satisfied himself that none would gather, he sighed and crossed the road with a light, carefree step.

That same step brought us to my room. I moved to unlock the door. Tendulkar motioned for me to stop.

He turned around to face his impromptu entourage: "Please, you must wait here."

Then he nodded to me. I unlocked the door and he and I went inside. Closing the door behind us, I looked up into many pairs of questioning eyes.

I gestured towards the bed, near the telephone. Tendulkar sat down, and within ten seconds of him doing so, ringing filled the void. When the BBC say they will call at 7.05pm, they don't mean 7.06pm.

"Yes, this is Sachin. Good evening."

For the next ten minutes I watched and listened as Tendulkar answered questions, several of which dealt with the 127 not out he had scored in his most recent innings. It was his 18th one-day century, which took him past Desmond Haynes' record.

Tendulkar spoke calmly, with good manners and with understated insight. If he understood all the fuss and bother, he wasn't letting on that he did. To have been able to think that he would play another 265 ODIs and score another 31 centuries in the format would have done my head in. That he would become the first player to win 200 Test caps? Even the man from the BBC wouldn't have believed that.

"Thank you. Goodbye."

Tendulkar replaced the receiver, stood up, and used his hands to smooth the bed cover where he had sat.

"I'm so sorry to invade your space like this," he said, extending a hand.

This time, I couldn't find the brainpower required to nod. I simply stood there and stared. Did I shake hands with him? Can't remember. Possibly not.

Quite who and what I was staring at I was no longer certain. I thought I had been in the company of a rarefied being from a galaxy far, far away. Instead, he was just another bloke on the phone, trying to make his way home.

Tendulkar was, after everything, human. But what kind of human doesn't blink at being followed around by a crowd of people who look on him as a god made flesh?

Perhaps, after everything, he wasn't human. Surely not, because he went willingly to the closed door, turned the knob, smiled a farewell at me over his shoulder, and stepped back out into the madness.

Yes, the crowd was still there, waiting.

Telford Vice is a sportswriter based in Johannesburg

A LAD AGAINST LIONS

HARSHA BHOGLE

In an otherwise nondescript little town called Lahli, Sachin Tendulkar is battling away against bowlers who were not born when he started playing international cricket. He is now winding down. I never thought I would use that expression about him. But he is. He is near 41, he is rich and famous beyond compare, and nobody will play as many Test matches as he has.

Tendulkar is prodding and pushing, tucking the ball off his pads sometimes, driving gently through the off. I shut my eyes. It is about 22 years since he played his most defining Test innings. He drove down the ground that day. And he punched through the off side to the most distant boundaries the game would allow. His feet were light and his eyes looked for opportunities to grab runs. While the rest were negotiating a short-term lease at the crease, he was laying the foundation for a great career.

At home, when I was not yet a teenager, we had a book called *I Was There*. Great sporting moments were brought alive in words that gently coated them. Perth 1992 was an "I Was There" moment. It was unforgettable. Sepia surrounds the edges of the frames from that day. The little notebook in which I recorded scores has worn away. Vast numbers of Tendulkar fans weren't yet born when he walked out to bat at No. 4.

If you play your best innings before you are 19, it might give the impression that everything has been downhill since. Not true. There have been many great ones since, drawing gasps from opponents. But every match that followed that day in Perth had expectation accompanying it. The young man was used to it as he went from gymkhana to maidan in Mumbai, sometimes both on one day, riding pillion on his coach's scooter, but after Perth 1992 it has been different.

So let us put that innings in perspective by looking at what came before. Tendulkar had played 15 Test matches for 837 runs at what now seems an underwhelming average of 39.85. Only one of those 15 Tests, and only one innings in it, had been played in India. From 16 and a bit when he went to Pakistan, Tendulkar had played in New Zealand, in England and in Australia, each with conditions that presented different challenges. Seasoned pros take time to adjust. It was actually an outstanding batting average.

He had made two centuries. One on a good pitch in Manchester, saving a game that was lost, and another on this tour, in the third Test, in Sydney, when Merv Hughes apparently told Allan Border, "This little prick's going to get more runs than you, AB." But never could Tendulkar have seen pace and, more crucially, bounce like there was in this surface at the WACA.

Up against him was Craig McDermott, a wonderful bowler who was to take 31 wickets in that series at 21.61, and Hughes, who gobbled his fair share too. And while he had batted at No. 4 for India in limited-overs internationals, he had only acquired the batting position that was to define him one innings earlier. It came on the last day of the Adelaide Test, where India were hoping to mount a chase. Dilip

Vengsarkar was pushed down a slot; Tendulkar was pushed up two. The change in status told a story in itself.

Alongside him were experienced players who were falling short. The lower half routinely outscored the top half in Australia that year. When a batting order crumbles as a matter of habit, it affects everyone; the flames of negativity envelop all. It was against that backdrop that Tendulkar walked out to bat at the home of fast bowling on day two of the Test.

Australia posted 346, India were 69 for 2. Tendulkar was not yet 19 and he was 5'4", plus or minus a bit. But almost like he was levitating, he seemed to find the inches to get on top of the bounce and hit the ball down to Perth's square boundaries. It wasn't yet fashionable to bring the rope in, and so the square boundaries there were an autorickshaw ride away, at least double the length of the boundaries on the maidans of Mumbai. But the ball kept finding them and it was a riveting contest. Those who were there knew they were seeing something rare.

In later years, maybe forced by reflexes and experience, Tendulkar might have tried to wear the bowling down. But here his mind harboured no such thoughts. Fifty-five were scored in the first hour on day three as India tumbled from five down to eight down. Tendulkar made 42 of those. By lunch he had made 81. This was not survival, he wasn't a boxer on the ropes, he was batting the only way he knew. He was taking on the bowling.

Close to 22 years later, I sought out my match report for the day. This is what I found:

His timing was divine. The kind that would have had lesser mortals tearing their hair in agony. And one shot typified that. To a ball from Whitney that was just short of length, Tendulkar stood up and just caressed it with his bat, like he were wiping a speck off a china dinner set. It went to the boundary like Clive

Lloyd had unleashed his might on it. With Tendulkar attacking majestically on the off side, Whitney tried to cramp him by bowling close to the body on the leg side. Tendulkar's response was to get inside the line and force the ball behind square.

There were other shots where bat came down on ball with ferocity. And when the bowlers bowled straighter, to deny room for the cut, he drove and flicked to leg. If a veteran had played that way, we would have been overjoyed. To watch someone so callow do so was to be aware that this was the blossoming of a rare talent. I turned, as I often do, to my friend Peter Roebuck's thoughts, and this is what he wrote that day:

Sometimes it is a privilege simply to be there. Perth yesterday was one such occasion. To see Sachin Tendulkar batting was, for two hours, to be transported from our humdrum world and taken to a distant land, a land of magic, an impossible land in which a boy of 18 summers can bat as man can seldom ever have batted.

And the fatherly Richie Benaud, who had already seen more generations than most, said on commentary that it was an innings that deserved a crowd of a hundred thousand.

Now, many years later, as Tendulkar bats in Lahli with a man who was born on the day he made his Ranji Trophy debut, I ask myself: where does this innings sit in the company of the many stirring ones that his bat conjured? In those years Tendulkar took bowlers apart and occasionally ground them down. He waltzed to the pitch of the ball and played the paddle sweep. He played the upper cut and, even if rarely, a pull shot of great ferocity. Across the world and against the greatest he scored runs, he built monuments.

But because that day in Perth, as a young man, he compelled us to watch, he ordered our senses and he captivated us, I still believe this would have given him the greatest satisfaction.

If I had to choose an "I Was There" moment, I would choose this.

Harsha Bhogle *is a cricket writer, commentator and presenter*

"I TEND TO GET OVERCONFIDENT VERY EASILY"

INTERVIEW BY ROHIT BRIJNATH

Let's face it. Sachin Tendulkar and Brian Lara are the two most exciting batsmen in the world. Tendulkar has an average of 52.71 in 35 Tests. Lara's is 57.06 in 19 Tests. In one-day internationals, Tendulkar's average is at 36.40 and Lara is marginally ahead at 40.22.

And finally, Lara has three Test centuries plus two world records which he set last year – 375, the highest Test score ever, and 501, the highest first-class score of all time. Tendulkar, in comparison, has scored eight centuries, with 179 his highest.

But being great players is not easy, for pressure, expectation and public scrutiny follow them every minute, everywhere.

This interview was first published in *India Today* magazine in 1995

You both come from cricket-crazy countries, and the expectations, therefore, can be unreal. How do you manage that?

Tendulkar: It's hard, but there's no way out of it. You just have to keep your cool. While playing even a Test match you'll hear the crowd chant "We want sixer." Many times they don't understand that it is more important for me to stay at the wicket, and that's when it sometimes disturbs my concentration. It's irritating when you're not doing well.

Lara: It's easier on my part because I'm playing with a team that has been successful for a number of years. For Sachin it's a bit different. He's playing with an Indian team that's recognised at home, but away from India they need to improve their record. And he would have that sort of problem with the public that is expecting him to change India's fortunes throughout the world. But the expectation is great for me because life in the West Indies is surrounded by cricket and people talk about the West Indies team as the only unifying factor in the West Indies.

How do you cope with the pressure of being the best batsmen in your teams?

Tendulkar: It's good in a way. I'm very happy the team is expecting something from me. I wouldn't like to be considered one of those players who might get runs once in a blue moon. I hate to be like that. The team expects things from me because I'm capable of doing it. And I have to do it.

Lara: It's a great feeling. Playing with the West Indies, you're talking about holding the same position as Sir Garry Sobers, as Viv Richards . . .

and here comes Brian Lara and they look upon you in the same light. But the thing about the West Indies team is that you're kept on your p's and q's because if you don't perform, someone is willing to take over the mantle from you.

Who do you mainly take advice from?

Tendulkar: Mostly I speak to Mr Gavaskar, and the other person is my brother Ajit.

Lara: I talk to Sir Garry a lot.

Form is very fickle. How do you feel when you are out of form?

Tendulkar: Sadly, the evenings become very miserable. The important thing is for a player to stay alone and analyse what happened. But just for a little while. Because if one stays like that all the time, it's very hard to come out of. It's more important you work it out on the field rather than just doing the theory and forgetting about practical things.

Lara: How I feel? I've lost a lot of confidence. But I felt it's something special this year. I've been out of form before this, but this year's been such a big success for me that I don't personally think it was my form. Sometimes I felt good batting, but some other force outside of just my natural batting ability was maybe getting me out or didn't have me as focused as I wanted to be.

Do you ever find yourself becoming arrogant against weaker teams?

Tendulkar: Sometimes, when you're getting runs, you try something extra which you shouldn't. And that's the worst thing that can happen to a player. Because you might be in good nick, but you have to play within your limitations. And if you want to see how far your limitations are, then you find yourself going back to the pavilion.

Lara: No. In a Test match, most of the time you want to cash in. It's a weaker team yes, it's a batting track yes, but there are going to be times when you can't score any runs. So make the most of the opportunity and score as many runs as you can.

I suppose Kambli is a good example, when he cashed in on a couple of poor teams, and although he had a poor series against the West Indies, I'm sure his batting average is still over 50. Which is damn good. I don't see it as becoming over-arrogant. In fact, I remember Richie Richardson telling me, "You're going to have times when you can't score runs. So when you meet teams that you can score against, you better score a lot of them."

What do you like about each other's batting?

Tendulkar: One thing I've observed about Brian is that he doesn't like to give it up that easily. Even though he has got so many runs under his belt, the determination is there. And that is the kind of sign you'll only see in a great player.

I feel most of the guys are talented, that's the only reason they get to this level. But when talent meets talent, I think it's determination and the mental approach that counts. So that really separates him from the rest.

Lara: My concept of Indian batting, what I've heard before or what I've seen, is that when there is more life in the pitches, they tend to be a bit scared. But Sachin believes in himself, and it doesn't matter what opposition he comes up against, he seems to have the resources to perform well. And for a 21-year-old to be thinking like that . . . I think he's a tremendous player and he's going to score a lot of runs. What's going to be even better for him is if his team does well. It's going to help his confidence, playing with a winning team often.

And he is the backbone of Indian batting. It's simple to see that and he knows that and I think he is capable of handling the job even at this tender age, and he is capable of winning matches for India. Maybe one day I'll be giving him a call to congratulate him on breaking my record.

What do you aspire for eventually?

Tendulkar: In the long run, towards the end of my career, after I stop playing, more than the spectators, I think former cricketers should say I was a good cricketer. I think there are very few people who really understand what's going on, and so only the player can judge how the player is. That will be the greatest thing.

Lara: I'd just like to stay consistent. One of my dreams is to maintain the unbeaten run the West Indies have had, at least through my career.

Do you aspire for records?

Tendulkar: I'm not really bothered about them. If you're good enough to break records, you won't have to worry about it. If you're not good enough, you have to.

Lara: No. I sit back and think about the amount of hassle I've had breaking these two world records. There has been a lot of pressure. I'm not in a hurry to break any records. I just want to maintain a certain level of consistency, and at the end of my playing days I wish I could be considered a great player. I don't think I am right now, just because you are breaking a few records and people go crazy and start comparing you with the great players of the past. Which I think is stupid.

Which was your best innings, the way you played, the circumstances you played it in?

Tendulkar: Maybe in Perth against Australia [1992] in the fifth Test. I got a hundred when we were something like 120 for 6 and I just went all out. On that kind of hard and bouncy fast track, I batted very well. I was so confident I thought I could face any bowler.

Lara: 277 in [Sydney] Australia, definitely the best. As for the 375 [against England], we already had the series 3-1 and you're going into the last Test match on a very flat track and it's kind of "help yourself". While in Australia, we were one Test down and the third was in Sydney, and the West Indies don't have a good record in Sydney. But I enjoyed that innings and we went on to win the series, so the value of that innings I cherish more than anything else.

When you are playing your best cricket, timing the ball perfectly, is that the best moment of your life?

Tendulkar: That's the worst moment in my life. Because I tend to get overconfident very easily. It's the biggest problem I'm facing right now. Like in the first innings [in Chandigarh, against West Indies], I tried something more than I should have. Because I was striking the ball so well – in 40 I had scored nine boundaries – I tried for a stupid shot I shouldn't have. And that really scares me a lot.

Lara: Yeah. Because my whole concept of it is, when you're doing well, cash in. Don't play stupid shots because when it's your time, it's your time. I don't think you can manufacture that time, I don't think you can make it happen. When it's your time, you realise that when you're scoring runs you are going to get a world of luck. In April-May [1994], after the 375, 1 went to England [for county cricket] and I was just scoring runs. In the 501, I got bowled off a no-ball, an easy catch to the wicketkeeper was dropped, and then I went on to break a world record. It's the best time of life and I cherish it and I doubt it will ever happen again.

Do you have a private life? Does anyone respect your privacy? How tough is it being a star?

Tendulkar: It's very tough. It's very irritating because you get no privacy. Like when I got engaged, I didn't want my photo to appear in the papers. It was a personal thing and my fiancée and I refused. I requested the press not to make it a big issue. Yet after that, for 10-15 days, the photographers were following my fiancée. They think it's a very common thing that because you're public property, everybody should know. But everybody should know about my cricket and nothing else.

Lara: Yes, it's tough. Your private life, I think, should be yours. You play cricket on the field, you perform on the field, and regarding the private aspect of your life, you should at least be given the liberty to live your own life and do the things you want to do outside of cricket.

Every time you go out to bat, people expect you to score a century. Even if you score 85, they say, "It's good but he

missed a century." Is that too much?

Tendulkar: That happens, I know. But there's no answer to it.

Lara: People say that now. You know, looking back, I look at this series and say, well, if a ball beat me outside the off stump, someone is already writing about it. Because you've done so much that people are looking at every single delivery, looking at every single move you make and want to make a report about it. That was a lot of pressure. What I've realised in the last innings [Lara scored 91], when I went out to bat was that you can't do worse. You've come to India and disappointed and I found myself batting, more freely.

That wasn't happening before. I was worried about the ball and what people were thinking. I have to go back to my old days when a Test fifty, a Test 60, was good. I've lost that part of my game, all I want to do is score hundreds.

What is the stupidest thing ever said or written about you?

Tendulkar: That Shilpa Shirodkar and I were having an affair. Because we don't even know each other at all.

Lara: My not wanting to field in the English county season. That was the stupidest because I'm one who enjoys his cricket and one of the better aspects for me is fielding. People said I was a prima donna and that I wanted to just bat and not field, which was completely untrue.

How do you think you've matured from the time you began, both technically and mentally?

Tendulkar: Things have really changed. When I was playing my first Test in Pakistan [1989], I was going for each and every ball outside the off stump, and I was getting beaten by the pace, the bounce, the swing. Because I hadn't faced this kind of quick bowling – Waqar Younis and Wasim Akram – and the wicket had a little bit of life in it. Then I thought it was my first and last Test and that I would never again play for India.

I was hoping I would be picked for the next match, and luckily I was. I had decided that even if I don't play well, it doesn't matter because I have nothing to lose. And I just stayed there and got 59 and from then on I started feeling very confident.

I think if you stay at the wicket for long, you get to learn a lot of things. If you don't stay there, you don't learn. So fortunately I stayed there. I've been getting runs, so it's nice. Also, now is the right time. Not many guys get the opportunity to learn at the age of 21, so looking at it I feel each and every moment on the field is precious for me, it is very important for the future and I should learn.

Lara: I've matured a lot. Over the years, I've been very inexperienced and sometimes I give away my innings, and looking back at it you say you could have done better in the situation. I don't think technically I do anything better. Mentally, I've grown up many more years. I've gained in strength and I can hit the ball a lot harder than before. My self-belief and confidence going out against any opposition has improved and that is most important.

Who is the one batsman and bowler you admire?

Tendulkar: The batsman is David Boon. He's got runs wherever he's gone, against all kinds of attacks and he's been very consistent over four-five years. He played superbly against us in Australia and he looked very determined, very mean, the way a batsman should be. The bowler is Courtney Walsh. I just like him.

Lara: The batsman is Jimmy Adams. He is the most dependable batsman in our team and will remain so for a long time, for his stability, his strong defence, his strong mind. I admire that. And Curtly Ambrose is the bowler, of course. There's no doubt he's the best.

Lastly, is it personally very important for you how you get your runs?

Tendulkar: It is important how I get my runs, but people only remember it for a year or so. But how many you get, that they remember for a lifetime. So the scoreboard speaks for itself.

Lara: Yes, you set a certain standard and you wouldn't like to be fishing and find yourself with a hundred. Sometimes you like to show a bit of the class that you believe you have, in a little flamboyant way. And sometimes you like to play shots and look good, but you can't do it all the time.

Rohit Brijnath has written on cricket and other sports for over two decades

MY 4AM FRIEND

YUVRAJ SINGH

Whenever I see Sachin Tendulkar and a plate of biscuits in the same room, it makes me laugh. Yes, I know it's not the right thing to say first up about a cricketer of his stature. But it won't go away. The first thing Sachin ever said to me was: "Excuse me. Biscuit pass *karna*."

This was November 1990. I was a schoolboy in shorts, taken to Chandigarh's lovely old cricket ground, the Sector 16 Stadium, to watch an India match live for the first time, a Test against Sri Lanka. My father had ended his first-class career for Punjab by then but the Sector 16 Stadium was still his home. He got me into the dressing room – which in those days you could do – and I tried to be invisible.

Sachin and his buddy Vinod Kambli were there, teenagers acting their age, joking and fooling around. I was standing in a corner, by the food table when Sachin turned to me and said, "Excuse me. Biscuit pass *karna*." As much as I remember him saying that, I can't remember what I said to him. I could barely speak.

Later Kapil Dev, Chandigarh's own hero, introduced me to Sachin. "This is Sachin Tendulkar, the new boy in the team." He looked like a boy, like one of my seniors in school. This was the boy who had scored a Test hundred at Old Trafford a few months ago. A Test hundred! I remained wordless.

I remained in awe of his batting and his achievements. He brought out the cricket lover in everyone. On another occasion, Dad had Sachin and Vinod to our home for dinner during a Challengers Trophy match. They were piled into our car and Dad told me that because there was no room, I should walk home. I was slightly peeved, but maybe it was for the better. They would have thought Yograj Singh's son couldn't speak. Sachin knows me better today and he will confirm that this is *so* not true.

In my junior cricket days, Sachin did pop up now and again. I remember him giving a pep talk to Kailash Gattani's Star CC just before we left for our tour of England in 1996. By the time I was picked for the Indian ODI team in 2000, for the ICC KnockOut, which later became the Champions Trophy, he was without any doubt the best batsman in the world. Numero Uno. Top of the Tree. And I would share a dressing room with him. The very idea scrambled my mind.

When I was asked to take the seat next to him in the team bus, I was too much in awe to think I could. It was at that time, however, that I met the real Sachin Tendulkar, past the biscuits, the records and the reputation.

His batting came close to technical perfection. Foot movements, body position when attacking or defending, the utter stillness of his head – it was flawless. It was like a dancer moving only the part of the body that is meant to move. You couldn't copy it.

What I found as astonishing as his mastery, and even more, was that it came from a regular, grounded guy. Not some moody genius. Often moodiness is explained as the result of genius. Not with Sachin, and we got proof in the dressing room. It is a very big deal because in cricket, a high-pressure workplace, it is routine for people to fluctuate. Their worlds change, depending on how they are doing. Success and failure make them different people. Attention and acclaim can change them completely.

Good times, bad times, runs or no runs, Sachin's approach towards the game and people around him never fluctuated. He loved the game, understood that there would be ups and downs, and treated everyone with respect and attention. It is a very simple thing but hard to master. He had found a way.

Later I learnt that he could be naughty, a natural prankster. Sourav Ganguly told me of the time Sachin engineered a stunt when they were both at an under-15 camp in Indore. When Sourav was asleep in his room, Sachin and his pals poured buckets of water under his door to flood it. So when Sourav woke up, he found his feet in water. He says it was ankle-deep, Sachin says not that much. Anyway, Sourav's kit and his bats were at a safe height.

As youngsters in the Indian team, however, we were spared that treatment. Sachin was very aware of his role in the team set-up. He was quick to break the ice with younger players and quickly identified those too tongue-tied to speak to him. Like I was very early. He would then voluntarily step in to help you out and try to make sure you spoke freely. He was a patient listener, no matter what the problem was: your grip or your stance or your training. He wanted the person speaking to him to do so without inhibition. He wanted that to be a natural way in his dealings with everyone. It didn't matter if you had played 100 Tests or zero.

His response to any question was always to offer a suggestion. Never an order, never a command, never a lecture. "What works for me . . ." he often said. If you had half a brain you'd pay attention because there was a very good chance it would work for you too. Not because he was Sachin Tendulkar, superstar, but because he spoke from very long experience.

He treated everyone with equal respect – from the captain to the board president to the newest player to the dressing-room attendant, the baggage man, the guy driving the bus, the coach, everyone. You may have heard that he is humble and rooted, but it is another thing to experience this quality first-hand.

Everyone knows you can't imitate his batting no matter how much time you put in in the nets. But you could learn from his manner, and that is what I tried to do. I think that has been the foundation of my friendship with Sachin: that I could speak openly to him and not be judged on the basis of my averages or my experience. He became my 4am friend through everything. The guy I could call no matter what. He would always make time to listen, or to meet and try to sort it out. This was crazy, given that he was always surrounded by people who wanted a piece of him, but he would do that for friends.

When I was undergoing my cancer treatment in the US, India was playing its Test series in Australia. He was going through one of the toughest times in his career. The time difference was crazy, but he was in regular touch. Always he would try to keep me motivated when I was feeling down and defeated by chemotherapy and its brutal side effects. When the treatment was done and I took a break in London on my way back home, he flew over to see me.

Every so often in the course of our conversation, he would get up and come over to hug me. Later he told me that when he saw me, worn out, bald, eyebrow-less, he had come very close to crying but had managed to keep his emotions in check. That evening was one of my best memories from my cancer journey. I can't tell you how happy it made me, how energised.

I've often tried to understand what kept him going for so long. Everyone says early success makes you crazy. He had success very early, and fame and celebrity, and he didn't go crazy. For 24 years. He has often said to me that his close friends and family were those who kept him grounded. It is this core group that has shaped him as a person. His brother Ajit and wife Anjali, I think, are integral parts in his life who have made him the person he is. He learnt how to tolerate the fallout of his success and how to manage his failures. He managed to remain detached and keep things in his control. He carried his greatness as a cricketer lightly. Not many can.

Much of it had to do with his utter dedication to cricket over and above all else. Whether he was getting runs or he wasn't, his practice regimes, his intensity and his application to his work never changed. There were never any shortcuts. It is like he treated his talent like a gift and then did everything he could to polish it to perfection. To watch him go to work every day was an education in itself.

Sachin's example is very, very hard to follow. In many ways, cricket is a hard, unforgiving and ruthless sport. During a bad patch once, I got out early and was totally fed up because I had worked like a donkey. No use. I got into the dressing room and threw my bat. After I had cooled down, he came over and said, "This bat is your identity. It has given you name, fame and put food on your table. It is responsible for the life you are living. Don't insult it. Never do that again. Never take this game for granted."

I understood almost immediately what he meant. It was a simple truth and he had always followed it. I felt silly. I promised myself I wouldn't ever take *my* anger over *my* mistakes out on my cricket bat or equipment.

It is not that we didn't see the aggressive side of Sachin, but his aggression was measured. In a team game, passions can run high, and in the heat of the moment many of us step out of line. There have been times people have gone at each other in the dressing room. Sachin knew exactly when to get in and settle the issue. When he was around, you didn't see too many arguments – most of these things happened in his absence.

He had amazing control over aggression and channelled those

energies for the use of the team. He has gone hard at opposition teams, as much as most of us, but he had a very good understanding of when and where to stop and rein it in. Probably because he had good control in every area of his life, he could do the same in cricket. He said to me once, "Cricket *josh se nahin, hosh se kheli jaati hai.* [Cricket is not played with mere passion but with complete consciousness]." Those words of advice have stayed with me.

I know all this must make him sound almost saintly, but only saints are saints, not cricketers. Sachin did have his faults. I think the younger members of the team could definitely offer him tips on dress sense. Let us say he is not a fashion natural. Secondly, in the changing room he would play this utterly horrible music. He told us it was from the 1980s, but who knows, it could have belonged to the '60s or earlier, when pop music was just being invented. Whenever we begged him to change it, he would say to us, most seriously, "*This,* guys, is *real* music. Not that stuff that you listen to nowadays." We put it down to the generation gap and gritted our teeth.

Maybe the only positive of his retirement is that we can play our own music. When he played his, we had to just endure it. It could not be changed. Not ever. But *paaji,* never mind the faces we made as your music played on. The fact that we didn't change it was our funny way of telling you how much we loved you.

Sachin has been synonymous with Indian cricket and what was good and stellar about it for 24 years. All of us have our Sachin stories. It is going to be difficult to imagine an Indian team without him, but it will happen. Like I read somewhere, there will, of course, be another batsman who will take his place in the XI. But who can possibly replace the man in our dressing room? Our mentor, our friend, our North Star.

Yuvraj Singh played 198 international matches in the same side as Sachin Tendulkar

WAKING UP TO SACHIN

SANTOSH DESAI

It was a summer's day in Mumbai in 1998. The heat was falling off our bodies in the form of balls of sweat, and Sachin Tendulkar was batting. Actually, he was pretending to bat as we set about shooting a Pepsi commercial with him. He was just back from a dream run in Sharjah, at the very pinnacle of his form. The script required him to swat cricket balls contemptuously with a fly swatter, while drinking Pepsi. He refused – as has become famous since – because he felt that would be showing disrespect to the game. Of course, later in the afternoon he showed no qualms about heaping disrespect on bowlers in the nets as he swatted them contemptuously to distant corners. His ability to keep a sense of perspective in the midst of all the madness around him was never in greater evidence than at that particular moment.

Sachin came at the right time in more ways than one. In 1989, the first set of economic reforms had already occurred in India, but by the time the second wave hit us in 1991, Sachin was well on his way to becoming a legend. His success caught fire commercially because of its timing, as it coincided with the opening up of the market. More important, it gave wings to a growing self-confidence that began to replace the nagging sense of inferiority the country had been bedevilled by. The coming of the market and the availability of hitherto unavailable options freed the spirits of a middle class burdened by the knowledge of its own inadequacies. In cricket and in Sachin, they found an accelerant of their growing aspirations, a symbolic assertion of the new confidence with which they felt ready to take on the world.

As a vehicle for Indian self-image, cricket was the perfect choice. It was the primary unifier of the country, more than even cinema, and had sufficient history behind it as a familiar presence in everyday life. It gave the country a sense of being competitive on a global scale, and because only a handful of countries played the game, it provided that sense with relative ease. Importantly, these few countries included a few developed western ones, which legitimised the sport as being global in Indian eyes. This allowed cricket to become a receptacle for national pride; indeed, it became the primary site for a display of patriotism, as Team India became synonymous with the country, and carried with it the burden of representing what the nation could or could not achieve. It also elevated the game to a level where it was that much more attractive to marketers looking for a national platform that could allow them to reach a country that is otherwise far too diverse and media-fragmented to be able to aggregate.

The unique ability of cricket, particularly in its one-day format, is that it allows advertisers to reach a defined target audience with a degree of certainty not available before. Structurally, cricket allows for advertising to insinuate itself every few minutes, given the natural punctuation offered after every over. It also holds the viewer's attention over an entire day, allowing for more opportunities to plug an ad, whereas traditional content, however popular, could not deliver for anything much more than an hour. When a tournament is involved, an advertiser can speak to a captive audience over weeks, making it an ideal platform to launch new campaigns or brands. But while cricket in India might have been, in theory, a great vehicle for the market to hitch a ride on, it needed a spearhead to catapult the game into something much more significant. It needed a glue that ensured that beyond national loyalty, viewers would come back and continue to make an emotional investment in the game.

In Sachin, we found just that. A guileless destructive force that was as endearing as it was dominant. In not looking the part, in looking absurdly young and speaking in an adolescent's voice, he became everyone's mascot; all of India felt they had some stake in him. He represented the idea of a young nation, seething with talent and ability, ready to take on the world and dominate it. Sachin reconciled hunger with innocence; he seemed to be acting without a larger agenda. While Indian fans, and even the team, displayed an increasingly aggressive attitude that revelled in finally being able to give back as good as they received, Sachin himself was the still point of a turning universe, intent only on his next innings. Not for him the mouthing off against the sledging opponent or the prolonged angry stare or the shirt-waving expressiveness of his captain Sourav Ganguly – his focus was only on the task in front of him. He ignited a larger need for self-respect and validation that sprang up around him by appearing completely unmindful of it. He did not seem to need that as extra motivation, though – just being able to go out and dominate bowlers seemed enough.

In doing so, he seemed to capture the essence of a young market in all its youthful exuberance. For the market, Sachin underscored the power of a currency with universal access and deep emotional power. In some ways, the idea of the brand ambassador in its modern form was constructed by Sachin Tendulkar. To be sure, there had been other cricketing superstars who had been used commercially. Sunil Gavaskar and Kapil Dev had a clutch of endorsements, but in their time, cricket was not the commercial force it became later. As pioneers in this space, they played the grittier role of extracting commercial value from their sporting achievements. The idea of the "professional" player looking to create commercial opportunities for himself by monetising different aspects of his persona was very much the dominant reality of an earlier era.

In Sachin's case the market exploded around him. When Mark Mascarenhas signed Sachin for what was then the unimaginably high figure of Rs 45 crores, the transition was complete. I remember the utter sense of disbelief that this number evoked at the time; it seemed that the larger-than-life Mascarenhas had made a serious mistake by overreaching himself dramatically. But he had instinctively grasped the potential that Sachin and cricket had in a country that was beginning to explode with growth. In a single action, the power of Sachin and that of cricket as a commercial engine multiplied. Five years later, when the contract was renewed for Rs 100 crores, no one blinked. By that time the power of cricket and Sachin Tendulkar had become an accepted fact of life.

More significantly, the idea that brands needed a face that exemplified what they stood for became standard industry practice. The market for celebrities was in many ways constructed by people like Sachin Tendulkar and Shah Rukh Khan, whose presence at a key time in India's resurgence and whose role in shaping a new, more self-confident narrative for the nation was pivotal in making consumption the force it has become. The idea of conflating achievement and popularity as represented by a celebrity with products and brands made consumption an act of assertive aspiration rather than of self-centred materialism. "*Yeh Dil Maange* More" was not so much about greed as it was about a yearning for more freedom and room for self-expression as a generation uncoiled itself from the restraints imposed on it by a restrictive past.

The market has not looked back since, certainly, nor has the commerce surrounding cricket. The IPL has taken the numbers surrounding the game to stratospheric heights, and cricket teams now attract valuations that large corporations would be proud of. The coming of T20 cricket has made the game even more attractive commercially, and it has helped that the new Indian team seems to be crackling with talent. The fiery brilliance of Virat Kohli and the cool command shown by MS Dhoni are helping them rack up endorsement deals of a kind that even Sachin in his heyday might not have seen.

And yet, as evidenced by the kind of farewell received by Sachin, there was something special that happened around him, something that no amount of money can replicate. Sachin helped create a new set of meanings around a game that India has always loved, and shaped the way it is followed, consumed and exploited. There are times when the commercial success of the game appears to be to the detriment of the spirit of the game, as it becomes more commercial vehicle than sport, but that is a story for the future. As far as Sachin is concerned, he woke cricket in India and he woke us to its many potentials, not the least of which was to believe so completely in a young boy with a big bat.

Santosh Desai is an author, columnist, and the CEO of Future Brands

STRICKEN BUT SOARING

TANYA ALDRED

Yesterday I went for a run. Halfway round, where the river bends and the plane trees come into sight, three crows flapped alarmingly close to my nose, as simultaneously three ducks were dragged downstream and a line of geese honked in the sky.

A head is full of moments like this, scraps of random stuff pushed chaotically into an overloaded cranial pocket. Many memories are more intensely personal – a kiss, a fight, a birth. But others are about being somewhere, when someone else did something, something unforgettable. And I was there on May 23, 1999, when Sachin Tendulkar put on his pads in a small dressing room in the south-west of England, picked up his bat and walked out to be extraordinary.

It was the seventh cricket World Cup. The organisation had been chaotic, the opening ceremony a damp handshake of broken microphones, enveloping firework smoke and mutterings that the organisers were absurd in trying to put on an international tournament during the notoriously wet English late spring. England were still employing roly-poly bits-and-pieces players in their one-day team and were duly knocked out at the first hurdle. The tournament song was released the day after that. Luckily, the cricket itself saved the competition.

That May Sunday, I got an early train down from a shared house in north London to Bristol, where India were playing Kenya in a Group A match. Nevil Road was a small, undeveloped ground crammed in by housing and bordered by trees. It was my first World Cup – the first in England since 1983 – and I was thrilled to be trusted to pick up a pencil and write about it.

The ground filled up. The crowd was curious. There were the people commonly spotted at cricket matches – the older couples with their picnics, the middle-aged man with his floppy hat, scorecard and selection of coloured biros, each with the correctly corresponding cap. Then there was a scattering of Kenyan painted faces and flags, but the majority of the fans were British Asians supporting India. They wore replica shirts, had home-made posters and posed in orange and yellow and green wigs. And they made noise, lots and lots of noise.

In 1999, British cricket grounds weren't used to this type of din – the exuberant West Indian supporters that places like The Oval could attract during the 1970s and '80s had largely disappeared and people mostly watched either in respectful contemplation or with drunken chanting. This was different. This was bawdy, uninhibited, joyful, constant rabble.

The game itself proved to be a no-contest. Kenya were valiant, Steve Tikolo made a crackling 58, but India won by 94 runs. Rahul Dravid, slow, reliable Dravid, made a century off 107 balls. But all that anyone could talk about, all I remember from that day really, is Tendulkar. Brilliant, mourning, awe-inspiring Tendulkar.

He had just returned from India where he'd been at the funeral of his father, Ramesh, who had died unexpectedly from a heart attack, aged 69. His flight back from Mumbai had only arrived in London the day before – he had determined to stay at home but had been told to return to his team-mates by his mother and sister. He was 26 and had been playing Test cricket for nine and a half years – a young man forced by his astonishing ability to become an elder statesman when really he was little more than a boy.

I'd never heard a British-Asian crowd in full voice before. India won the toss and batted. The sound surged around the ground, a swarming multitude of bees hungry for sweet boundaries. When Tendulkar walked out at 92 for 2, there was an atmosphere of anticipation and reverence; as he unveiled shot after shot, there was one of community: "We got tickets. Aren't we lucky! Did you see that? And that? Wow!"

The placement was astonishing, the shots breathtaking, and oh the fluency – 50 off 54 balls, 100 off 84, finishing on 140 not out off 101 deliveries. Two shots I remember well: a reverse sweep like a plummeting falcon, and that six off the last ball, a pull over deep midwicket, full of mastery and utter domination.

He was short, this master, his stocky little legs dressed in pale blue pyjamas, his dark blue helmet with the Indian sun pulled over his black curls. When he reached 50, and then again a hundred, as the crowd roared with animal delight, he looked up searchingly to the sky. Just watching felt like an intrusion on his private grief.

Everything that day was heightened – the breeze that buffeted shirts, the constant riddle of the ice-cream van, the spring sunshine where it fell on your cheek. The deep green of the grass, the haze of the sky. The Kenyans, plucky but predictable, had not a chance of actually winning the game.

Tendulkar, at the end, dedicated the innings to his father. Those of us there paid a kind of homage too. To me it rewrote what cricket could mean.

I had started going to cricket matches in the mid-1980s, when England weren't very good. Botham was already past his brilliant prime. Gower, a lackadaisical genius, and Gooch, a hard-working, upright run machine, fired haphazardly. And although I'd seen wonderful things – Gooch's 333 at Lord's against India, Darren Gough's hat-trick in Sydney, Viv Richards swaggering to the crease to make a quick fifty for Somerset – this was on a different level. It felt like greatness.

Some would argue against sporting performances being great – but they're wrong. It's not just a physical triumph of being better than your opponent, but of operating entirely on a different level, dancing on the roof when they're stuck down in the cellar. It is having the discipline, skill, talent and mental fortitude and, putting all those things together, producing something startling. Something that causes those watching to wonder in disbelief and delight.

The Tendulkar who batted on that cloudy day in Bristol seemed capable of cheating the turn of the clock. He saw the ball earlier, had time to deliberate over where to put it, and was mulling over his evening while the fielders turned to see where the ball had gone. He was engulfed in grief but somehow found a path through. I'd bet every one of the 8508 people who walked out of the ground that day, scraps of autographs stuffed in their pocket, souvenir programmes in their hand, felt an emotional connection to what they'd just witnessed.

More than that, we had seen an all-time great bat like an all-time great. Not a black- and-white photograph but a real flesh-and-blood man, a man just two months younger than me, walk in the footsteps of the giants.

Tendulkar undoubtedly played better innings against stronger attacks in more high-pressure situations. I saw him again in dusty Ahmedabad, during England's 2001 tour, when the wasteland outside the Sardar Patel stadium was flooded with rickshaws and scooters as people arrived in hordes to watch him bat. Nasser Hussain tried to tame him by packing the off side with eight fielders and asking his faster bowlers to fire ball after ball a couple of feet outside his off stump. He thought he'd bore him out. Tendulkar put up with it until after lunch, when he suddenly launched into a perfect counter-attack. He just picked up the balls and shot them back through the leg side to the boundary. The crowd, obsessed, convulsed with joy and appreciation. His 27th Test hundred was a truly wonderful one.

But that day in Bristol, those circumstances and his reaction to his terrible sadness, wormed its way into my brain. And there it sits, fighting its corner still, along with the other flotsam and jetsam.

Tanya Aldred is a sports columnist for the Daily Telegraph

THE ENTHUSIASTIC IMP

SIDHARTH MONGA

During his great innings at Newlands in 2010-11, Sachin Tendulkar, having reached his century, responded to a Dale Steyn sledge. A bemused Steyn couldn't believe his ears: Tendulkar was having a chat with somebody during the play. "You're talking to me?" Steyn said. Unlike in *Taxi Driver* – although Steyn could have fit the role Robert de Niro played – he stressed not the "me" but the "you".

Tendulkar was supposed to be above chatter. People didn't sledge Tendulkar. Except for when he was standing up for a team-mate during Monkeygate, Tendulkar was a saint. People didn't give him send-offs, except Taufeeq Umar, who mouthed off after Tendulkar had put up an exhibition in Centurion in a World Cup match. People left him alone. People thought it would be nasty to try to break his concentration with verbals. How could people be nasty to such a nice man?

People, of course, forgot Tendulkar the bowler. With the ball in hand – remember when he was young? – Tendulkar was a little rascal who mocked batsmen, waved them goodbye after taking their wickets, celebrated in their faces, and annoyed the hell out of them. The way Andrew Flintoff laughed after he asked Tino Best to "mind the windows" was regular fare for Tendulkar after he got the better of batsmen with his allsorts.

It's quite a cliché to invoke Tendulkar's childlike love for the game, but the boy found that complete, unadulterated, pure expression when he bowled. As a batsman he never showed you the man behind the visage, not even against spinners, after the early '90s. No fear, joy, satisfaction, humility, arrogance. Nothing. As a bowler he got angry when he was hit, exulted if he took out the man who was hitting him, and was extremely excited when he did what he wanted to do with a delivery.

The long sleeves rolled up to the elbows, the hat off, the hand sorting the hair out, the fist waggling to settle the bracelet, the field adjusted, the mind up to devilish tricks – that Tendulkar was more accessible, more us, more imperfect yet beguilingly good, than the focused Tendulkar under the helmet could ever be. And the man could bowl. Everything. Seam, swing, cutters, legbreaks, wrong'uns, offbreaks, topspinners. He didn't have the flipper, but how many specialist legspinners do? And he could make up for that with a quick seam-up delivery that tailed in towards middle and leg.

Sanjay Manjrekar, with and under whom Tendulkar played a lot of his domestic and international cricket, is of the view that if Tendulkar had the physique – height mostly – to go with his bowling skill, he could have been another Garry Sobers. Both Manjrekar and another Mumbai and India team-mate, Ajit Agarkar, say Tendulkar was more passionate – if that is possible – about his bowling than his batting.

There were three sides to Tendulkar the bowler. The first we saw with our naked eye. The iceman who could come on to bowl with the scores level and deliver a tie, who could come on to bowl with 5 needed in the final over and concede just 3, who could make a nuisance of himself when big partnerships – especially involving Inzamam-ul-Haq – were frustrating India. He was always confident of bowling at a crucial juncture.

In Perth, West Indies were 126 for 9 once, in reply to India's 126 all out, when all four specialist bowlers were bowled out. That's when Tendulkar squeaked: *"Mere ko ley, main nikal deta hoon* [Get me on, I'll get the wicket]." Sure enough he did. When he came on to bowl during the famous last over of the Hero Cup semi-final, someone suggested, "Why don't you bowl offspin to these South Africans?" Until then the world knew only Tendulkar the seamer and the legspinner, but he said, "Okay, I'll bowl offspin. What's there?" Mohammad Azharuddin, the captain, appreciated the confidence but asked him to take the safe route of seam. It worked.

Over longer spells, Tendulkar relied on mind games as much as on his skill. "Always wanted to play with the batsman's mind," Agarkar says. "He tried to look ahead from a batsman's perspective, and a great one at that. Where he will try to score, where he will try to manoeuvre certain balls. And most times he was right. He used to think out of the box a lot of the time."

Tendulkar's list of victims is illustrious. Inzamam was his favourite – eight times in international cricket – followed by Steve Waugh, Brian Lara, Andy Flower and Moin Khan, at four each. His mind games would always surface against Pakistan. In Multan in 2004, he and Rahul Dravid – remember the controversy about the declaration earlier in the match? – talked about getting Moin bowled round the legs because he swept a lot. How the joy on Tendulkar's face papered over the bitterness of the previous days when the dismissal came to pass just so. In one ODI in Kochi, he got them so confused he took out five, bowling legspin from round the stumps. Even specialist legspinners don't have the heart to be pitching more than a foot outside leg regularly in an ODI.

Also in Kochi, in 1998 he took a five-for through pure skill, and stole a game that was lost. The five wickets this time were Waugh, Damien Martyn, Darren Lehmann, Michael Bevan and Tom Moody. When he came on to bowl, Australia needed about 110 in 20 overs with seven wickets in hand. He gave the ball some serious rip that afternoon, after having been dismissed for 8.

By the time Dravid became captain, injuries had restricted Tendulkar the bowler, but Dravid knew when to use Tendulkar. "You wanted to use him when there was a partnership that needed to be broken, and when you wanted to bowl to tailenders," says Dravid. "With partnerships, you felt he brought you a bit of a change, and you thought people might take him a bit lightly, but he was better than that. He had certain skills, and when he got them right, he was as good as specialists. He could spin the ball a long way, especially. He had a variety of tricks. I don't think tailenders read him very well."

Agarkar gives Tendulkar's mind a lot of credit, which brings us to the second aspect of Tendulkar the bowler. The one that was always in the bowler's ear whether he was captain or not. The problem sometimes was that he expected the bowlers to be as good as he himself was as a batsman. It didn't help that he knew the things he demanded could be done – because he had done them himself.

"He just felt you could do everything easily," says Agarkar. "'Why can't you do this?' I wish we could. I wish we were all geniuses like him, but it wasn't the case. With his batting it was amazing. Some days he used to be still, some days his front foot used to go in front, some days his first movement was back, and he could do it all easily. 'Why couldn't you bowl an inswinger?' You try, but sometimes it is unrealistic for normal people to do. I could see the ideas. It was interesting because he thought so far ahead of the batsman, not many would think of that."

It's not that it didn't help. In fact, it helped more than it annoyed. Agarkar says he has worked too many batsmen out with Tendulkar to remember but fondly recalls when they got Mark Waugh out in Sharjah during the desert-storm series. "The night before the final we were having dinner. Bumpers were not allowed then," Agarkar says. "Mark Waugh was opening the innings. Not that he struggled with the bumper, but people targeted him with the short ball. He was more than okay to play it. We had a chat that night. 'Look, I know it is a no-ball, but let's bowl one or two to him and try to get one wide.' I bowled one to him. He tried to pull, it landed in front of fine leg, and he got a couple or something. The next ball was really wide and he nicked it. It looked on TV to be a terrible ball that got a wicket, but it was thought of."

It's Manjrekar who tells the fondest stories of Tendulkar the bowler, of the third variety: the Tendulkar of the nets and of the domestic game. The nets were where Tendulkar expressed himself best. Both Manjrekar and Agarkar fail to remember a day in the nets – before injuries got the better of him – that Tendulkar didn't bowl when he was not batting. You couldn't take the ball out of his hand.

"Whatever he chose to do, technically he was brilliant," Manjrekar says. "When it came to swing bowling, seam-up, offspinners . . . with legspinners he would actually embarrass a lot of specialist bowlers in the nets. I have seen spinners saying there is no turn in the wicket, and when Sachin would bowl, suddenly there would be turn.

"Incredible gift. Just loved bowling. When he was fitter, younger, he would just take the ball and start bowling to everyone. He would create problems. He used to bowl no-balls. About two-three feet. We didn't mind because he gave us good practice. He loved bowling, especially to me, being friends and all that. The rivalry was always there. He was always a cunning bowler."

"He used to swing the ball miles," Agarkar says. "The release. That's what he emphasised when we were bowling. Someone watching probably tells you better. Where your wrist is. When he batted, he watched it so closely it was unbelievable. Every time he got something right he was super-excited about it. He used to bowl to good batters and try to out-think them. That got him quite excited. That got him more excited about his bowling than his batting. He hit sixes, he was okay with it."

Agarkar remembers that fast bowler's attitude from the old days. "I remember when I joined Shardashram [the school both of them went to] he was passing out so I never really played against him, but I had heard he loved bouncing people. That probably got him into bowling. Those are the stories I heard about him, that he loved to hit people."

Agarkar also believes Tendulkar's bowling played a big part in his staying fit over such a long career. "To bowl an hour, an hour and a half, two hours, in the nets every day . . . he didn't much love running or anything. Just the batting and the bowling aspect of it. He was so match-fit. The bowling to a large extent over the first ten, 12, 14 years of his career helped his fitness."

In domestic cricket Manjrekar would often use Tendulkar. "When I was captain, I would never give him more than two–three overs. Because he seemed to get a little bored if he didn't get a wicket. For me, his first over was about getting the rhythm. Most dangerous overs were the second and third. If he got wickets, he was fine. If he didn't, he would try everything. Because he didn't bowl as regularly as normal bowlers, the odd loose ball would come in.

"Didn't have the discipline to bowl 12 overs outside off. I tried to get him to do that sometimes – just bowl, this is a flat wicket, don't do anything – but after a couple of good-line deliveries, he would try the inswinger. It was against his nature."

Once, though, Tendulkar surprised everyone. It was a Duleep Trophy game against Central Zone on a dry Chennai pitch when West Zone realised they would need an offspinner and they didn't have one in the squad. Up comes Tendulkar and tells the captain, Ravi Shastri: "I will bowl offspin." Neither Shastri nor Manjrekar had seen him bowl offspin until then. Fondly Manjrekar recalls, "And the idiot ended up bowling 25–30 overs. First over, like a typical specialist spinner he wanted silly point, short leg. He did his job. First time ever I saw him bowl offspin." Tendulkar's figures: 21-9-35-0 and 11-1-49-1.

Possibly, then, Manjrekar's theory is correct. Had Tendulkar had the physique and the easier schedule, he might well have been a Sobers. He would have had to bring the rigour of his batting to bowling, though. A lot of bowling is about the mundane. And Tendulkar the bowler didn't do the mundane. "This trait of his could be seen when he gave bowling-machine practice too," Manjrekar says. "When he finished batting, he loved giving bowling-machine practice. Typically I would tell him I want short of a length outside off. He would set it, and I would say, 'Okay that is perfect, keep bowling there.' He would bowl four–five balls there, and quietly when I was not looking . . ."

Times changed. Injuries took their toll, including to the toes, which you need to pivot on when bowling. Tendulkar's batting became more meticulous than instinctive, and it needed more work.

Agarkar feels Tendulkar didn't remove the pads even after he was done with his batting because if he did he would not be able to stop himself from bowling and aggravating something. Manjrekar has always known bowling to be such an integral part of Tendulkar's cricketing life that he was almost shocked at learning Tendulkar didn't bowl in the nets any more, towards the end of his career. "So what does he do after his net?" he asks. "Takes throwdowns," you tell him.

Oh well. There are prices to pay.

Sidharth Monga *is an assistant editor at ESPNcricinfo*

THE MAN WHO MADE YOU PLAN
FOR WEEKS

ALLAN DONALD

The Cape Town Test, 1997. We had won the Durban match, bundling out India for 66 in the second innings. Before the second Test we discussed Tendulkar in the team meeting. We said that the best way to tackle him was to bowl a bit fuller, with more of an angle at the crease, because we wanted to attack the stumps a bit more. But we had to be precise in terms of our execution.

In Cape Town, Tendulkar started by missing a few balls. I remember there was even an inside edge that beat Dave Richardson behind the stumps. The pitch was not as fast as the one in Durban, and in the end it turned out to be an absolute belter. He might have made a double-century if not for an unbelievable catch by Adam Bacher on the fence. So that was a plan we did not execute very well!

We were a little bit too greedy, trying to knock him over, and we lost our lengths and lines. And he switched gears as well. He played some shots I never saw him play before. One shot that stood out came after tea. It was against a back-of-a-length delivery. He just stood up and hit the ball on the top of the bounce through extra cover for four. It was just an unreal shot, and it was an example of the challenge Tendulkar posed.

My first encounter with him was during the short trip to India in 1991 – our first international after readmission, the ODI at Eden Gardens. I had seen pictures of him in the *Cricketer* and *Wisden Cricket Monthly* magazines. We missed a run-out when he was on very few. Richard Snell dropped the ball and missed the chance. I ended up with a five-for, but Tendulkar made sure his innings would hurt us. We lost the match by three wickets.

We knew then we would need to keep an eye on this kid, who most of the cricket world was talking about. Fast bowlers have this memory bank, where we log that kind of performer: you know that the next time you play against him, you're going to have to be on the money.

Technically, Tendulkar is the best I have ever seen. He had balance, he had flair, he had all the shots in the book. Through my career, at least through my best years, I saw Tendulkar grow from a boy into a man and an amazing batsman.

His technique was so pure; when Gary Kirsten joined South Africa as coach after his India stint, he pointed out that Tendulkar could adjust his technique to any surface. That is a major thing for anyone to be able to do. For example, he opened himself up on pitches with extreme bounce. And that is how he could score hundreds anywhere in the world, making subtle technical changes.

His balance was the best among the top-order players I had the opportunity to bowl to. You had to be spot-on in terms of your length, not to mention your lines. If your length was slightly off, he would take advantage. He was a short guy, just sat in the crease, and he was such a good back-foot player, with quick feet. That was the difference between him and the rest: Tendulkar could adjust.

Brian Lara had amazing flair. When he was on, he was an absolute genius. He could play shots to good deliveries, similar to Tendulkar. But Tendulkar did it without any fuss. Lara had a huge trigger movement across the crease. Tendulkar was uncomplicated – he had subtle things that bowlers never really picked up. And that is part of what Gary meant about him being able to adjust his technique.

If you ask Tendulkar how many coaches made a difference to his career, he probably might point out one or two. Mostly he worked things out himself. That is the greatest attribute he will ever have: he made sure he figured it out himself, and he did not rely on other people to do it; and how quickly he did that was amazing.

You didn't work Tendulkar out in days. You had to plan for him weeks in advance. Otherwise, he could frustrate bowlers. When Hansie Cronje was the captain, our thinking was that the first 20 balls we had to make Tendulkar play every single one, even if we leaked runs. We also decided that we were not going to test him with the short ball early on: it was an easy way for him to get himself into his innings. We wanted to make him sweat as much as we could.

I think that plan usually worked pretty well. At Eden Gardens during the 1996 Test, I bowled him with a ball that just sort of nipped back a little bit. The length was spot-on. He sat back in the crease. Not just him, even Lara, when he got out early in his innings, was lbw or bowled, because he sat back expecting us to bowl short.

Tendulkar was never really a guy to get a big stride when he first came in. He was happy to sit back and defend on the back foot. Yes, he had quick feet, but the majority of the time he was comfortable just sitting in the crease and letting balls go by, either on bounce or on length.

You know that when there is a batsman you as a bowler haven't had success against over the years, he has some sort of a hold over you, and you will feel that pressure. Take Dale Steyn. When Dale spoke about Sachin, he would get really grumpy. When a Lara or a Tendulkar walks up to the crease, you tense a little bit. You get a little apprehensive, because you know they will fight fire with fire. You know you have to be brave and put your head on the block for the team and give it everything, and if it does not come off in the first few overs, so be it.

I know Dale said that he just could not wait to bowl to Tendulkar and run over him. When he bowled to him, he changed gears from three to six and his speed went up from 140kph to 148. Tendulkar brings the best out of his opponent. That shows the greatness of this man, that he had a hold over so many of the best fast bowlers of his time.

It was the same with me. I always said to Hansie: when Tendulkar comes in, I want to have a crack; if I am in the sixth over of my first spell and someone gets a wicket and he comes in, just give me some more overs. The thinking was that psychologically Tendulkar would respect the No. 1 fast bowler in a team. And that got my tail up. It inspired me when he walked to the crease. I felt that I had a good chance. I always did my homework against him, and I thought it was a matter of execution.

When a great batsman is in form, that is when you get really challenged as a fast bowler. Tendulkar turned that bowler's ego to his advantage. We saw it dozens of times, when he counterpunched really well. He had that ability, when the bowler was at his best and in fantastic rhythm and bowling at his optimum pace, to come in and change the state of the game, to hit you off your line, get you out of the attack. He was careful, but if you offered him half a chance he would make you pay. With Tendulkar you were always working with fine, fine margins.

Once I was discussing him with Curtly Ambrose and Courtney Walsh. They thought you had to keep it full and angle it back in, to make sure Tendulkar played. What they kept harping on about was the length: keep it on the fourth-stump line, hitting off stump, because if you slid the ball towards the leg side he could work it away well. So if there were two seamers on, you had to target his stumps, make him play as many balls as possible. You didn't want him to leave the ball. If you made him play, you had a chance of getting him caught behind.

My favourite Tendulkar stroke was the straight drive. Nothing annoyed me more than seeing him lean on it – he did not hit it. I remember two back-to-back boundaries he hit in the final Test match at the Wanderers in the 1996 series. There was no big stride; he just leaned on it and it beat me.

I've always liked Tendulkar for his humility, his respect for the game, his respect for his team-mates, his respect for the opposition. He would never take his position in the team for granted. I will give you an example of the difference between Tendulkar and others. We played West Indies at home in 1998. Hansie had made it clear he wanted bouncy, hard, green wickets. We played five seamers then. What I found was that Lara did not respect the way his team was. He was the one player who could have made a massive difference, but as good as he was, he was going to play his way, not for the team. That was the only way he knew – to attack.

Tendulkar had the knack of attacking, being respectful when necessary, reading the situation better than anyone else, and then kicking on from there. That is what set him apart, besides his ability to make big scores on any deck. And he could keep his partner going, make him believe they could get through a sticky situation. As much of a genius as he was, Lara would think: if I am going to go down, I am going to go down firing.

Another challenge Tendulkar posed to bowlers, especially in his final decade, was when he cut out some of strokes, like the pull, which he stopped playing after his tennis-elbow problem. For him to decide that it was hurting him and he was going to cut out a few strokes and go under bouncers was great thinking. That is demoralising to the bowler: if the batsman keeps going under short balls, it is a waste of time for you. Such moves alter your thinking and tactics as a bowler.

I have always judged professional athletes on what they are as people, and it is the same for Sachin Tendulkar. He always played with a smile. He played hard, he played fair, and he kept the same demeanour at all times. He never went over the top. He always kept the same face.

Allan Donald took the wicket of Sachin Tendulkar ten times in the five Tests and five ODIs in which both figured

WHEN HE WAS TOLSTOY

SURESH MENON

After the loss of the French port Calais in the 16th century, the queen of England, Mary I ("Bloody Mary"), said, "When I am dead, you will find Calais written on my heart." It is not difficult to imagine Sachin Tendulkar saying something similar about Chennai 1999, where despite one of his best centuries, India lost a Test match to Pakistan. And Sachin himself, quite undeservedly, picked up a reputation for – to quote those who speak in absolutes – "never being able to see India through to a victory".

Heroic failures are the stuff of sporting legend. Sunil Gavaskar's incredible 96 on a turner in Bangalore couldn't prevent a loss to Pakistan by 16 runs in an earlier series. Before India began to win with any degree of consistency, the heroic failure was compensation for their supporters. Tiger Pataudi's 148 in Leeds, Vinoo Mankad's innings of 72 and 184 and bag of five wickets at Lord's, Hazare's 116 and 145 in Adelaide, Polly Umrigar's 172 not out in Trinidad, had all come in losing causes. Defeat was the norm, victory merely an unexpected bump in the cosmic order.

Yet it says something for the altered mindset of the Indian fan that while the defeats in the pre-Tendulkar days were accepted as the standard and any crumbs of consolation taken gratefully, the loss in Chennai was seen as being a personal betrayal by Tendulkar.

The little man from Mumbai had played the major role in changing the mindset. In a decade of international cricket, Tendulkar had managed to make the fan feel that winning was the default result for India, at least at home. In a year, Sourav Ganguly would take over as captain and extend that philosophy across the world, as India began to win Tests and series abroad more often.

The nation recovered faster from that loss (by 12 runs) in Chennai than Tendulkar apparently did. Years later he told an interviewer, "I think my knock of 136 against Pakistan at Chennai was my toughest. The wicket was deteriorating and the quality of the bowling attack was outstanding."

A rush of blood with India just 17 runs from victory saw Tendulkar swat at Saqlain Mushtaq outside the leg stump and lead-edge a catch to Wasim Akram. As three more wickets – those of the Karnataka bowlers Anil Kumble, Sunil Joshi and Javagal Srinath – fell for four runs, Tendulkar's early repair job was forgotten. He had taken India from 82 for 5 to 218, adding 136 with wicketkeeper Nayan Mongia. At 254 for 6 chasing 271, India were nearly home when disaster struck.

Perhaps great innings are like great novels, containing a wider range of emotions and invoking greater responses than the average good innings or novel. Love, disappointment, betrayal, reconciliation, temptation, anger, frustration, elation, conflict resolution are elements of both. Tendulkar played a Tolstoyan innings in Chennai that day, ending in suicide in the manner of Anna Karenina.

It is possible that stroke for stroke, back spasm for back spasm,

Tendulkar's innings of nearly seven hours was the best he played. The context alone would justify that claim. India versus Pakistan. Chasing a target before a packed stadium. Wasim Akram, Waqar Younis, Saqlain Mushtaq and Shahid Afridi bowling. And then the gradual change in texture as the innings is lifted from a deep hole and placed on the road to victory. And that's before considering the physical pressure, as Tendulkar's back threatened to give way; singles were difficult to run, so he hit boundaries in a cricketing version of feasting on cakes when bread is not available.

Yet, great innings sometimes carry with them the seeds of their own future fall from grace. And that was the tragedy of Tendulkar's 136. Had India won, it would have been merely the inevitable conclusion to such an effort. But they lost, and in the illogical manner fans and critics have of attacking the most visible target, it was agreed that Tendulkar was responsible.

In sport, of course, one team's tragedy is another team's success. And, importantly, you get another chance. Tendulkar had to wait for a decade before redemption. That came with another century, at the same venue, this time unbeaten and against England. Set 387 to win, India won by six wickets, Tendulkar top-scoring and laying a personal devil to rest. The batsman had the honesty to confess later that visions of the earlier chase had risen in his mind. "I did think of it," he said matter-of-factly.

The Pakistan tour ran into trouble from the start when the Shiv Sena, the Hindu right-wing allies of the Hindu right-wing Bharatiya Janata Party which was in power dug up the wicket at the Feroz Shah Kotla in Delhi, where the first Test was scheduled. The match was moved to Chennai, amidst a veiled threat from the BJP that it wouldn't mind losing a political ally and dropping the Shiv Sena if it "continued to embarrass the government". Despite a half-hearted effort before the Chennai Test, it was clear that the Shiv Sena's writ did not run in South India.

Pakistan's 238 in the first innings of the Chennai Test was given greater respectability by India's reply of 254. A smashing 141 by Shahid Afridi in the second innings (21 boundaries, three sixes) took Pakistan to 286 and set India a target of 271. As so often happened throughout his career, when Tendulkar scored runs, he tended to make everything else appear a bit ordinary. In a Test where neither team passed 300, the bowlers obviously called the shots. There was Saqlain's 10 for 187, Venkatesh Prasad's spell of five wickets without conceding a run en route to claiming six for 33, and in the first innings of the match Anil Kumble's 6 for 70.

Yet on day four, which began with India scoring just 40 in 21 overs, all that was pushed into the background. Tendulkar's 50 came in a team total of 93, after which he began to open out. A paddle sweep off Saqlain and a pull off the same bowler to a delivery that wasn't really short proclaimed his form and intention. At 160 for 5, wicketkeeper Moin Khan not only dropped Tendulkar but also failed to stump him as he stepped out. Tendulkar showed his gratitude for this double by sweeping and pulling for boundaries. Waqar Younis with the new ball was sent screaming past extra cover, and a perfectly respectable delivery from Wasim Akram was pushed for a gorgeous straight drive to the sightscreen.

It was an innings that combined caution and abandon to a marvellous degree. An innings of remarkable restraint and delicious boundaries (Tendulkar hit 18 in all) that fell just short of a happy ending for the spectators in Chennai. But it had succeeded in briefly erasing the historical baggage between the two countries as well as the boorishness of those who had dug up the wicket in Delhi.

In a gesture that was spontaneous and inspiring, the crowd rose as one man to give the visitors from Pakistan an ovation the echoes of which continue to reverberate today. Akram responded by leading his team on a lap of honour that had a message for the politicians of the two countries if they cared to read it. Akram said later it was his favourite cricketing moment.

Great innings do that. They appeal to that part of ourselves that makes us great.

Suresh Menon *is editor,* Wisden India Almanack

DAVID TO A THOUSAND GOLIATHS

MARK NICHOLAS

For the past two decades, the fall of the second Indian wicket has created an unparalleled frenzy. This comes first from the crowds, who at once animate a mild sadness at the departure of one man and an unbridled joy at the entrance of another. In homes all around India, families alert one another to the moment and gather close to their television screens.

At the ground itself, the cameramen have switched their focus from the pitch to the Indian dressing room, where a small, strong man is reacting. Still sitting, he pulls on his arm guard and rubs his hands as if drying the palms. Before standing he puts the first batting glove on his right hand and then, as he rises to his feet, carefully positions a protective helmet upon his head, eases the strap under his chin and tucks almost 3lbs of bat under his left arm. As he begins the walk to the middle he pulls on his right batting glove. He is now ready for the calling that has been his life.

This article was first published on ESPNcricinfo in November 2013

Sachin Tendulkar is 40 years old. He first played for India when he was 16. He made a hundred for India when he was 17 years and 112 days old. He has made 51 Test hundreds and 49 one-day hundreds. He, along with his captain, MS Dhoni, and a couple of film stars, is the best known person in a land of more than a billion people. But even his recognisable peers do not carry the hopes of that nation each minute of every day. Tendulkar is a victim of himself and so powerful is the impact that adoring followers hyperventilate around him.

He is unarguably a great cricketer and a near-perfect ambassador for modern, progressive India. He likes popular music, clothes and cars, and he has worn jewellery. Yet he retains an old-fashioned perspective. His wife is a doctor, his children like cricket. The family takes holidays behind walls or disappears into cities on faraway continents. He is unfailingly polite, angelic almost. He is as much a part of the fabric of India as the Red Fort, the Pink Palace, the Maharajas, and Diwali. Indians like cricket but they truly love Sachin Tendulkar. He has been David to a thousand Goliaths. He may, or may not, be the second-finest batsman to have played the game. To many Indians, he is a god. Or God. And now he retires from the game that has defined him.

Twenty yards from the pavilion, he stretches his back and rocks his torso from side to side. He rolls his shoulders and swings his arms before linking his bat to his body with a series of left- and right-handed movements. He rehearses some strokes. The bat looks too big for his body. It always has. He twists his mouth and contorts his jaw. He squints and then opens his eyes, wide as they will, to the brighter light. He looks to the heavens, as if acknowledging a friend.

The television director brings the statistics of a life's work to the screen: 15,837 runs at an average of 53.87; 67 fifties, 51 hundreds; highest score 248 not out. The commentators talk lavishly of his achievements and of the legacy. The excitement is at fever pitch. The spectators stand and roar their appreciation. The airwaves fizz. The viewer feels a shiver through his spine.

Tendulkar takes guard, marking a line in the crease with a forceful rip of the spike in his shoe. I think back to Karachi in 1989 when he did this for the first time in a Test match. The attack against him was Imran Khan, Wasim Akram, Waqar Younis and Abdul Qadir. He may have never faced better. He looked boyish then because he was a boy. He still appears boyish now. In those days he had set records at school, club and state level. India wondered if the kid could cut it. Now they know. In one Test of that first series, Waqar floored him with a short ball. Tendulkar refused the idea that he should retire hurt, dusted himself down and made a fifty. He may never have achieved more. But he did.

Now, in Kolkata, in the only innings of his 199th Test, he looks around the field. Is this for fielders or for gaps? He blocks convincingly off front foot and back. Then he drives Shane Shillingford through the gap at midwicket. The ball rolls over the boundary rope. Two balls later, he hits the same gap. The ball speeds over the same rope. The crowd goes apoplectic. He fiddles with his thigh pad, pushing one way and the other and then he squats, stretching out his groin, before repositioning his protective box and settling deliberately back into his stance. These fidgets, these idiosyncrasies, have never changed. Ball after ball, match after match, year after year they have remained the same. *Plus ça change, plus c'est la même chose.*

I think back to the catch at Lord's on his first tour of England. An athletic, running effort that hinted at real talent. I think of his match-saving hundred in the next Test, at Old Trafford, when, aged 17 years and 112 days, remember, he appeared to marshal his senior partner, Manoj Prabhakar. I think of the way in which hard-bitten Yorkshire embraced him as their first overseas cricketer. I think of his smile and of the sense of fun that burst from his youth.

Oddly, this makes me think of his bowling, which always looked like a release from the strain of true responsibility. I think that I remember him saving a match with the ball. I look it up. He did, using a quirky mix of swing and spin to restrict South Africa to just three runs when six were needed from the last over of the Hero Cup semi-final in Kolkata. Mohammad Azharuddin was his captain then.

Tendulkar plays quietly forward. It is an aesthetically pleasing push/punch. His hands hold the lower part of the bat handle, revealing the butt at the top of the grip to be covered by a different colour of rubber. In the push/punch the blade of the bat is exactly straight, showing its whole face to the bowler. It was ever thus.

He went to that first hundred at Old Trafford with a wonderful boundary past mid-off from his back foot. It is about the most difficult stroke there is and it is a Tendulkar trademark. That, the straight drive that misses leg stump at the non-striker's end, and any number of wristy leg-side moments that draw intakes of breath from opponent and audience alike. Then I think about the slaughter of Shoaib Akhtar during the 2003 World Cup in South Africa and the almost primeval approach to that innings that set him apart. Even Virender Sehwag has not played an innings of such brutality. Tendulkar has said that he was once like Sehwag. But we all run out of years.

He dips at the knees in that squat once more, shuffles his box and settles into another perfect stance. Side-on, eyes level, bat tucked behind the right foot. He watches the ball closely of course, a prerequisite of good batting, and has uncanny balance in all his strokes. I think of the systematic attack on Shane Warne and the Australians in India in 1998 – pre-planned, well practised and brilliantly executed – a performance of which Ian Healy said: "Bradman must have been good if he was better than him." I think of the double-hundred in Sydney – a considered and controlled performance that came from a chronic elbow injury and the desire to succeed in spite of it.

A tweet from Brian Lara flashes across the screen: "The only man

I would pay money to watch," says Lara of his old adversary. Was one a better batsman than the other? Perhaps the West Indian was the greater match-winner, the Indian the greater technician. I think of two innings at the Kensington Oval in Barbados. Lara's unbeaten 153 to outwit the Australians and Tendulkar's 92 on a really bad pitch, a dangerous pitch (one of the few on that fine field) against Curtly Ambrose and Ian Bishop. The most revered right- and left-handed batsmen of the age. I imagine them at the wicket together, a kind of nirvana.

The age of Tendulkar has seen five unarguably great batsmen. Lara had an arrogance, Viv Richards an aura. For Jacques Kallis' statesman think Ricky Ponting's streetfighter. But there is no single thing that can be attached to Tendulkar. You cannot say he has a style, and he reveals little of his personality. Perhaps this is a conscious approach, designed to give the opponent no clue. Summarising his emotion is impossible, he doesn't do drama. If anything, there is a sense of vulnerability that makes him attractive. We still see him as the underdog, and this a man who has become a national symbol of optimism and pride.

Now he is in his stance again. Shillingford rolls in and delivers the doosra. It beats our hero on the back foot and hits him around the upper thigh. Shillingford and other West Indians appeal ferociously. The English umpire, Nigel Llong, gives it out. Ye gods, Nigel, what were you thinking!

My mind goes to Cape Town in 1997 and the post-lunch partnership with Azharuddin. I have never seen such batting. Nor, one suspects, had President Mandela, who had come to say hello. Of the first 12 balls of the session, 11 were hit for four or six. In 40 overs they put on 222. It took a remarkable catch to finish Tendulkar on 169. I was as disappointed then with the man who took the catch, Adam Bacher, as I am now with Umpire Llong.

I stay in a Cape Town sort of mind for the innings less than three years back, when a spiteful pitch encouraged Dale Steyn and company. I asked Sachin about this and he rated the 146 that day among the best. I asked if the standard of bowling had diminished during his time in the game and he thought it had changed in method rather than quality. The bowlers defend better than earlier, thus his own game has retreated from aspiration towards attrition.

I recall Perth in 1992, when the free-thinking 18-year-old model flayed Merv Hughes and Craig McDermott on the world's fastest pitch. Incidentally, he thinks Steyn is as good as anyone, which, given a list that begins with Imran and incorporates Malcolm Marshall, Wasim Akram and Allan Donald, is high praise.

The crowd reacts with shock to Llong's decision. Tendulkar appears resigned to the moment, as if he has seen it before. The DRS would have saved him but he and his colleagues have not supported it. With typical dignity he begins the long walk to the dressing room. The crowd rise to applaud, more than aware of the dying light. It is hard to be sure when greatness slipped away from Tendulkar but the World Cup win in 2011 seemed to provide the perfect final chapter to an extraordinary story. He chose to write an epilogue but it has lacked the possibilities of the previous narrative.

Suddenly he has gone from view. As he will next Monday, for ever. A piece of us goes with him. I have seen, either live or on television, every one of the innings remembered here and many more. Each of his journeys to the wicket has led to a nervous excitement and each performance has given immense pleasure. India's most precious son has been a gift to the rest of the world too.

Mark Nicholas, the former Hampshire captain, presents the cricket on Channel 9 in Australia and Channel 5 in the UK

A BIT OF HIM IN FOREIGN FIELDS

DAVID HOPPS

To describe Sachin Tendulkar as Yorkshire's first overseas player sounds little more than an insignificant footnote in a distinguished career, but it does not quite capture the scale of his challenge when he arrived, still a slip of a lad at 19, to play a season of county cricket in England.

Transformation was in the air. Yorkshire's decision to abandon their reliance on players born within the county boundaries had finally arrived after years of tumult. That only Yorkshire folk could play for Yorkshire remained for the traditionalists – a vocal and sizeable minority – a stubborn article of faith, a symbol of purity, of not taking the easy way out but producing your own talent, a defiant expression of commitment to the good of the game.

But the county was in decline: since its last Championship title in 1969, when the careers of Brian Close, Raymond Illingworth and Fred Trueman were passing into history, Yorkshire had finished in the top six only four times in 23 years. There had to be change, but for many that change was embraced grudgingly.

This was a county languishing in its memories, proud of its past but unable to promise much of a future: debilitated by internecine strife and increasingly impoverished. As the years passed, Yorkshire's home-grown stance began to sound uncomfortably close to racism. There were many observing from afar on the *Guardian*, where I had been recently employed, promulgating the same assumptions. An attack on Yorkshire's home-grown policy was a convenient mind cleanser for many of a liberal disposition.

But the policy was not based on racism; if it had been, Tendulkar would never have prospered. Individual prejudice, of course, was always easy to find. But the no-outsiders policy drew strength from Yorkshire cricket's stubborn belief in its great history, in the northern emphasis on self-reliance, on not taking the easy option, on nurturing your own, on preferring tradition to change, however illogical that tradition might have become.

But those traditions were under assault. The Yorkshire leagues, themselves heavily reliant on overseas imports, were no longer producing enough players. The world was also a more mobile place. Finally, the recognition that a generation of failure could eventually bring about bankruptcy forced a change. Yorkshire's committee voted 18-1 in favour of employing an overseas player, although Fred Trueman, refusing to yield until the end, called it "a bloody disgrace".

It felt no sort of place for an Indian teenager, even one as evidently accomplished as Tendulkar. By then he was already 16 Tests into his career, his average already top side of 40, a wonderful, counter-attacking 148 not out in Sydney in the New Year Test of 1992 providing confirmation of his extraordinary talent. But this was a county that had not long before emerged from years embroiled in the Geoffrey Boycott Wars, a rancorous power struggle centred upon one individual, a place where a lapse back into Machiavellian politics, mistrust and blame was always possible if the wrong overseas player was chosen.

But the right overseas player was alighted upon – with Boycott a prime advocate. Tendulkar quietly guided Yorkshire into a new, saner era. He did not particularly achieve that by weight of runs, although he made a highly respectable 1070 first-class runs at 46.52. Neither did he make any eloquent speeches, although to his credit he was impeccably researched. As his Yorkshire captain, the former England batsman Martyn Moxon, reminisced: "He knew more about Yorkshire's history than most of us did."

In those days, covering Yorkshire was a year-round job: cricket and politics in the summer, just the politics in the winter. One journalist claimed that a night never passed without a dead-of-night phone call from somebody with an axe to grind. I presume he was exaggerating – even in Yorkshire there would be peace on Christmas Day, surely – but goodwill would not automatically be granted to an imported cricketer, no matter how talented he might prove to be.

Yet Tendulkar's fond memories of Yorkshire survived an entire career. That much was evident when Yorkshire qualified for the Champions League in 2012 and faced Mumbai Indians, Tendulkar among them, in Cape Town. The match was eventually abandoned because of rain, just another forgettable game on cricket's treadmill, but when Moxon introduced the Yorkshire players to Tendulkar, fond memories were exchanged. "He was still the same Sachin after all these years – he remained very humble," Moxon said. Nobody who knew him had doubted that it would be any other way. To be seemingly impervious to fame has been one of Tendulkar's great lessons.

Moxon had argued for Yorkshire's first overseas player to be a fast bowler. His view carried impeccable cricketing logic because it was in quick bowling that Yorkshire's own resources had so often been found wanting, especially after the switch to covered wickets, which reduced the effectiveness of Yorkshire's medium-fast seamers.

Initially, the county accepted Moxon's logic by signing the Australian quick Craig McDermott, only for McDermott to withdraw with a groin injury barely a month before the start of the season.

What followed was back-of-an-envelope stuff. On Boycott's suggestion, Yorkshire approached Solly Adam, who was a great provider of overseas players to the local leagues: more than 400, all told. Adam, who also ran a sports shop, had come a long way since he arrived in England from North India in 1963, at a similar age to Tendulkar when he made his debut, with £3 in his pocket. He bought a petrol pump in 1972, stayed open all hours, and eventually, as his business improved, explored his first love and began pumping cricketers into the local economy rather than petrol.

Agents were not so common in cricket in those days and Adam's involvement was voluntary. He loved his connection with the cricketers as they ate at his home, then, homesickness dispelled, made runs on a Saturday. He loved watching them progress into international players and knew if he ever needed a ticket for an international, no matter how much in demand that match might be, he would have a grateful benefactor able to return the favour. Adam suggested that Yorkshire sign Tendulkar, as he had just signed his school friend Vinod Kambli to play in the Bradford League. He was confident he could persuade Tendulkar that it would be a valuable experience.

Tendulkar was playing Test cricket at the time in Australia and told Adam to give him a week or so to think about it, as he wanted to speak to his parents about the move. Yorkshire, resistant to overseas players for so long, were by now desperate for him to say yes. About a week later, he did just that.

Adam protected and guided him that summer as if he was his own son. He was in the crowd for Tendulkar's farewell Test, in Mumbai. Before he went he told me: "It will be my last glimpse of genius. I'm 68 now and I won't see another Sachin as long as I live. He was put on to this earth to play cricket and to entertain the people."

In ten Tests in the West Indies, Tendulkar scored only one century, but fans there loved him almost as much as they did Sunil Gavaskar in his day.

You know the man is coming out to bat when the noise levels increase tenfold. Fans in Bangalore make themselves heard during the 2001 Test against England.

Can't get up close to the real thing? Madame Tussauds a trip too far even? Fear not, substitutes are always available.

If you're the owner of a small business in India, you could do worse to get customers into your shop than hold up a picture of Tendulkar at the entrance.

Everyone's a phone-camera-wielding fan when Tendulkar's around. Security personnel not excepted.

An appeal for good exam results? A prayer for an India win? No matter what the cause, lay your petition before the altar of Tendulkar.

Never mind that he never did manage to make a hundred at Lord's, the egg-and-bacon tie brigade at the MCC love him too.

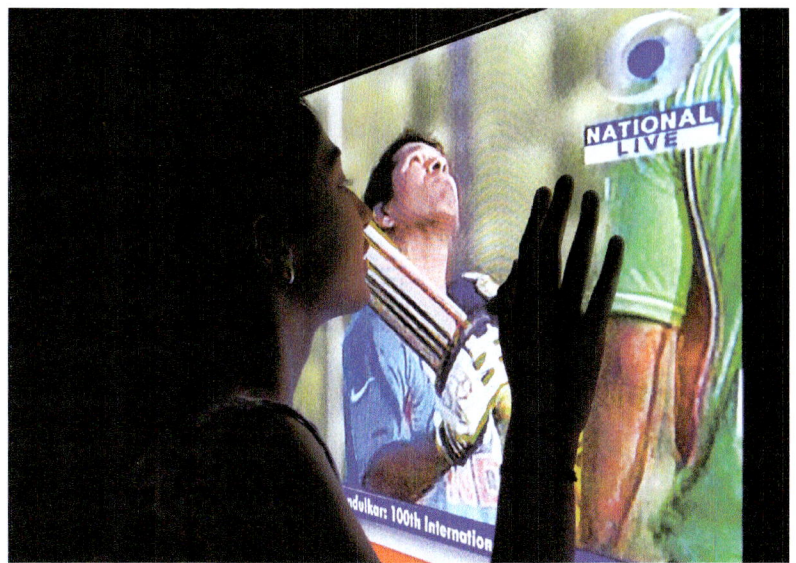

Tendulkar's success helped cricket in India expand its reach to include new fans. It brought a whole generation of followers to the game in the 1990s.

You can't be a Tendulkar fan without wearing your passion on your person. The little master was a merchandiser's dream.

We've all heard the one about cricket being a religion in India and Tendulkar god. Occasionally, devotees get opportunities to worship in the presence of their deity.

Australia has been the scene of some of Tendulkar's most famous innings: Sydney and Perth in 1992, Melbourne in 1999, and Sydney in 2004.

It's not just commoners who fall under the Tendulkar spell, as this picture from a reception at Buckingham Palace in 1999 shows.

There are fans and then there's Sudhir Gautam, the Indian team's unofficial mascot, who has made a vocation out of Tendulkar worship.

If so, perhaps he was also put on the earth to sort out Yorkshire's mental confusion. Supporters and players all adored him. He was only 19, and his batting approach remained developmental, but he was polite and dignified. Yorkshire could not afford any bad publicity and Tendulkar suited their public-relations need ideally.

More to the point, Tendulkar was willing to fit in. Yorkshire might have signed an overseas player, but they were not about to change the habits of a lifetime. If there was any social adjusting to be done, it would be Tendulkar who would have to do it. They adopted him as an honorary Tyke, and because he was so young and easy-going and valued the experience, he had no qualms about it. That much was evident at his introductory media conference, when he patiently posed for a stereotypical photo in Yorkshire flat cap, brandishing a pint of Tetley bitter, the sponsors' local brew. It was an early lesson for him in the hackneyed nature of most advertising campaigns.

It is doubtful whether it ever crossed his mind that, if Yorkshire wanted to attract a more multiracial audience, there were many more people of Pakistani origin in the county than Indian, and that being so, brandishing pints of bitter was not the best way to attract them. But the picture was not intended to communicate Yorkshire's open-door policy to its minority ethnic population; it was intended to communicate to Yorkshire cricket followers that Tendulkar was an honorary Yorkshireman, and that if revolution really was in the air, it would be a painless one.

On the pitch, nothing much changed. Yorkshire still struggled to bowl sides out and finished third from bottom, but if Tendulkar failed to create an immediate miracle, he left something longer-lasting: an imprint of professionalism, a tacit message to Yorkshire that if they so valued the talents of their own stock then a mature attitude, a desire to learn, a basic belief in the unity of the dressing room should be part of the deal. The lesson Tendulkar left behind was one of standards. His team-mates only had to watch him strap on his pads – pads that always seemed slightly too bulky for him – to recognise his maturity, to be taken by the way he went about things and his determination to succeed.

Even when he was 19, Yorkshire's players loved to bat with him. Moxon had won the last of his ten England caps by then, and his 30th birthday was behind him, but he relished it as much as anybody. When asked for his strongest memory of Tendulkar at the crease he chooses the way he played Phil Tufnell, the England left-arm spinner, on a turning wicket against Middlesex at the outground in Uxbridge.

Tendulkar repeatedly struck Tufnell over mid-on. Against a left-arm spinner it was not the done thing in county cricket at the time: the MCC coaching manual didn't approve of hitting against the spin. When Moxon began his coaching career, at both Durham and Yorkshire, memories of that stayed with him and he was an enthusiastic convert to the Indian belief that he must learn how to hit into the spin. Tendulkar was, by his example, already challenging all Yorkshire's opinions on batting.

The genius of Tendulkar's appointment, for Yorkshire, came in his youth, his placid nature, his overwhelming sense of decency. He went about his business in a way that showed a dedication to his profession, a desire for self-improvement and an even-handed approach to life. He reminded Yorkshire that success required diligence. He was wary of celebrity even then and asked for his name to be removed from his sponsored car so he would not draw much attention to himself.

Yorkshire supporters smiled benignly upon him from the outset. Even the county's affronted cricketing historians, who clung to the home-grown rule more keenly than most, felt obliged to tone down their opposition. When he completed his final game for Yorkshire, a Championship match against Nottinghamshire in the coastal town of Scarborough, the standing ovation was inevitable. The Yorkshire public had come to love him.

The borders breached, Tendulkar paved the way for others.

Michael Vaughan, for one, was grateful that his life was simplified. Vaughan was schooled in Yorkshire, his potential first spotted while he played on the outfield as a child during the tea interval when Yorkshire visited his home city of Manchester. But Vaughan, then in Yorkshire's 2nd XI, had been born across the border in Lancashire. He had reason to be grateful when he made his Yorkshire debut without a whiff of opposition the following summer. He went on to lead England and now sits on the Yorkshire board.

There were others, too. When Adil Rashid, Bradford-born, became the first player of Pakistani origin to play Championship cricket for Yorkshire (Ajmal Shahzad, of similar stock, had made a one-day debut the previous summer), the Scarborough crowd was bathed in smiles as his legspin won the game by bowling out Warwickshire at Scarborough. I drove across the Wolds with my son that day in the hope of witnessing a historic moment and I did.

These days, Yorkshire's production line of young players is hailed by the ECB as second to none. Multi-ethnic sides are taken for granted, overseas players come and go, and occasional signings are made from beyond the Broad Acres. It is now appreciated that Yorkshire's strength is drawn not from border controls but from maintaining their own standards.

It was a lesson taught to them, taught quietly but taught well, by a young man from Mumbai. Who knows, it might be an exaggeration to suggest that deep down a little bit of Yorkshire remains in Sachin Tendulkar, but a little bit of Sachin remains in the history of Yorkshire cricket and it is all the better for that.

David Hopps is ESPNcricinfo's UK editor

YOUNG, POISED, CLOSE TO PERFECT

GREG CHAPPELL

Ring the bells that still can ring
Forget your perfect offering
There is a crack in everything
That's how the light gets in

—Leonard Cohen, "Anthem"

A good innings from the young Tendulkar was as close as anything that I have seen to cricket perfection.

One that encapsulated Tendulkar's genius for me was his 15th Test century, at the Chidambaram Stadium against Australia in 1998. Two balls from Shane Warne summed it up. The first, from around the wicket, was full. Tendulkar slog-swept it for four through wide mid-on. The second was slightly shorter. Tendulkar stepped back and slapped it through extra cover for four more.

Tendulkar had taken it upon himself to repel Warne in that series, and that assault was his opening gambit. None of the Australian bowlers had an answer to the maestro that day. Here was a champion in his prime, full of confidence and set to bat forever.

I have reflected on Tendulkar as a batsman recently, and dwelt on how he compares with other greats that I have seen. I consider myself fortunate to have watched the best batsmen of the past half-century of Test cricket from close quarters.

Each of the champions had a method distinctly his own, and distinctive traits that defined him. Neil Harvey was wristy and light on his feet, Garry Sobers languid and yet explosive, Rohan Kanhai feisty and classical, Graeme Pollock brutal and driven, Sunil Gavaskar surgically measured, Barry Richards erect and imperious, Viv Richards powerful and disdainful, Brian Lara artistic and bold, Adam Gilchrist dominant and pulverising, and Ricky Ponting deceptively strong and measured. Tendulkar sits easily in the company of these batting titans.

What characterised a Tendulkar innings for me was balance and efficiency. He was rarely rushed, and even the best bowlers found it difficult to keep him quiet for long.

A Tendulkar innings was poetry in motion. Each time I watched him, I was struck by the simplicity and symmetry of his batting. His poise meant that the bowler had a very small margin of error. Anything other than a perfect line and length would be dispatched with disdain.

Tendulkar had power, but not the brutal kind. Even big hits were executed with minimum effort. His method was simple, but his shots were powerful and precise because he never committed to a static position until he had ascertained where the ball would be.

That early method was an excellent example of how critical intent is to the art of batting.

Sachin's intent was to seek to score – unless forced to defend. This meant that his whole being was focused on scoring runs. This created the ideal active-neutral position that all of the best players have in common.

His pre-ball movement was consistent and based on what his eyes were picking up, which in turn allowed his brain to synchronise with the rhythm of each bowler. He would not have thought consciously about these movements or their timing but would have trusted his brain to compute these for him.

His little back-and-across movement was made as the bowler landed his back foot; then his front foot hovered momentarily as he picked up the line and length. If the ball was pitched up, his weight was perfectly positioned on the ball of his back foot. This allowed him to pounce on the full ball. If he perceived that the ball was still in the bowler's hand past the point where it could be a full delivery, he would plant on to the ball of his front foot to push himself back and up to his full height, to deal with the shorter delivery.

Because Sachin is not a tall man, he operated in a tight zone just in front of the popping crease or marginally behind it. This meant that bowlers had to be precise with their length or he could punish them with ease. What might have been a good length to a taller player became short enough for Sachin to push on to the back foot to punch down the ground or through the off side.

Of his many shots, I favoured his square cut, his straight drive, his pull shot and the shot to leg off the full ball sliding on to his pads. All of these shots were played with a minimum of fuss and with exquisite timing.

The cut was my favourite because he always took the ball at the top of the bounce and struck it with a slightly downward blow, with his weight coming back into the ball. He rarely mistimed the stroke, which says that his reading of length was impeccable. His pull shot destroyed the confidence of the best bowlers. It was a stroke that he was more likely to play to spin, but it was used with great effect against the faster bowlers early in his career.

My first memory of these two shots was at the SCG in 1992, when he became the youngest batsman to make a Test century in Australia. This innings was in Shane Warne's first Test and nearly destroyed the young spinner before he had begun. Merv Hughes, Craig McDermott and Michael Whitney all suffered similarly at the hands of Tendulkar in Perth in the same series.

The next two Australian bowlers that I saw get the treatment were Michael Kasprowicz and Damien Fleming, who received a mauling in the ODIs in Sharjah in 1998. Sachin made two centuries in that series and exasperated the Australians.

As his bat's weight grew in mid-career, the pull and the cut largely disappeared from his repertoire. It is the main reason why he had to work much harder for his runs in the latter stages of his career. Thankfully the straight drive and the deflection to leg remained constant, as did the punch off the back foot through extra cover.

Before the heavy bats, Sachin was quick to pounce on anything marginally short or wide, and bowlers were forced to bowl fuller to keep him quiet. But anything that was slightly overpitched or that drifted slightly into his pads was treated contemptuously.

The straight drive is one of the great shots in the game and Sachin was a master at it.

Nothing demoralises a bowler more than having a delivery driven back past him faster than it went down. None but the very best bowlers will pitch the next one up if this happens to them.

This suited Sachin down to the ground. If the bowler over-corrected, he was likely to suffer at the hands of the punch through the off side, the cut or the pull.

The other shot that destroyed many bowlers was the one through the leg side that was played to either full or slightly short balls. The full ball was dispatched effortlessly from straight midwicket to backward square leg, while the shorter delivery was clipped off the hip and usually went just in front of square or just backward of square.

The shots played to the fuller deliveries were often to balls that would have hit the stumps, and were often the result of Sachin manipulating the line by shifting his body towards the off side during his initial movements. This was guaranteed to frustrate the bowler, who would then go wide of off stump and suffer again.

As Tendulkar's career stretched into its second decade, injury, heavier bats, and an understandable conservatism meant that he did not move as quickly into position and score with his earlier ease. In this period, the youthful exuberance that I so loved in the first decade was not so obvious, other than in 50-over cricket.

The weight of expectation no doubt had its impact on that exuberance. When so many hopes ride on one's shoulders, it is natural to withdraw into a shell to some degree.

I wonder if Sachin actually realised what impact the heavier bats were having on his batting in the second half of his career. They forced him to pick the bat up earlier in his load-up. This meant his weight was forced on to the flat of his feet rather than on the balls, as before.

Because one needs to have the weight on the balls of the feet to move quickly, the speed of his reactions was affected. Balls he had pounced on previously were that much harder to get to. He gave back to the bowlers some of the advantage that he had had over them before.

In the final stages of his career, probably because his bats were even heavier then, he actually held the bat up as the bowler approached. This further restricted his movements and made it harder for him to load the bat because he was not cocking the wrists naturally, as part of the take-away. In turn, this meant that he did not coil his body, as his old method had allowed.

By not using his body as efficiently, he was forced to rely on his arms more. This caused him to push at the ball rather than hit it, which in turn made it harder for him to time the ball as exquisitely as previously done. Consequently, the initial speed of the ball from the bat was reduced, allowing fielders to cut off balls that had once raced past them.

If Sachin had maintained his early bat weight and his youthful exuberance, I think he could have put himself ahead of all the greats except Bradman. I believe it was the heavier bats, and self-doubts, that caused the crack in his perfection, and stopped Tendulkar from placing himself in a class all of his own.

Greg Chappell, *one of Australia's finest batsmen, coached India in the mid-2000s*

OUR QUEST FOR THE REAL SACHIN

RAHUL BOSE

Which is your favourite Sachin? The child who scooter-pillioned from maidan to maidan, playing three matches a day? The boy who stood on a deck set on fire by Waqar and Imran? The son of India whom Lata Mangeshkar kisses on the forehead?

My favourite Sachin is the boy who scampered after the ball with the enthusiasm and delight of a cricketer playing his first inter-school match. The delight, the glee at having an open field to run in, a ball to chase, a day to spend under a cloudless sky – that, I believe, is the essence of Sachin. We all have our favourite and it is of that favourite we ask: is this the real Sachin?

Perhaps one way of finding out is by imagining Tendulkar having played a different sport and then asking ourselves – would anything change? Would he be different? What if he was a tennis player? What, for example, if he was a tennis contemporary of one of his childhood heroes, McEnroe? Imagine McEnroe playing Sachin in a tennis match. John spewing and cursing, Tendulkar stoic, determined, aggressive.

John thinking he'd steamroller this meek Indian kid through sheer intimidation, only to find Sachin, after a quick adjustment of his shorts, rifling forehand after forehand past him. (Would he play left- or right-handed?) Would Sachin ever exhort himself with a Murrayesque "Come on!" on breaking McEnroe after being a set down? Would he change his shirt to catcalls in the break? Pump his fists and thrust his crotch in a Becker hip-stutter when he took the fourth set to make it two-all? Would he collapse on his back, crying, when he won 9-7 in the fifth? Throw his wristbands and towels into the stands? What would his exultation be like when he lifted the cup at Wimbledon? Would he have, a few minutes before, clambered up clumsily to hug his trainer, his girlfriend, his mother? Or would he simply play controlled, aggressive tennis, emotions in check, VIP gallery unmolested, trophy kissed for the cameras, autographs for the ball boys, a ball or two hit high into the stands?

Would his playing another sport have revealed the "real" Sachin to us? For the answer we have to turn our gaze inwards. Towards us. To our insolent impatience, our speed of dismissiveness, our tendency to fawn, our alacrity to scorn, our delusion in claiming greatness through our idols. Would you risk showing any more emotion than Tendulkar did if you were faced with the most volatile, excitable, mercurial crowd on earth? Would you risk being skinned one day and crowned the next? What would that do to your equilibrium, your focus, your sanity? And what if this extended into every corner, every millisecond of your private life? Would you air your opinions freely knowing they could start a riot? Take a stand knowing people might immolate themselves?

And so, when you retired, would you change because you feel the pressure lift? Or, having descended one step below the pedestal, would the protective gild of idolatry lose one coat, making you 10% more vulnerable and open to the sharks? Would you breathe easier because you don't have to step into a cauldron of 50,000 people every week, or would it be suffocating to not ever play under a summer sky bleached by an Indian sun?

It was easier for McEnroe when he retired. Much easier. All he had to do was sober down. He gentled down. He relaxed, and so did we. It was a relief. Now, just to keep us interested he plays the odd exhibition match where he stokes the "You cannot be serious!" myth by giving us theatrical displays of mock anger.

With Sachin the question is different: do we really want to see him with his guard down? Because then there might have existed the possibility he would not have quite commanded the unquestioning respect of a young-blood Indian dressing room despite his records, his incredible cricket brain, his intense desire to maximise everybody's abilities. He mightn't have been listened to as intently as he sorted out technical glitches in tens of India debutants, batsmen and bowlers. Captain after captain might have quietly and ever so slightly discounted his counsel to change the field, shuffle the batting order, effect a risky bowling change. Because he would not have had the aura. The halo.

You can ask as much as you want for a more "human", more "feelable, touchable" Sachin. But it's my bet he's never going to change. He's going to be the Sachin we've always known – considerate, gentle, fiercely determined, careful, kind, well brought up.

Lightning rods of a country's hopes and dreams don't have options, they have responsibilities. Thank your stars he never forgets that.

Rahul Bose is a writer, actor, and former rugby international for India

"I DON'T LET MY NATURAL INSTINCTS GET CONFUSED BY UNWANTED THOUGHTS"

INTERVIEW BY SHARDA UGRA

Just before he began a TV interview, Sachin Tendulkar requested the two technicians sitting just behind the camera in front of him not to move. If they did, it was possible he would get distracted and look at them rather than his interviewer. The men nodded and the conversation began. Something else happened for the next 45 minutes. Seventeen other people in the room behind the glare of lights on Tendulkar's side also froze – in instant obedience.

It is what Tendulkar has done over 20 years of international cricket: striking the ball, scoring runs, giving India floods of joy, bursts of hope and a renewed shower of spontaneous respect.

Just before his 20th international season began, he spoke to India

This interview was first published in *India Today* magazine in 2009

Today *about his international career, his opinions on the modern game and his hunger and competitiveness for cricket.*

November will become the 20th year in international cricket for you. Only Garry Sobers has played non-stop international cricket for that long a period. Do you remember it all? Does it feel that long?

I feel that time definitely flies. I remember on my first tour Kapil Dev challenged me. He said, "You play for ten years." It was a healthy bet, which I won. When I completed ten years, Kapil Dev was the coach, so I caught him and said, "I've won our bet." I'm glad today I'm very close to doubling that. I remember things clearly, even though time has flown. I remember most of my dismissals and I don't think any cricketer forgets that . . . I remember the great shots too.

What part of your 16- or 20-year-old self would you like to have in your game today?

Mentally it's different now. When I was younger, there have been times where I've gone out thinking of attacking from ball one, that wherever the ball is, I'm going to attack, wherever the ball is, I'm going to hit a six. Literally that kind of thought process. But I'm glad that doesn't happen today. You think differently in various stages in life and you react accordingly. So obviously I think differently at this stage and I don't feel like that, like I miss anything.

What would you say is the single biggest lesson cricket has taught you? One which would save younger guys a lot of trouble if they knew about it?

I think to respect the game and to respect fellow cricketers. I was made to realise that very early on by a friend. In the early years of cricket, you have done everything possible under the sun to achieve your target. All of a sudden you have the India cap and India T-shirt and you start thinking, oh I'm somebody special.

I remember just after I started to play for India, a very close friend of mine conveyed a message through another person. "Just tell him that I've noticed that he is probably starting to think differently. The sooner he realises that, the better it is." And I sat back and I realised that, yes, it was true. I normally tend to tell all the youngsters who get in the team, "I know that it's good that you are here but learn to respect the cricketers who actually played with you before." That would help you to stay on the ground more than anything else.

More than the runs or records, it is your consistency that has stood out for two decades now. What's the secret? If a young player asked you, "I've got the game, I've got the fitness, how do I stay consistent?" what would you say?

I don't know how to answer this. I wish I knew the answer. I've just gone out and played, and played with a lot of passion, and I spent a lot of time preparing myself. Not only physically but mentally, I spent time preparing. There have been ups and downs in everybody's career but I would much rather . . . when there are disappointments, I would much rather convert that negative energy into positive energy and use that somewhere else. In training harder or spending more time in the nets.

The setbacks have actually motivated me. My thinking is simple – I want to convert those disappointments into positive energy and use it and get even more determined. That is what I've done, nothing else.

They say as athletes get older their body starts to break down, give them trouble, but their mind gets sharper about

their game, they find out new things. What have you learnt as you've become older?

You discover a lot of new things and I've been able to do that. If earlier there were just a couple of ways to deal with a particular bowler, then today there would be four ways. You just know how to use what and when. It's about not accepting every little challenge thrown at you and going after that. Sometimes you hold back and when it's needed you go for it. You just calculate better and it comes with age and experience.

How much was opening the batting in one-day cricket a factor in your success at taking your game up another level?

Yes, I thought it was an important phase. I remember in 1994 when [Navjot] Sidhu was not fit for an ODI game in New Zealand, I walked up to Azhar [Mohammad Azharuddin] and Ajit Wadekar and told them, give me one chance. I told them, "I know I can hit the fast bowlers, and if I fail, I will not come and ask you again." They agreed and I scored 82 runs off 49 balls. From there on, things started looking different for me. Obviously it helped in a big way.

Why and how do you think that happened?

Because I was consistently facing the new ball and playing the first spells. And also had to play shots – there was that freedom too.

While doing that, I thought I developed a few shots batting up the order, like the punch off the back foot and the short-arm pull. I used to play those but opening the batting there was more opportunity to do that, so I did, and I started using that in Test cricket more than I would earlier.

The switch worked for me. To go out there and face the first spell and look to play shots . . . It was good for my game because I was always thinking positively. On very few occasions did I look to just play out the first spell. I was looking to hit the ball.

You say that essentially you express yourself when you're batting, but without a bat in your hand you're not really aggressive, you're quite calm.

Well, I was very naughty. In school days I was always very naughty, always up to mischief. If I get to know a person, I cannot be serious with them, I'm always up to something.

Then, I've always been competitive. It's extremely important for a sportsman to be highly competitive. One should not be able to take defeat just like that. I mean, I don't believe in, you know, oh, it is just another game. When I'm out competing, I want to go all the way to the end. I would want to compete hard but compete hard in the right spirit.

Do you ever think about your place in history? Where you will stand in the reckoning of the great batsmen who have played cricket for a hundred of years?

I don't know, honestly. I haven't thought about that at all, I've not . . .

Do you think you changed the way Indians bat? Did you wonder why the other batsmen didn't quite counter-attack like you did?

I don't know about that and I honestly didn't think much about the other players. Whenever I was made to take up the challenge, I felt that I can easily go and play a particular shot against a bowler. What's such a big deal? I would do it. I would not let my natural instincts get confused by various unwanted thoughts. I backed my natural instincts and I just went ahead and played my game. It wasn't like I was out there to prove something to someone. I was there to take the opposition on and put my team in a comfortable position.

You've said once that batting was actually about finding comfort.

I've always believed in that. In changing my stance, for example, I've always thought more about my comfort level rather than what looks good. Even if it's technically something that people say you shouldn't be doing. But if I'm comfortable and can adjust, then I will go ahead and do it.

My stance depends on the wicket – it has lot to do with feel. If I feel I have to do something differently, I just go ahead and do it. If I feel one particular position is suiting my bat-swing, my backlift and movement on that particular day I would just do it. It has nothing to do with the way I've been taught or how I've practised. It changes in between the innings also. One over I would be batting with a different stance. The next over if I feel another stance would suit me better, I will change that in between an innings.

A lot of other players say that you can get into the perfect state of mind when you are batting at will, into the zone.

I wish I could but I'm glad I give that impression to the opposition! But it doesn't come so easily – I would definitely have liked to be in that zone more often than not. But on various occasions I've been able to do that.

It's just a level of concentration where you forget about everything else . . . it happened to me in the Chennai Test match against England [in 2008]. I didn't know we had won the game. When Yuvraj [Singh] came running up to me and jumping up and the opposition came walking towards me, to shake hands, that's when I realised that, yes, we've won the match, because until then I was not looking at the scoreboard. That's when I realised I was in that zone.

That was quite an emotional innings for you, given the terrorist attacks that happened in Mumbai on November 26. Talk us through it.

We obviously wanted to win because if you look at a cricket match and compare that to what had happened, a cricket match is virtually non-existent. It wouldn't be right to compare the two things.

At the end of the match, I saw that the groundsmen were jumping, and the lady who sweeps the wicket came and she shook hands with me. I've never experienced that before, and I thought maybe that has to be because of what had happened.

I felt strongly about it and I felt that even for a fraction . . . for those people who lost their loved ones and dear ones, if we were able to divert their minds somewhere else even for a fraction of a second, then that would be our achievement. And we were able to do that as a team. So I think that particular match means a lot to me.

Did you try to understand why you were able to enter that mental state for that game?

It just happened. The concentration level was very high . . . there's no particular formula to that, that if you walk like this or that, it will happen, if you breathe like that, this will happen. Sometimes you make the effort and it doesn't happen. Actually when you start making the effort then your mind is conscious about that particular thing and it doesn't happen. But in Chennai, the concentration level was such that it just happened.

Have there ever been times in your career when you've thought, this is too tough, I cannot cope, I can't do this?

There have been tough times but at no stage did I feel that I can't do it. The only stage I've felt that I don't belong here probably was after my first Test. I felt, "This is not my cup of tea."

There have been situations where there was no hope, but you still go out and do what you can. You still try. Earlier in the interview I said that for a sportsman the spirit of competitiveness has to be there, no matter what. If that is not there, then you are going to struggle. I feel that the competitive spirit has played a huge role in making me what I am.

There have been tough situations where, like you said, there was no hope. Yes, there have been but you still go out and you want to do something which may not have an impact on that game but it may have an impact on the series. You have to look at that, you look at the bigger picture. If you do that, then you start approaching tough times differently.

In your career have there been times you've felt doubt or experienced insecurity or known fear first-hand?

Whenever I'm injured, those phases were quite difficult. All the injuries I had were related to my batting style or batting grip. Whether it was tennis elbow or a finger injury, or bicep and shoulder . . . all of that is needed for you to have the right bat-swing, things like that.

The tennis elbow was a tough one to deal with. I tried every possible thing and it didn't work. I also went to the extent where I said, "Give me a shot [of painkillers] before the Test match and I'll play." Of course I didn't have the knowledge that it would not work because you'll have certain kind of numbness – which is what a more knowledgeable guy told me. At the time I was just not able to lift a cricket bat, so I had to back off. Even in the recovery time I worked very hard and it wasn't the same, so I had to be patient and take things as they come. That was tough.

On a cricket field, what is the toughest thing you would say you've done, that you're most proud of?

Well, I'm proud that on my first tour, to Pakistan, I continued batting after being hit on the nose by Waqar [Younis]. When I came back, I realised that I'd broken my nose.

Everyone thought it was cut but later on I figured out the nose was broken. We managed to save that Test match. We were 38 for 4 with almost a day and a half to go. Before that we'd drawn three Test matches and this was the last Test and Pakistan was in a good position. I think that has to be it.

Why did you opt out of playing T20 for India? It's only about seven games more a year.

We had just reached England from Ireland in 2007 when I took the decision. I was struggling with my ankles at that time. I had twisted my ankle, my body was just not feeling right, at least for the T20 version. I thought, if I am part of this, it's unfair for my team-mates. I don't think I'd be able to sustain that pressure of running and I might damage something. So I said, "No I don't think I should be part of the team because I'm not in a position to give 100%." And the team did fantastically well and I said, "That's it. I'm not going to disturb the combination."

You don't regret that decision now?

No, not at all. Absolutely not, because the decision has come from my side. I felt I should not be part of the Indian T20 team. I was obviously also asked to be part of it afterwards, but I feel that the team has done well and I should not be a part. If I was 26, yes, I would have been back, but not at this stage. I don't think so. It's not right for me. My heart just doesn't allow me to do that.

Sir Don Bradman's Test average 99.94 is completely impossible to equal today. What according to you is a standard similar to that these days? Would, say, 15,000 Test runs be a peak that would be tough now?

Obviously getting to 15,000 runs will be something. I'm not talking about myself getting it – I'm just generally talking about the numbers. I feel that, yes, that would be some achievement.

I don't think anyone should be compared to Sir Don, because what he has, that's a phenomenal record. And you cannot compare eras either. But today, yes, one can say that 15,000 Test runs would be something special.

Could you talk us through what goes on in your mind in an over when you're facing any bowler of great quality, like, say, someone like McGrath?

Definitely alert. There are different strategies on different days, depending on the surface, depending on the position of the team. All those things. There would be days when I would play him out, there would be days when I would be normal, there would be days when I would want to go after him.

How did you succeed in bowling duels where your batting was completely tested? Which would you say were the best of the duels that you handled?

I thought in England in 2007 I played a spell from Ryan Sidebottom well. I was not playing any shot. I played almost close to six-seven maiden overs – I just kept blocking and leaving, and kept getting beaten also. He was bowling well, and I knew that that was the most important phase of that Test match. I thought that if we see through the spell then the doors are going to open for us, when we can play some shots.

That is what happened and that set us in a dominating position, and after that we had the upper hand and we ended up winning that Test match, the second of the series. That was a particular patch, I can say, where I was mentally strong. I got beaten on various occasions. The guy was bowling well, I was smiling at him, and I was saying, "Fine, you still have to get me out." It was a good challenge. And today I look back and feel, yes, I did that job.

People normally think of your attacking batsmanship. Any incidents of that kind?

You remember different kinds of incidents. Well, probably in Nairobi when we were playing the 2000 Champions Trophy. We had won the toss and batted in overcast conditions against Australia. The wicket was also damp, and the way Glenn McGrath bowled the first over, I told Sourav [Ganguly], "Just give me freedom for a couple of overs because I want to do something." I felt otherwise he's going to come and bowl six-seven overs, four maidens, seven runs and take two-three wickets, and we'd go down slowly but surely. I started stepping out and hit McGrath for a couple of sixes. He bounced and I hit him, exchanged a few words, disturbed him. I did something different and it sort of worked. I remember that particular match – we won it.

What criteria are paramount to you when you assess yourself or other players: that they entertained, won matches, were

masters of their craft, or played the game in the right way?

Playing the game in the right spirit is extremely important and then somebody who obviously gave his best for the team and was able to adapt to the situation. Adaptability is very important too.

A lot has changed in Indian cricket since you made your debut. What about Indian cricket has not changed in all these years, which disappoints you?

Yes, sometimes we used to feel that, you know, a lot of things are not right, but over a period of time a lot of things have changed, so I have no complaints. Most things have changed now. Right now if I have to say then maybe the only thing which needs to be worked on or looked into is providing facilities to players in rural areas to spread the game as much as possible and provide equal opportunity to everyone playing it.

I know it's not going to be equal because someone living in Mumbai or Bangalore or Delhi or the heart of Chennai will have better facilities than someone who stays in some remote place, but a certain basic standard has to be there.

T20 is the new format that has caught everyone's fancy. Do you worry that kids won't want to learn the basic skills of the longer game, like, say, the forward defence, because they're not going to use them in T20?

Well, I'd say probably even Test cricket is changing. Now very rarely will you see three maiden overs in a row. I mean, you know that if there are five-six dot balls, in the next over the batsman will probably walk across and do something to ease the pressure. It's just progression; the game has changed and that's fine. I feel it's fine as long as Test cricket doesn't get neglected. The innovations are going to be there. Now in one-day cricket people play over the keeper's head and past short fine-leg, and play the reverse sweep to fast bowlers. It makes the game exciting, it's fast.

The guys not wanting to play longer cricket because they are all looking at T20, since there is more glamour – well, for Test cricket you get a different crowd. For T20 there are so many who come there because it is exciting. They don't understand the game, but the atmosphere is such that they want to be part of it, and it is fantastic for the game. You want as many people inside the stadium as possible because that makes the match more exciting.

How would, say, your son Arjun take to this new environment? Is he going to want to learn the skills needed for Tests and long games when there's the glamour of T20 around?

Arjun actually likes both – he wants to wear whites and hit sixes! So it's a combination of both. I have to keep telling him that when you wear coloured clothing you can hit the ball up into the air and when you wear whites you have to keep the ball on the ground. But I basically want him to enjoy the game more than anything else – if he enjoys the game then he is willing to go to any extent to achieving his target.

Do you think coaches of the future will really want to teach older skills to kids who are going to come to the game in the next ten years?

I think it's extremely important for coaches to be teaching kids the right techniques, the right fundamentals. You can't be practising just forward defence for seven days. Maybe you do that for a day, then it's playing reverse sweep and over fine leg's head . . . maybe one day in a week can be set aside for innovation.

There are different kind of skills – to leave a ball outside the off stump and to know where your off stump is, that is an art. Similarly to beat short fine-leg is also an art, but that is considered an art in a different format.

As long as we respect formats, we should be okay. There is no mixing of formats because then there are always going to be bumpy rides. It good to be multidimensional, and that can only open various doors for you.

We've got to be realistic. Probably there are 25-year-old guys who know that it is difficult for them now to play Test cricket for India. Even one-day cricket might be difficult. So why not grab this opportunity to play for an IPL team where you get to play cricket that is exciting? It has the ideal recipe, it has recognition, following, the game moves at a phenomenal pace, and you also earn money out of it and you live your passion.

What do you think is needed to save one-day cricket?

I was thinking about it. I said, why not think of introducing a different format if everyone is talking about it, and maybe this thought came to my mind because of the 2002 Champions Trophy final. We played for a couple of days in the final against Sri Lanka. Both days Sri Lanka batted happily for 50 overs and when our turn came to bat we batted for five-seven overs and it rained. We ended up playing close to 110 overs and there was no result.

So why not do something which solves the problem all across the world, and give teams the chance to play their 50 overs in two lots? There are times in the afternoon when the wicket is on the slower side and the ball doesn't come on to the bat, so it's difficult to bat.

The spinners come into play, but at night the ball starts getting on to the bat and there is dew and you can hit through the line and the game changes.

Even if you score 280 you can still go and chase. So why not then give 25 overs to one team and then the other side can use the 25 overs the way they want to? If you want to exhaust all your ten wickets in the first 25 overs and score 230 runs, thinking that it might rain, you can do so.

So if you score 240 runs all down in 25 overs and the other side says, fair enough I'm going to play out and play 25 overs and score 150 runs, and again we start batting and it rains, you've won the game because you've scored more runs in the first 25 overs.

You get only ten wickets in 50 overs – use them whichever way you want. That makes it exciting. To know when to send which player is equally important, and the weather also becomes important. You're sure that if you get 40 overs therein, you will definitely have a result.

Would you like to see more technology in umpiring? What do you think of referrals now?

I think for the basic line decisions you have to have the laser or something like that. It is tough for the umpires to also watch the no-balls and watch what's happening in the front. They don't need to look at the line decisions, they just need to focus on what's happening.

The no-ball is like tennis . . . you can call it by the machine. They should use the Hot Spot for the bat-pad decision so the main umpire has to only make the lbw calls. We are still using technology for close catches. The umpire has to only concentrate on lbw decisions because for the caught behind and all, Hot Spot will come. Close-in catches . . . again the Hot Spot will come. For the bowled you don't need a machine, so only the lbw decisions is what the umpire has to concentrate on. Maybe we could have umpires doing a session each and so have three umpires for a game, so umpires do get time off also.

And the referrals?

I'm not particulary happy with the referrals because I'm not convinced of the angles and all. I'm not convinced. I wasn't happy when we first went through it, but I'm quite happy with the Hot Spot because that establishes the contact.

How should young cricketers handle what they think of Indian cricket today – that its fans are too fickle and too extreme, that its media has too many channels, and there is too much scrutiny?

Along with cricket, the things that happen around cricket have also changed. You just have to accept that. It will continue to change and you have to accept and take it in your sporting stride – that is how it is going to be in India. As long as nobody sort of interferes in your personal life, that is fine. I feel that a player's personal life should not be intruded upon by anyone else. A player's time with his family should always be respected.

What is your dream for Indian cricket?

Obviously I would like Indian cricket to be right at the top. Indian cricket should be regarded as the best cricket played in the world. It won't be right away but I think that with the introduction of IPL there are so many foreigners playing here, and domestic players get the chance of playing with and against them. That is going to eventually improve the standard of playing in India. There are one-day players and T20 players who are also playing IPL. Back-up bowlers and batters are also playing IPL along with and against the foreign players, so it will help Indian cricket in time to come. It has to help Indian cricket.

Sharda Ugra*, senior editor at ESPNcricinfo, was chief sportswriter at* India Today *from 1996 to 2009*

THE USE OF WEAPONS

JON HOTTEN

July 2011, England v India at Lord's, the 2000th Test. In his final game at a ground that has never been kind to him, in Test match terms at least – his highest score here is 37 – there has been more misfortune for Sachin Tendulkar. Taken ill on day four, he has been forced to leave the property, and as he makes his return, the television cameras are on him as soon as he steps out from his car by the Grace Gate. "Here comes Sachin," says the commentator, Nasser Hussain. "He has his bat with him. That goes everywhere with him, he never leaves it in the dressing room."

As any batsman knows, a bat is never just a bat unless it's someone else's. It's a totem, a prop, invested with hope and with dreams. It is all that he takes to the crease, all that he has between him and the bowler and the pressing field. For the professional, it is the tool of his trade, an organic, once-living thing to be fussed over, obsessed with, to be adjusted minutely with sandpaper and oil and new grips. It is a deeply personal relationship, and like any relationship, it evolves.

Trust grows and trust can leave; the end can mean heartache and uncertainty. When you find the one you love, you just know.

In his recent autobiography Ricky Ponting writes:

> Occasionally you'll meet a cricketer who doesn't give a toss, but most of us, particularly batsmen, are obsessed by our gear . . . Most of us arrive with an arsenal of bats: the lucky one, the one that's almost broken in, the one that's there and about . . . The secret to a good one is how it feels in your hands and the soft tonk a new ball makes on good willow. Your ear tells you. I suppose a guitar or a piano is the same.

Sachin Tendulkar may bat like an immortal, but taking his bat home with him, keeping that No. 1 within his sight at all times – that tells us something about the man. When he embarked upon his last great run, the rush that brought him to 99 international centuries and concluded with his towering 146 at Newlands in January 2011, he used one bat, a piece of willow that has probably scored more meaningful centuries than any ever cut from the tree. How he loved that bat, taking it to the crease again and again as its centre darkened and then blackened with the number of balls that struck it. If cricket has an Excalibur, it is this.

Ram Bhandari, the intriguing former stuntman who is said to have "modified" more than 20 of Tendulkar's bats, somehow kept it going, nursed it through its glorious dotage. Looking at the footage from Newlands, where Tendulkar duelled unforgettably with Dale Steyn either side of lunch on day three, the bat is deeply scarred, long cracks running down its face, the dye of the ball deep inside the grain of the willow. It is a remarkable sight, an image that defines the relationship between player and bat, a study in the psychology of belief.

Tendulkar's public presence has been an inscrutable one. Into the void of how little we know about him comes myth. He offers a canvas on to which others can paint. Rarely is this as evident as in the provenance of the bats that he uses. Even here in England it is rare to meet a bat-maker who does not let it slip that he has "done one" for Tendulkar. Rumours swirl like a spring breeze, some stronger than others. Somerset's Millichamp & Hall have a bat called The Master, supposedly based on the shape preferred by Sachin: they are said to have made him some bats. On the Sussex coast, Newbery's Tim Keeley is widely thought to have shaved pods for the great man's bag – the late, great CMJ implied as much in one of his *Telegraph* pieces. In India there has been a long relationship with Somi Kohli at BAS.

On the eve of Tendulkar's farewell, Kohli said: "Sachin has been associated with us for nearly 20 years and has not changed one bit. He is not fussy at all and seldom asks for changes in his bat." That may be because Bhandari is busy altering them, but then who except Sachin will know? The myth here is more interesting, and more enduring, than the truth.

I once received an email at my blog from someone who had been given one of Tendulkar's bats after his sister spoke to Sachin's wife. He sent me its dimensions: weight, 3lbs 2oz (1417 grams); edge at its thickest point, 1.25 in (317mm). In 2006, when Tendulkar was having a quiet spell, Bhandari said he reduced the weight of Sachin's bat from 1350g (3lbs) to 1250 (2lbs 12oz) and the runs resumed their flow. "Tendulkar was so happy that he asked me to give him bats of this weight only."

For his final appearance in Mumbai, Kohli sent the Little Master two new bats, "at least 35–40 grams lighter than normal" and also slightly shorter in length. Did he ask for them? Did he use them? What weight does he like? Again, only Tendulkar knows.

One thing is certain: Tendulkar has lived and played through the bat's golden age.

Over the course of his career, dead-straight, wafer-thin pieces of willow, pressed hard, oiled deep and dried to the colour of chestnut have become super-sized WMD: sexed-up, thick-edged, fully bowed, lightly pressed killing machines. In the hands of someone like Tendulkar, well, what would you expect of wood like that: the push down the ground that rockets to the rope, the ramp over the keeper that clears the sightscreen, the firm-wristed clip that buries itself in the boundary board. These have rung from his bat.

Because willow was once a living, growing thing its condition is not stable, even once it is cut and shaped, shaved and oiled and prepared. It has infinitesimal variations in density and moisture content, in the way its fibres lie together. Combined with human biorhythms, it means that the same bat in the same hands can feel different on any given day. As Ponting said, a relationship with it must change and grow, trust must be invested, the demons of luck fought and defeated. Even the great Tendulkar will have had times when he has cast one aside, left it behind, thought bad things about it, persuaded himself that a new start may be better.

Geoff Boycott would counter his tiredness by using a lighter bat after tea if he'd been in all day. Tendulkar's old friend Vinod Kambli became obsessed with the handle of his, at one point pulling nine grips onto it. Graham Thorpe decided that his handle was too long, sawed a bit off the top, realised it was now too short and tried to nail the piece back on again. Neil McKenzie began taping his bat to the dressing-room ceiling: his team-mates had first done so as a prank and he'd taken it down and made a hundred. Mark Ramprakash asked his bat-maker why he couldn't keep a handle and interchange it with a series of blades. Bats do strange things to the minds of batsmen, caused by the deep uncertainties of what they do.

When Tendulkar's legacy is considered, alongside the weight of runs we should set his mastery of equilibrium. He controlled the natural anxieties so well; in coach-speak he stayed out of his own way. How he related to his bats is just another mystery buried under his benign implacability.

The Australian kit supplier Harry Solomons perhaps came closest to answering the question of how so many bat-makers claimed a relationship with the era's greatest run-maker, in an interview during Sachin's last tour of Australia, a place where he batted so beautifully.

"A lot of manufacturers give him handmade bats because it looks good for them to say they made a bat for Tendulkar," he said. "He gets inundated – and then he gives them away to poor kids."

Jon Hotten *is the author of* Muscle *and* The Years of the Locust, *and writes the* blog *The Old Batsman*

SUPERNOVA INCIPIENT

AYAZ MEMON

Among several emotionally charged fans at Sachin Tendulkar's farewell Test was a forty-something lady from Amravati who, alas, had got to the ground after he had been dismissed. She was inconsolable. "I have not missed a single match of his since I was a teenager. Will I get to see him bat a last time?"

This was slice-of-life stuff, and imbued with some sadness, as it transpired. West Indies folded without a fight in their second innings and India completed a facile victory, by an innings. There was to be no "last time" for the lady from Amravati.

At a philosophical level this was a reminder of mortality. He had been such an integral part of our lives, our collective consciousness, for a quarter of a century, that his presence was verily assumed. That everything must have an end is often a painful realisation.

From a cricketing perspective, Tendulkar's farewell Test marked the end of an epoch. While there have been several significant stages in the history of the game, and a galaxy of outstanding performers, I believe there have been only three players who have defined specific eras by the impact they have had on people and the sport rather than just the record books: WG Grace, Don Bradman and Sachin Tendulkar.

In understanding this era, Tendulkar's early years are fascinating because they speak of the transition of a young, cricket-obsessed lad into the game's biggest draw card. Everything that was anticipated about him came true, almost as if it was divinely ordained. He was, to use a cliché, to the manner born.

When Tendulkar made his Test debut, on November 15, 1989 in Karachi against Pakistan, a curly haired, 16-year-old with a squeaky voice, he already had a world record under his belt. By the time he retired in the November of 2013, almost 24 years later to the day, you had to seek hard to find a batting record he hadn't appropriated.

This does not mean he is the greatest cricketer ever. Bradman's incredible average of 99.94 is never likely to be breached. Even if it is, it does not alter the pecking order. In any case, in my opinion Garfield Sobers sits atop this peak because of his brilliant all-round ability. Yes, ahead even of Bradman. But that said, Tendulkar, over a long career, still acquires extraordinary dimensions.

Just about a dozen players in the history of cricket have played so long – some like Grace and Jack Hobbs have gone on longer. But if you include Tests, one-day internationals, first-class matches et al., nobody has spent as many days on the field playing for his club or state side or country. But the Tendulkar saga is not just about longevity. Rather it's about a phenomenon that transcended sport, especially in India.

When he burst on to the scene, the country was turmoil-ridden in the wake of the Mandal agitations and the demolition of the Babri Masjid, and the economy was moving from a mixed to an open one. Tendulkar in many ways became a source of both solace and aspiration for an India experiencing massive churn.

It is beyond the scope of this article and the expertise of this writer to analyse why and how Tendulkar struck such a strong bond with a billion-plus people. Suffice to say that the impact he had on their psyche is worthy of serious research undoubtedly.

My first experience of Tendulkar's exceptional cricketing talent was 18 months before his international debut, when he was playing schools cricket at the Cricket Club of India in early 1988. He had by then already announced his arrival to the world with the 664-run partnership with schoolmate Vinod Kambli that found them a spot in the *Wisden Cricketers' Almanack*.

But this was only the high-water mark of a series of brilliant, often blazing, innings that he was to play at this level. Amol Muzumdar, his other mate from Shardashram High School, who has been among the most prolific first-class cricketers in the world, and was truly unlucky not to have played for India, recalls some early experiences that give a fascinating insight into Tendulkar's cricketing make-up.

"He was always a bundle of energy," says Muzumdar, "and by that I mean positive energy. Even at age 13, he was self-assured, he had poise at the wicket, and power and timing behind his strokes way beyond his years. Scoring big hundreds was like child's play for him. He never got tired, and all of us would be surprised if he failed."

By 1987-88, Tendulkar was already a much-talked-about youngster in Mumbai's cricket circles, in fact almost a young superstar, with unmistakable charisma, attracting big crowds because of his exploits. The trappings of such early fame did not seem to affect him much; what did were big scores, especially when the opposition was tough.

"In one of the school matches at Azad Maidan," recalls Muzumdar, "Sachin scored 178 not out against Anjuman Islam High School, almost winning the game all by himself. Not only did he bat with extraordinary control against an opposition that tried hard to unsettle him, but he even took on the crowds that had come to support the other team. The harder they tried, the more resolute he became."

Straight after this victory, Tendulkar, Muzumdar and others of the Shardashram team went to see the movie *Top Gun* as reward. Chips and colas were gulped down hungrily. After the movie, it was straight back to practice at Shivaji Park.

"What struck me about Sachin that day," reminisces Muzumdar, "was the utter ease with which he played the dual role – of an aggressive and mature cricketer on the field and a fun-loving teenager off it."

In spite of his prolific run-making, however, doubts existed in 1987-88 about Tendulkar's ability. Sport abounds with stories of prodigies who have fizzled out prematurely. Was he truly precociously talented or was this misplaced enthusiasm not uncommon in cricket-crazy India?

I suspect even Dilip Vengsarkar, then India captain and looking for fresh faces, had not made up his mind. One day in early 1988 I got a call from him at *Sportsweek* magazine, where I was employed. "This young fellow is poised to get another century," said Vengsarkar. "Let's go and watch him."

By the time we reached the CCI, Tendulkar was past his century but looked neither spent nor satisfied with the landmark. He seemed to want to bat on and on and on. Soon Vengsarkar wandered off to meet friends and colleagues and I joined Raj Singh Dungarpur, then president of the club and among the most influential people in Indian cricket.

Rajbhai, as Dungarpur was fondly called, was in thrall. "Watch this boy," he said. "He is not quite 15 but he has the mind of a 35-year-old cricketer." Ever the cricket romantic, Rajbhai was known to get hyperbolic when talking of players. But in this case the argument seemed well founded.

To stem the flow of runs, the opposing captain had scattered the fielders afar. Tendulkar started to push – rather than hit – the ball to take singles and twos: as soon as the field was brought in, he would clear the fielders to get boundaries. Whatever the field set, he could still maintain a consistent run rate. "Many international batsmen don't know how to beat a field," Rajbhai added for emphasis.

He had, in his own mind, already earmarked Tendulkar as the pivot of Indian cricket in future. The idea of a "Team of the '90s", as he was to title the side when as selector he made Mohammad Azharuddin captain in 1990, had actually begun to take root in 1988.

But while runs came aplenty for young Tendulkar, an India cap was some time in coming – and not without heartache. Late in 1988, some months past 15, he made his Ranji Trophy debut against Gujarat at the Wankhede Stadium and scored a century. In the weeks that followed, he made a hundred on debut in the Duleep and Irani Trophies too.

No batsman had had such a spectacular start to his first-class career in India, not even the redoubtable Sunil Gavaskar and Vengsarkar, both of whom had been unrelenting run-makers in school and college cricket. Tendulkar had eclipsed them not just at the school level, he had made a sizzling start to his first-class career, arousing the interest of the entire country.

By now he was a household name across India, and drew big crowds wherever he played first-class or even club cricket. With each successive century, his stock rose exponentially, and it would be fair to say that he was the most discussed player in India at that point: not just among fans but also those who ran the game.

In the ordinary course, Tendulkar would have been a certainty for the impending tour of the West Indies in early 1989. But the Indian selectors were cautious. "He is only 15," reasoned one of them after the team was announced. "West Indies have this dreaded pace attack. If he gets hit or injured, he might lose confidence forever."

This was, however, no solace for the bitterly disappointed Tendulkar. The actor Tom Alter and I interviewed him shortly after, for the sports video *Grandstand* brought out by *Sportsweek*. The venue was Hindu Gymkhana on Mumbai's spectacular Marine Drive.

Tendulkar came straight from a match, kit bag in tow and brother Ajit for company, shy, unrecognised by the crowd that had collected there to see Vengsarkar, the India captain, who was also interviewed.

Tendulkar waited patiently for almost an hour under a tree on the periphery of the ground, hardly even shuffling his feet, while the interview with Vengsarkar was being completed. When his turn arrived, Tendulkar was forthright: of limited words, sure, but with a mind startlingly his own for one so young:

Alter: Are you disappointed that you are not going to the West Indies?

Tendulkar: Yes.

Alter: The selectors were actually concerned about you, that you might get hit and lose confidence . . .

Tendulkar: (*with a distinct steely edge that came through despite his squeaky voice*) If I had got hit, I would have only learned quicker.

These words were to echo in my mind when Tendulkar was felled by a snorter from Waqar Younis in the last Test of his first series, in Sialkot against Pakistan in 1989. Wiping away the blood from his nose and brushing off protracted medical attention, he squared up to face Waqar again unflinchingly. The next ball was cover-driven to the fence for a boundary. Within minutes, as it were, the boy had become a man.

His Test debut three matches earlier had not been newsworthy, except for the fact that everybody was eager to see how the highly rated youngster would fare in international cricket. I remember Imran Khan making some preliminary enquiries before the first Test, in Karachi, but Tendulkar did not distinguish himself, scoring 15 in the only innings he played. Imran was generous enough to say, though, that he liked the boy's sense of belonging at this level.

Tendulkar did create a stir off the field, at night, to be precise. Former India stalwart Chandu Borde, manager on the tour, was to reveal that the youngster had a tendency to sleepwalk – muttering about cricket – which necessitated that somebody senior slept in the same room to keep guard!

The nocturnal waywardness was not the only matter of concern for Borde. Tendulkar's unusual grip, with both hands close together and the bottom one dominant while playing, made Borde take a close look. "He uses a heavy bat, which makes it even more difficult to understand how he does it. But in defence and attack he is so assured and polished that nobody should interfere with his grip or technique," said Borde.

Tendulkar had a hard-fought 59 in the second game, in Faisalabad, to suggest that his inclusion was not based on sentiment; that he was fundamentally strong, in technique, skills and temperament. In the third, he impressed again with an innings of 41, and he made 35 in the first innings of the fourth Test. But his pedigree and his absolute passion were to become evident only in the next innings.

The second-innings half-century in Sialkot – which included the aforementioned bouncer from Waqar – was among two memories from his first series that have stood the test of time; the second came towards the end of the tour, when he hit the brilliant legspinner Abdul Qadir for four sixes in an over at Peshawar in a one-day game.

The match was not an international, but Tendulkar seemed to have something to prove, if only to himself. After the first six, Qadir broke into a smile, as he often did when batsmen became aggressive, believing he had seduced his prey into folly.

When the next six went soaring over the ropes, the leggie looked at his captain, Imran, to assure him that everything was still under control. By the time he had been hit for a fourth, Qadir's face was wiped of its smile. Imran too was no longer looking on indulgently at his match-winner, but the crowds were in raptures.

It was a glorious end to a tour on which India had remained

undefeated in the Test series, but even more so because they had discovered a star. "This boy can bat," Qadir was to tell some journalists later. As events over the next 24 years were to prove, there could not have been a more prosaic description for a genius.

*Veteran sportswriter **Ayaz Memon** has covered six cricket World Cups*

AN AUSTRALIAN SORT OF HERO

CHRISTIAN RYAN

From the beginning, the relationship was about something bigger than admiration and affection. When Sachin Tendulkar set foot in Australia he brought with him rain.

Lismore, a place of board shorts and stubby coolers, on the far north hippie trail of New South Wales, was the strange location for Tendulkar's maiden first-class innings in Australia. Lismore hadn't seen rain – the kind of rain that wet your shirt – in months. The Indians arrived on a Friday, November 1991, and all that morning it poured, drowning out the net session they'd scheduled. They moved indoors and it poured some more.

Local politician Reg Baxter used a home-made Super Sopper to get play started. Conditions were grey overhead and green underfoot, which made predicting the ball's flight path tricky. The bowling was top shelf – Mike Whitney, Geoff Lawson, Wayne Holdsworth,

This article was first published on ESPNcricinfo in November 2009

Greg Matthews, Steve Waugh, Mark Waugh – and the batting a little gormless, all except for the one who was 18. Under the Oakes Oval pines he took careful guard, his head still, his footsteps like tiny, precise pinpricks, going backwards mostly, unless the bowler overpitched. Fifteen hundred people saw this, the great Alan Davidson among them. Davo was dumbfounded: "It's just not possible . . . such maturity."

Tendulkar hit 82 that afternoon, when no one else passed 24, then 59 out of 147 in the second innings. When Australians hear Indians grouch about their hero going missing in an emergency and having no appetite for a scrap, it always comes as a shock.

The Tendulkar Australians got to know, the one with the baby footsteps, had played cricket in six countries already. Still he looked like his team-mates' little brother. He ran faster than them all, a gammy-legged bunch, and as he ran, his eyes would be wide and round, and darting, as if alert to the danger that his team-mates' barely muzzled huffiness might distract him from important things. And what was important to Tendulkar – and here Australians saw in him something rare and precious, a single-mindedness they fancied they recognised in themselves – was run-getting.

Every bolt and screw in the Tendulkar technique seemed put there to aid the getting of runs. Tendulkar was a run-getting machine, except no machine could also be so graceful – or instinctive, for that's what it was, instinct, which told him that the way to bat was to attack. He didn't learn this. He knew it, inside himself. Runs were what counted. So nothing outlandish would be tried for the sake of outlandishness. Those footsteps were only as big as they had to be, for footwork was simply the thing that moved your body from its starting position to its ideal hitting position. Once you got there, you kept out the good ones and hit the loose ones hard. And when you hit hard, you did so along the ground – because you cannot get caught and get runs.

This is the way of Bradman, the way of Hill, Trumper, Harvey, the

Chappells and the rest. Give him a pair of bushy mutton chops and paint a weathered furrow or two on his brow, and Tendulkar could pose for the cover of *How to Play Cricket Australian Style*.

Tacky facial add-ons, or some bleach-blond spikes, say, have never been Tendulkar's go, and Australians like that about him too. Australia takes its cricket seriously. Your after hours are for sombre reflection and practising your forward-defensive, not for phonechasey with sheilas or motel-room hijinks in your Playboy undies. You occasionally hear it said wistfully that Tendulkar is the Australian Shane Warne could have been. It is a neat line but it undersells what they have in common. For, if any two modern cricketers might be soulmates, it is Warne and Tendulkar, grandmasters of their arts. Bowling legspin comes as naturally to Warne as batting does to Tendulkar, which is to say, as naturally as the rest of us find breathing.

Two sublime Tendulkar hundreds lit up his first trip: one, in Sydney, as serene as a stroll through rhododendrons; the other, in Perth, more pugnacious, less repeatable. He didn't tour Australia again for eight years. But he visited. He went, with Warne, the two of them in beige suits, to see Sir Donald on his 90th birthday. Tendulkar got as excited as any Australian boy – "I consider myself one of the luckiest guys on earth" – and he asked Bradman the questions any Australian boy would ask, stuff about his stance and his grip and his bats.

When next he came to play cricket he was captain of India, and perhaps that did distract him from the really important things. But it lost him no admirers. Asked his views on sledging, he replied: "One should expect that at this level. You are playing Test cricket, not club cricket."

Always when he went to the wicket, Tendulkar's was the scalp on which the afternoon's destiny hung. Fieldsmen dived further, getting hands to quarter-chances that would normally have eluded fingertips. Umpires concentrated harder – too hard probably, if you tally up the bat-pad rulings that never got a feather, the creative licence applied to some leg-before-wicket interpretations. One never-to-be-forgotten day in Adelaide, Tendulkar was adjudged shoulder-before-wicket. "You almost want him to get a few runs," Mark Waugh once remarked, "just to see him." Odd how a cricketer so Australian as Tendulkar could provoke such un-Australian sentimentality.

He has toured Australia on four occasions, as many times as Bradman toured England. Like Bradman, he has never gone home without a Test hundred to his name.

One particular hundred – Sydney, 2003-04 – might outlive the others. When someone bats for 613 minutes, strung across three sweltering January days, the mind can wander, and as Tendulkar trudged on, making do without the cover drive, for it had caused his downfall too many times already, this mind wandered to Leichhardt and Giles and the famous explorers, who made do without company, without water, surviving on single-mindedness and instinct. He could do things to your imagination, this boy who knew how to make it rain.

Christian Ryan *is a writer based in Melbourne. He is the author of* Golden Boy *and* Australia: Story of a Cricket Country

MAN-CHILD SUPERSTAR

RAHUL BHATTACHARYA

Sachin Tendulkar comes to the ground in headphones. He might make a racket in the privacy of the bus, who knows, but when he steps out he is behind headphones. Waiting to bat he is behind his helmet. The arena is swinging already to the chant "Sachin, Sachin", the first word long and pleading, the second urgent and demanding, but Tendulkar is oblivious behind his helmet.

At the fall of the second wicket, that familiar traitorous roar goes round the stadium, at which point Tendulkar walks his slow walk out, golden in the sun, bat tucked under the elbow. The gloves he will only begin to wear when he approaches the infield, to busy himself against distraction from the opposition. Before Tendulkar has even taken guard, you know that his quest is equilibrium.

As he bats, his effort is compared in real time with earlier ones. Tendulkar provides his own context. The conditions, the bowling

This article was first published on ESPNcricinfo in November 2009

attack, his tempo, his very vibe, is assessed against an innings played before. Today he reminds me of the time when . . . Why isn't he . . . What's wrong with him!

If the strokes are flowing, spectators feel something beyond pleasure. They feel something like gratitude. The silence that greets his dismissal is about the loudest sound in sport. With Tendulkar the discussion is not how he got out but why. Susceptible to left-arm spin? To the inswinger? To the big occasion? The issue is not about whether it was good or not, but where does it rank? A Tendulkar innings is never over when it is over. It is simply a basis for negotiation. He might be behind headphones or helmet, but outside people are talking, shouting, fighting, conceding, bargaining, waiting. He is a national habit.

But Tendulkar goes on. This is his achievement, to live the life of Tendulkar. To occupy the space where fame and accomplishment intersect, akin to the concentrated spot under a magnifying glass trained in the sun, and remain unburnt.

"Sachin is God" is the popular analogy. Yet God may smile as disease, fire, flood and Sreesanth visit the earth, and expect no fall in stock. For Tendulkar the margin for error is rather smaller. The late Naren Tamhane was merely setting out the expectation for a career when he remarked as selector, "Gentlemen, Tendulkar never fails." The question was whether to pick the boy to face Imran, Wasim, Waqar and Qadir in Pakistan. Tendulkar was then 16.

Sixteen and so ready that "precocity" is too mild a word. He made refinements, of course, but the marvel of Tendulkar is that he was a finished thing almost as soon as he began playing.

The maidans of Bombay are dotted with tots six or seven years old turning out for their coaching classes. But till the age of 11, Tendulkar had not played with a cricket ball. It had been tennis- or rubber-ball games at Sahitya Sahwas, the writers' cooperative housing society where he grew up, the youngest of four cricket-mad siblings by a distance. The circumstances were helpful. In his colony friends he had playmates, and from his siblings, Ajit in particular, one above Sachin but older by 11 years, he had mentorship.

It was Ajit who took him to Ramakant Achrekar, and the venerable coach inquired if the boy was accustomed to playing with a "season ball" as it is known in India. The answer did not matter. Once he had a look at him, Achrekar slotted him at No. 4, a position he would occupy almost unbroken through his first-class career. In his first two matches under Achrekar Sir, he made zero and zero.

Memory obscures telling details in the dizzying rise thereafter. Everybody remembers the 326 not out in the 664-run gig with Kambli. Few remember the 346 not out in the following game, the trophy final. Everyone knows the centuries on debut in the Ranji Trophy and Irani Trophy at 15 and 16. Few know that he got them in the face of a collapse in the first instance and virtually out of partners in the second. Everyone knows his nose was bloodied by Waqar Younis in that first Test series, upon which he waved away assistance. Few remember that he struck the next ball for four.

This was Tendulkar five years after he'd first handled a cricket ball.

Genius, they say, is infinite patience. But it is first of all an intuitive grasp of something beyond the scope of will – or, for that matter, skill. In sportspersons it is a freakishness of the motor senses, even a kind of ESP.

The wonder is that in the years between he has done nothing to sully his innocence, nothing to deaden the impish joy, nothing to disrupt the infinite patience or damage the immaculate equilibrium through the riot of his life and career.

Tendulkar's genius can be glimpsed without him actually holding a bat. Not Garry Sobers' equal with the ball, he is nevertheless possessed of a similar versatility. He swings it both ways, a talent that eludes several specialists. He not only rips big legbreaks but also lands his googlies right, a task beyond some wristspinners. Naturally he also bowls offspin, usually to left-handers and sometimes during a spell of wristspin. In the field he mans the slips as capably as he does deep third man, and does both in a single one-dayer. Playing table tennis he is ambidextrous. By all accounts he is a brilliant, if hair-raising, driver. He is a champion Snake player on the cellphone, according to Harbhajan Singh, whom he also taught a spin variation.

His batting is of a sophistication that defies generalisation. He can be destroyer or preserver. Observers have tried to graph these phases into a career progression. But it is ultimately a futile quest, for Tendulkar's calibrations are too minute and too many to obey compartmentalisation. Given conditions, given his fitness, his state of mind, he might put away a certain shot altogether, and one thinks it is a part of his game that has died, till he pulls it out again when the time is right, sometimes years afterwards. Let alone a career, in the space of a single session he can, according to the state of the rough or the wind or the rhythm of a particular bowler, go from predatory to dead bat or vice versa.

Nothing frustrates Indians as much as quiet periods from Tendulkar, and indeed often they are self-defeating. But outsiders have no access to his thoughts. However eccentric, they are based on a heightened cricket logic rather than mood. Moods are irrelevant to Tendulkar. Brian Lara or Mohammad Azharuddin might be stirred into artistic rage. Tendulkar is a servant of the game. He does not play out of indignation nor for indulgence. His aim is not domination but runs. It is the nature of his genius.

The genius still doesn't explain the cricket world's enchantment with Tendulkar. Ricky Ponting and Jacques Kallis are arguably not lesser cricketers than he, but they have nothing like his following or presence. Among contemporaries only Shane Warne could draw an entire stadium's energy towards himself, but then Warne worked elaborately towards this end. Tendulkar on the pitch is as uncalculated as Warne was deliberate. Warne worked the moments before each delivery like an emcee at a title fight. Tendulkar goes through a series of ungainly nods and crotch adjustments. Batting, his movements are neither flamboyant nor languid; they are contained, efficient. Utility is his concern. Having hit the crispest shot between the fielders he can still be found scurrying down the wicket, just in case.

Likewise, outside the pitch nothing he does calls up attention. In this he is not unusual for the times. It has been, proved by exceptions of course, the era of the undemonstrative champion. Ali, Connors, McEnroe, Maradona have given way to Sampras, Woods, Zidane, Federer, who must contend with the madness of modern media and the sanitisation of corporate obligation.

Maybe Tendulkar the superstar, like Tendulkar the cricketer, was formed at inception. Then, as now, he is darling. He wears the big McEnroe-inspired curls of his youth in a short crop but still possesses the cherub's smile and twinkle. Perhaps uniquely, he is granted not the sportstar's indulgence of perma-adolescence but that of perma-childhood. A man-child on the field: maybe it is the dichotomy that is winning. The wonder is that in the years between he has done nothing to sully his innocence, nothing to deaden the impish joy, nothing to disrupt the infinite patience or damage the immaculate equilibrium through the riot of his life and career.

Rahul Bhattacharya *is the author of* Pundits from Pakistan *and the novel* The Sly Company of People Who Care

APT PUPIL

JOHN WRIGHT

In the days following the news of Sachin Tendulkar's retirement it started to happen again. People in New Zealand asking me what Sachin was like and what coaching him was about. During the many chats, it struck me that despite a very public career, it was the unseen parts of Sachin's life that made him the cricketer he is. Or, as we will say it now, the cricketer he was.

There was an eight-year gap between my leaving the India job in 2005 and joining Mumbai Indians in 2013. Much can change in eight years of a cricketer's life – form, circumstances, the person himself. As a coach you notice it in the smallest things.

When I came back to India, Sachin was in what turned out to be the last few months of his playing career. The Champions League Twenty20 was our last tournament together as player and coach. In the nets, Sachin was batting as well I'd seen him bat in the previous six months. He had obviously put work into it and was timing the ball well, but he still wasn't having the best time in the middle, and his reflexes weren't as consistently quick as they had been. God knows when you get to 40 you are not as sharp as you were even in your mid-thirties. Time just starts to catch you out.

Whatever else had changed for and around Sachin, fundamentally he himself had not. He was the same guy who loved cricket and was fun to be around. Whatever he did around the game was thorough and meticulous, as before. The day before a Champions League Twenty20 match in Jaipur, he was in the nets for an hour and a half. Justin Langer, coaching Perth Scorchers, made his young team stop training to watch. A 90-minute net the day before a T20 match from a player in his 25th year in competitive cricket. That says something.

Conventionally, this could be called a reflection of Sachin's work ethic, but I don't think the word "work" applies. Work is labour and industry. While doing his practice, Sachin was involved in something other than merely toil. Ed Smith, the cricketer who is now a writer, once quoted me a line from the poet WH Auden: "The first criterion of success in any human activity, the necessary preliminary, whether to scientific discovery or artistic vision, is intensity of attention or, less pompously, love."

In the nets, Sachin took to cricket with that "intensity of attention", like painters and musicians do with their craft. Sachin loves Mark Knopfler's guitar-playing, and I imagine Knopfler didn't learn to play guitar overnight. In order to get close to perfection or even to sense what it could feel like, the great masters practise and practise and practise. Similarly, in training, Sachin looked for constant refinement and even comfort. He could make adjustments to his game with an ease that demonstrated that he was in touch with the game at a level slightly removed from that experienced by most other cricketers.

As players we are so attached and dependent on muscle memory that our stance and grip become sacrosanct, like a golfer's swing. When they do not give us the results we want, changing them takes months. Sachin could often make those adjustments in practice the night before a game. What he was looking for was ease and calm, and he was capable of retooling himself to find it.

The great players have an acute awareness of how they want to prepare and what makes them play well. Sachin had that in spades. Amidst all the craziness and noise that went with every India match, he wanted to find a touch or a feeling that would indicate to him that he was ready to play. VVS Laxman's word "flow" to describe what he was looking for is perhaps the best description.

On the outside, Sachin is stoic, controlled, thoughtful. With his cricket, though, he was a man who completely trusted his instincts. Through stance, grip, hands, feet, head, in his training he looked for the best nesting place for those instincts. So that during game time, they could take flight. From there, he could make high-risk shots look safe. And create amazing angles, using a nimbleness of his body, and his head position and hands, to hit the ball where he wanted to while still playing with the full face of the bat. No matter where he had positioned himself.

Sachin always knew what he wanted out of training, what he needed, how much: whether he wanted to bat first or second or later, whether a long net or a short net or no net at all; the kind of bowlers he wanted to face, or if merely throwdowns would do. During the 2003 World Cup, he didn't have a single batting session in the nets, only throwdowns to groove his shots. What he did do in the nets was bowl heaps, so much so that he had to be stopped for fear of injuring himself.

No matter what the format – Tests, ODIs, or T20 in the IPL, he trained always in the same way – with Auden's "intensity of attention". He had a very good idea of what he needed to feel like in practice so he could feel like that in a game.

A net practice to Sachin was a learning, part of his development as a batsman, which extended to what happened at the game that followed. He was his own coach and his own trainer; his brother

Ajit, who knew his game inside out, was his fallback. Sachin was a reflective batsman and once his innings was over, he was able to debrief himself and knew where he had to go with his mind and his technique.

The time he spent with cricket, he spent with utter focus. His respect for the sport was grounded in the fact that he was never late – whether for the bus, meetings or nets. It was like going to church or to school; there's no negotiating those timetables. So it was with Sachin's training. The nets were his laboratory, his studio, and once there, he immersed himself.

Working with Sachin for me was about watching and asking questions. If I felt his head wasn't as still as it could be, I would ask him how he felt about his batting. If he said all was well, I kept my observation to myself. If he said things didn't feel quite right, you'd ask: "Is your balance feeling right? How's the head, you think?"

Everyone knows the story of how he didn't play a cover drive all through his Sydney double-hundred in 2004. I have another: during my second match in charge of India, in Nagpur, Sachin said he was going to get a double-century without hitting a shot in the air. He could have lofted Grant Flower or Brian Murphy any time he wanted, but he didn't. It was about reining himself in and exercising discipline. He got the double.

Early with India, when we were trying to get guys hooked on the importance of training and the gym, Sachin found his way there on his own. He had to be convinced that what he was going to do would not hurt his game. Once he was convinced about its benefits, he bought into the idea. If we did go running – and he was not a fan – he and I would be at the back, which suited me just fine!

Once, after he got a big score – I can't remember which one, but it is a while back – I brought up the figure of a hundred hundreds. It wasn't about sowing a seed; I just thought back then that if he wanted to, he could do it. Coaching often is a series of conversations with players. Sometimes they remember some things, sometimes they don't. Sachin and I did talk about longevity in the game, that the longer he stayed in, the more he was going to have to devote to staying in physical condition. To hire a personal trainer, to pay more and more attention to his body. He did that admirably, dealt with his injuries, adjusted his game, worked out what bat weight suits him best, what he should and should not do.

One morning, early in 2010, when I heard over the radio that he had become the first man to get 200 in ODIs, I laughed aloud. He was two months short of his 37th birthday and was being politely called a bit too long in the tooth. That 200 smelt like justice.

Coming back to work with him in 2013 was like seeing an old mate again. We just popped back into a familiar working relationship, where we could talk about cricket and batting and music. It may sound fairly humdrum but it is not. Success and fame can be a dangerous thing. It goes to the head and alters people. We see that happen all the time in sport – it is virtually the norm. Sachin experienced huge amounts of success and fame but dodged their bullets and retained both his sense of self and a sense of his place in cricket. He mastered the game better than anyone in the last 50 years, and was always confident of himself and his ability. Yet he always understood that the game is there to stretch you. Over two decades he remained a learner and a seeker – for more knowledge about the skill he possessed and what he could possibly do with it. Often players confuse expertise with knowledge, believe they are inter-changeable. Sachin understood the difference.

To respect the game beyond your own part in it requires a certain core of humility. With Sachin, there was never anything excessive about his game, and there is nothing excessive in his personality. After that T20 game in Jaipur that I was referring to earlier, he came over to me and asked if he could be excused the next day as he was going to Mumbai for his son's birthday. Not many players do that, particularly not those touched by that thing called stardom. Sachin was always consistent: not merely in his run-scoring but in his basic decency as a man, as a professional colleague and with his pride and passion for cricket.

Transfer his career, in performance and longevity, on to some other big names in cricket. Ask yourself if they would have never bragged, lost their temper or composure. In the time we spent in the dressing room together, I never saw him lose his rag, never saw him take cricket for granted. Maybe this absence of brashness was a quality that Indians loved as much as the aggression in his batting and the flamboyant range of his strokes. This essential unpretentiousness, I believe, was part of the fuel that kept him in the game.

Twenty-four years is a long time. Many in cricket have been touted as the next big thing, "the new Bradman". For about half a century, it never happened because it requires more than brilliant strokeplay. You need the mental capability to maximise what you have been given, to stick to your game and the values that have taken you to the top.

Cricket has had many great batsmen, their international careers lasting ten, maybe 15 years. Sachin has done 24: think about it. His career, now ended, is most great players' careers twice over.

---

*Former New Zealand batsman **John Wright** coached India from 2000 to 2005, and also worked with Tendulkar at the Mumbai Indians IPL franchise*

THE FIRST OF A HUNDRED

AYAZ MEMON

"Oh the places you'll go! There is fun to be done! There are points to be scored. There are games to be won. And the magical things you can do with that ball will make you the winning-est winner of all."

– Dr Seuss, *Oh, The Places You'll Go!*

Waiting for something special to unfold can be as thrilling as experiencing its arrival. Tension, fraught with anticipation, can both delight and devour: when the magical moment actually comes, it is to be cherished and never forgotten. This could be your first taste of ice cream, your first kiss, your first car, or in this case, watching Sachin Tendulkar's first century.

Casting my mind back almost a quarter-century, the prologue now seems as important and eventful as the story of the hundred itself. After protracted turmoil between senior players and the administration, Indian cricket was being made over, and the 1990 tour of England was seen, apart from all else, to be a test of new policy.

Mohammad Azharuddin had been unexpectedly elevated to the captaincy for the New Zealand tour earlier that year, and young players like Anil Kumble, Sanjeev Sharma and – above all – Tendulkar had been inducted in the preceding 12 months.

His numerous achievements as a schoolboy cricketer had made Tendulkar a rising star in the cricketing universe. But was he really a metaphor for the Indian team of the '90s or was this misplaced hype? Could he bat as well in England as he had done in the subcontinent? Just how good was he?

It was a star-studded team that reached England. Navjot Sidhu, Ravi Shastri, Sanjay Manjrekar, Dilip Vengsarkar, Azharuddin, Kapil Dev, Manoj Prabhakar and Kiran More were proven and classy performers. But the cynosure was Tendulkar, for several reasons, not least his youthfulness: to the English, 17-year-old Test players were rare.

Among the Indian press corps on the tour, a great deal of the conversation centred on when Tendulkar would make his first Test century. Now, a maiden century is a significant landmark in the life of any batsman, but in India, given the obsession with records and milestones, it is accentuated further.

Tendulkar's career till then had been defined by a hunger for high scores. In his schoolboy years, he had plundered single, double- and triple-centuries with mind-boggling regularity. He had centuries on debut in the Ranji and Irani trophies, and after the England tour, in the Duleep as well.

So when he became the youngest Indian Test cricketer, making his debut at 16 against Pakistan, expectations that he would break Mushtaq Mohammad's record as the youngest century-maker hogged headlines in the subcontinent. He had a modest first Test, and made two sturdy half-centuries in the series to show mettle, but Mushtaq's record (he was 17 years, 82 days old when he made his first century) was intact.

A couple of months later, the record came under grave threat when India played New Zealand in the second Test in Napier. Unbeaten overnight on 80, Tendulkar had nearly the entire country waking up at an unearthly hour to follow his progress on radio. But after two boundaries, he drove Danny Morrison to the off side and was caught at mid-off for 88.

The disappointment in India was huge. The next Test was to be played only in late July, in England, when he would be more than 17 years and 82 days old. A Test century had seemed ordained from the time he had held bat in hand as a ten-year-old. But it had now been seven Tests since his debut.

There was a hint of scepticism: was he was too flashy to succeed in international cricket with any degree of consistency? Not every child prodigy necessarily makes it at the highest level in any sport. Did he have the wherewithal and the discipline to make the quantum jump from first-class to Test cricket?

Tendulkar himself was unfazed – indeed even uncaring – about it. I remember interviewing him at his house for a magazine in the period between the New Zealand and England tours. He regretted missing the century in Napier, but not the record. He said playing attacking shots, dominating bowlers, gave him greater satisfaction.

His prized possessions then were a new music system on which he could listen to his favourite bands (Dire Straits topping the list), a new Maruti car, which he loved to drive even though he was underage, and a pair of used pads gifted to him by Sunil Gavaskar.

Curiosity about Tendulkar in England was obviously high. Given the attention and expectations, his team-mates and team management, and even the Indian press corps, were fretful about him: who he met, what he ate, what he said, and most importantly, was he still sleepwalking, as noticed by his first manager, Borde, in Pakistan nine months earlier?

He wasn't. But other unusual aspects of his cricketing persona were emerging: for instance, the half-squat before settling into his stance that was to become a signature mannerism in subsequent years. Not that Tendulkar fussed when team-mates pulled his leg about it, I was told by one.

In the first Test, at Lord's, Graham Gooch was dropped on 36 and went on to make 333, followed by another century in the second innings. Azhar, he of the tensile wrists and whiplash on-drives and sizzling cuts, made a dazzling 121 that many critics rated as the best knock played in England by an overseas batsman in half a century, perhaps more. There were attacking tons from Allan Lamb and Robin Smith too. Then there was Kapil, hitting Eddie Hemmings for four sixes to avoid a follow-on. The match saw six centuries in all, but India lost – to some extent because they made runs too quickly in their first innings, giving England enough time to force the issue.

Two Indian players in the limelight for different reasons failed to capitalise on the placid pitch. Vengsarkar, looking for a fourth successive century at Lord's, managed a sketchy 52 in the first innings. Tendulkar had scores of 10 and 27, looking good both times, then throwing it away. He had one terrific moment in this match, though, which is an abiding memory for me: taking a steepling catch after running in about 20 yards from wide deep mid-on, to dismiss Lamb in the second innings. In my opinion he hasn't done better in the field since.

The Lord's Test lost, the Indians were despondent and desperately seeking some inspiration. A fortnight later came the second Test, at Old Trafford. It was a better contest than the first, bitter in the cricketing sense, making huge demands on the technical skills, commitment and temperament of the Indian players.

The bowling, alas, did not have enough depth, and England's

batsmen were in roaring form again. Gooch, like a run-hungry ogre, hit his third successive century, and put on 225 with his opening partner, Mike Atherton, who also scored a hundred. Smith rubbed salt into India's wounds with a 121 that had the bowlers and fielders running for cover. Batting first, England made 519.

However, the track was still a belter. Manjrekar and, particularly, Azhar revelled. But when Manjrekar fell for 93, India were 246 for 4, the threat of a follow-on still hovering uneasily over them. Precipitate batting collapses were not unknown in Indian cricket.

I can't quite remember Tendulkar's first scoring stroke, but I do recall that it took him nearly an hour to get off the mark. Once the shackles were broken, the runs came freely, marked by an uncanny ability to pick gaps in the field and backed by clever running between the wickets with his captain.

Tendulkar's 68 didn't compare with the rhapsody of Azhar, who made a scintillating 179. But he showed resolve and a nuanced strokeplay, which were to become the hallmarks of his batting over the next quarter of a century. His half-century also set up the second-innings opus that was to save the game for India.

On the last day, after another bout of batting mayhem by England, as we trudged into the Old Trafford press box the big question was whether India would lose this Test too, and the series. Gooch's intentions became clear when he declared 20 minutes into the day, leaving India the improbable task of scoring 408 for victory – or the more excruciating one of surviving about 90 overs for a draw.

After four days the pitch was showing signs of wear and tear. Hemmings, the offspinner, would be a serious threat. But the early damage was done by the pacemen. Angus Fraser had Sidhu caught for a duck, Devon Malcolm got Shastri for 12, India were on the edge. Manjrekar and Vengsarkar steadied the innings, but after lunch Hemmings snaffled both on the same score (109).

I'll refrain from a Hitchcockian narrative, because the outcome is only too well known. But back then, every over, every minute was pulsating with twin-track suspense: could India save the Test, and would Tendulkar be able to score his maiden century?

Before writing this piece, I refreshed my memory of Tendulkar's century with a 20-minute clip on Youtube, and the marvel of that innings was revived. The gumption, technical certitude, joy, temerity and intelligence, given his young age and relative inexperience, make it more extraordinary in hindsight.

Unlike in the first innings, he didn't adopt a dour approach. Rather, he attacked the bowlers – especially Hemmings – to hit them off their length and make them lose rhythm. Gooch set attacking fields that Tendulkar cleared with chipped shots. When the close-in field was reduced, he pushed for singles and twos to keep the runs coming, or pierced it with sizzling drives on either side.

Every now and then he would walk down the track to his doughty partner, Manoj Prabhakar (with whom he added 160 runs to draw the match), for a bout of animated discussion. Prabhakar was to say later that Tendulkar was advising him rather than the other way around.

He had a stroke of luck on 10, when Hemmings muffed a simple caught-and-bowled, but that apart, Tendulkar showed a masterly, dominant touch, the highlight being a series of breathtaking cover drives off the back foot, rising on his toes. One of these, off Fraser, about 40 minutes before the close, went past mid-off and took him to the coveted three-figure mark. He was all of 17 years and 112 days old.

Plaudits for Tendulkar – from team-mates, opponents, fans and critics – were profuse and generous. This boy is indeed special, seemed to be the consensus. Bishan Singh Bedi, the irrepressible Indian manager on the tour, added a hyperbolic exuberance to this, saying every female in England, from 16 to 60, loved him.

Tendulkar, though, had clearly set his sights far beyond such distractions.

You knew that you were in the presence of something glorious but had no way of knowing that 99 more would follow. Twenty-four years later, you realise that was the moment the first brick was laid.

*Veteran sportswriter **Ayaz Memon** has covered six cricket World Cups*

THE REINVENTIONIST

AAKASH CHOPRA

When in the winter of 1989 a petite, innocuous-looking Sachin Tendulkar first walked down the pitch to bat against mighty Pakistan, who would have imagined this teenager would become the very reason for millions of Indians to watch and play cricket?

I was all of 12, and he 16, when I first saw him hold that bat and play the ball, on my family's new colour television set. There's a different kind of romanticism around young prodigies, which is what makes people love them so much. A young boy taking on the big, bad world brings out the deepest emotions in those watching.

Sachin had already become a rage by the mid-1990s. Little boys wanted to bat, dress and wear their hair like he did. I remember watching an advert for a cola brand that featured about a dozen boys playing gully cricket, wearing Tendulkar masks. That commercial captured the popular sentiment. Everyone wanted to be like him.

Parents would walk into cricket academies with their kids in tow, demanding the coaches train their boys such that they could play for

India, at 16, "like Sachin". Their logic was that if Sachin could do it, their son could. Little did they realise that Tendulkars are born, not made.

I distinctly remember my coach, Tarak Sinha, turning away scores of parents, telling them that he didn't "make Tendulkars". If you want your son to learn how to play cricket, you're welcome, he would say. Otherwise, please search for a different coach or academy. Unfortunately, Mr Sinha's problems didn't end there, for even the ones who weren't trying to become the next Tendulkar emulated his technique, almost as if unconsciously.

Back then, Tendulkar used to lean quite heavily on the bat while standing in his stance. His backlift came from the gully region and he wasn't shy of playing shots to balls that he couldn't get his feet to. If you pull out videos of his first tour to Pakistan, you'll see him flay at a fast Waqar Younis delivery way outside off. Watching Tendulkar bat like that, many of us started to lean on our bats while standing in the stance, and to play on the up without worrying too much about reaching the pitch of the ball with the front foot.

There was, of course, a minor thing that we overlooked: Sachin was exceptionally quick with his hands and feet, and he would invariably get the bat down in time even while playing across. His innate ability to pick the length earlier than most allowed him to compensate for any errors he made in picking the line. When you're leaning too much on the bat in your stance, you often fail to read the line of the ball well. You think that the ones that are outside off are on off stump, and the ones that are within the stumps seem to be drifting down leg. That makes you susceptible to fishing outside off and to playing across to the ones pitched in line. While the world wished for Tendulkar to succeed, bowlers in opposition teams had started to plot his dismissals: bowl within the stumps, make him play across and he would fall. Or so they thought.

Tendulkar's first big – perhaps his biggest – leap of improvement came about soon after he started playing international cricket. The longer he played, the less he leaned on the bat. He began to stand upright with his knees slightly flexed to provide the right balance, and in the end it evolved into the perfect batting stance: both feet comfortably apart, head in line with the toes. Once that foundation was laid, the rest started to fall in place.

More than the actual improvement, it was the intent to improve that stood out. During Tendulkar's first tour of England he was guilty of reaching out to the ball initially. That's when Sunil Gavaskar advised him to let the ball come to him. He did that not only in that series but also in every one thereafter.

When you're making your way to the top of the game, a lot of advice comes your way. You need to be prudent enough to know what to pay heed to and what to quietly duck under. While there is no dearth of people who want to offer advice, not many ask for it, especially at the top. Tendulkar, though, liked to discuss his game – like he did with me, a rookie who was cutting his teeth in international cricket, on the tour of Australia in 2003–04. During practice sessions and breaks between games, he would ask me questions about his technique and various aspects of his batting. Initially, I thought these sessions were meant to make me comfortable with him and the rest of the senior players, but as the days went by, I realised Sachin genuinely looked for feedback. And what I told him never put him on the defensive; he listened to every word with a keenness that you rarely see in players today. He seemed to thrive on criticism, and that's a hallmark of greatness.

A lot of people would probably have told him how flawed his grip on the bat was. Until you're successful, not one coach will advise you to hold the bat at the base of the handle – that's how a kid will typically hold a bat two sizes too big for him, and it has its dangers. It allows you more control but it reduces your flexibility, or so it is believed. Holding the bat nearer the top of the handle gives you a wider range of strokes, especially off the front foot, for it increases your reach. The lower down the handle the hands are, the smaller the curve in the downswing, and so the smaller the reach. But Tendulkar challenged that belief and wrote a new chapter in the coaching manual. His low hands allowed him to play the horizontal-bat shots, but somehow he also managed to be equally fluent off the front foot.

Through his career, Tendulkar showed acute awareness about his game. When he started, he was an aggressive batsman who wouldn't hesitate to fight fire with fire, revelling in duels and going after bowlers from the start of innings. While never rash, he would happily take the aerial route and play slightly high-risk shots regularly. But as time went by, his role in the side changed from that of the aggressor to the most dependable batsman. If he had to consistently succeed at the highest level, he needed to abandon some of the more risky options and play percentage cricket more often.

So he stopped dancing down the track to a fast bowler or going over the infield just because he could. He started finding different, less risky, ways of scoring the same number of runs. The lofted shot over the spinner's head was replaced by a paddle sweep played very fine. The ones that went along the ground past the fielders at mid-off or covers adequately replaced the extended airborne straight drive over mid-off.

Some of it was also due to injuries he sustained over the years. The wear and tear of playing international cricket meant he needed to shelve a few shots: his shoulder, wrist and elbow simply didn't allow him to display his full range. That's when his ability to put mind over matter came to the fore.

Batting, they say, is at its best when you're in the zone – the space when you aren't thinking about anything except reacting to the ball, the space in which you allow your instincts to take over and your skills come to the fore on their own. Ironically, one of Tendulkar's best innings, his 241 not out in Sydney in 2004, which I saw up close, came when he intentionally didn't allow himself to slip into that zone.

I was sitting next to him in the dressing room for that Test match and when he came back in after the innings he asked me if I noticed that he didn't play a single cover drive. I thought he was joking, but he wasn't. I realised it was true that he hadn't played a single drive through the covers off the front foot. He had been fishing outside off through that series, and so, though he was batting well, he didn't get a big score till the last Test match.

The Australians had looked to target him outside off in every innings, and in any case full outside off with two or three slips and a gully is the most obvious line and length to bowl in a Test match, especially on hard and bouncy Australian pitches. As natural as it is to bowl to the off-side trap, it's just as natural for a batsman, if not more, to allow his body to react aggressively to a half-volley. One can understand restraint early in an innings, for that's what most batsmen are conditioned to exhibit, but monk-like discipline once fully set? Sachin's mind fought a battle with his body and won.

The next innings after that knock in Sydney brought forth another facet of Tendulkar's character – the ability to rein himself in and play the supporting role. Virender Sehwag was on a roll and, though in good form himself, Sachin didn't mind being second fiddle in Multan.

After almost two decades of his debut, he made another major adjustment to his backlift, choosing economy over extravagance. He would no longer take the bat high up in the backlift to every ball bowled to him, only to those he thought he could hit. To the rest he presented a near dead bat, with no momentum whatsoever. This was quite visible even in his last Test match.

When you tweak your natural backlift and downswing, you sacrifice a bit of flamboyance. The Sachin of old could change his shot at the last minute, and the momentum from the backlift helped him do this. Later those decisions were made in advance. Ashish Nehra told me that it was impossible to bowl a slower one to Tendulkar in the nets, for even if he picked it a little late, he would simply make a last-minute adjustment and hit over the inner ring. That stopped happening in the last lap of his career. Also, the pull, another instinctive shot, went out of his quiver.

As the shadows started to get longer, you saw that Tendulkar was human too. He started getting bowled fairly often. While his technique was still the same, I thought his reflexes slowed down just a shade. In his last first-class match, he was still on the move when a Mohit Sharma delivery hit his elbow before going on to hit the stumps. Though he came back strongly in the second innings, it was clear that he was not the player of old.

The last innings at the Wankhede turned the clock back and provided a taster of most of what Tendulkar had done over the last 24 years. The balance while playing the straight drive was still there, he was still standing tall on his toes while dispatching short balls through cover, and most importantly, he was picking the line and length early. Of course, he didn't play the pull or the lofted shot down the ground, but to expect that during the last few overs of a long day's play was foolish.

The final hour of his career seemed like a montage of his life on the pitch – he came in with the team in a slightly precarious situation, wrested the initiative in his own inimitable style, passed the baton to a few able men, and left the scene after ensuring that his team was in a stronger position than when he came in.

Aakash Chopra played ten Tests for India in 2003 and 2004

FOREVER ICON

ED SMITH

Change is constant, but the pace of change is wildly inconstant. Some lives are played out in the context of continuity and stability; others must adapt to dizzying change and upheaval. Endurance, perseverance and resilience are all relative concepts: standing your ground is much harder when the sands are shifting all around you.

In 1989, when Sachin Tendulkar first took guard for India, cricket was mostly played in whites. The dominant team in the world was West Indies. ODI cricket was emerging but Test cricket firmly remained the game's gold standard. T20 was an accidental form of the game, a solution used only when rain shortened the duration of play. When the England Test team played away from home, it still wore the egg-and-bacon colours of the MCC, a strip invented in the 19th century. India was a passionate cricketing nation but a marginal

This article was first published on ESPNcricinfo in November 2013

player within the game's power structure and governance – money and influence lay elsewhere.

Twenty-four years later, as Tendulkar lifts his bat for the last time in Indian colours, survey the contours of the cricketing world today. Many more cricket fans love and understand the white-ball version than the red. India is the game's great superpower; it commands such huge television contracts that every other country wants a slice of the goodies. A whole dynasty, the Australian machine of the 1990s and 2000s, one of sport's greatest empires, has risen and retreated. T20, once a mere entertainment, drives the commercial imperatives of the sport.

When the final history of cricket is written – for our purposes here, let's call it the age of Tendulkar – his period has been seen as one of deep change and constant uncertainty. Yet throughout Tendulkar has adapted and endured. He has found answers to every new question – his 49 ODI hundreds are arguably the more remarkable achievement than his 51 Test centuries. And yet he has also belonged to the great, timeless tradition of pure batsmanship. Modern and classical at the same time, Tendulkar has been a cricketer for every stage.

It is a truism that he has faced a unique burden of expectation. That is partly because the changes in Indian society between Tendulkar's first Test and his 200th have trumped even the revolutions in cricket. In 1989, the Indian economy languished from protectionism and introversion. The beginning of India's economic recovery was the moment of Tendulkar's emergence as a global talent. That Tendulkar's career coincided with the emergence of India as an economic power was just that – a coincidence. But the subliminal link between the "Little Master" and a resurgent India provided yet another dimension of pressure and expectation.

So in celebrating Tendulkar's achievements, we are partly paying testament to the weight he has carried. When India won the 2011 World Cup final, Virat Kohli captured a deep truth: "He has carried the burden of our nation on his shoulders for the past 21 years. So it is time that we carried him."

Despite all this – all the many ways in which Tendulkar is admirable and impressive and inspiring – I have found it very difficult to gather together my thoughts about his retirement. My feelings about his career will not settle into a shape or a narrative. I can see the achievements but not the thread. I can list the feats and accolades, but the personality that achieved them eludes me. When I describe him as an enigma, I feel a failure on my part, as a writer. It is my job to find the man underneath the enigma. And I regret that I cannot.

When we watch athletes perform hundreds of times, we nearly always get to know them. Not from their quotes and their interviews but from the sporting performance itself. "An artist is usually a damned liar," DH Lawrence wrote in *Studies in Classic American Literature* "but his art, if it be art, will tell you the truth of his day." Change the word "artist" for the word "sportsman" and the same point holds: trust the runs and wickets, not the press-conference quotes.

We see into a sportsman's character by watching him play. We know when they relish the battle, when they allow themselves to enjoy it, when they are anxious and unsettled, when they are confident or in the zone. With players we care deeply about, we know and understand them almost as close friends. Knowing and being known, the mask slipped from the face: that was the playwright Tom Stoppard's definition of the emotion that sustains meaningful relationships.

But there is a strange paradox at the core of Tendulkar's career. The more he has played, the less we can see the real man. The mask has not slipped, it has risen. The carapace has not shrunk, it has grown. In a strange way, less is known about Tendulkar than ever before. The icon has supplanted the man.

Only a handful of human beings can understand what it has been like to be Tendulkar. Bob Dylan, writing in his autobiography *Chronicles*, said the hardest thing to handle was not criticism but deification. When they called him a prophet, hero and saviour, Dylan replied, "I'm just a song and dance man." Dylan drew upon his innate savvy to wriggle free from the straightjacket of being a redemptive hero. Sportsmen, sadly, find it harder to escape the traps of idolatrous celebrity.

I used to think that Tiger Woods had experienced the weirdest of all sports careers. In his heyday, Woods treated his own humanity almost as a flaw, like a kink in his backswing that needed to be ironed out. Woods wished to ascend from human frailty into machine-like invulnerability.

Now I realise that becoming a machine is much easier than being turned into a god – as Tendulkar has been. Perhaps he had no choice but to go along with what a billion people yearned for him to be. But I cannot avoid the feeling that the god has gradually displaced the man.

I try to understand men; gods leave me cold. Perhaps that is why, when I write about Tendulkar, for all my admiration and awe in the face of his great achievements, the words will not come.

Ed Smith is the author of Luck: A Fresh Look at Fortune

ENOUGH ABOUT THE 100TH

SHARDA UGRA

All right, everyone, he's not having fun himself, you know. It's bloody 2005 all over again. When room service carries in his dinner or housekeeping changes the sheets and towels, they all give him sheepish, respectful smiles and mention just one thing. Hello, sir, wishing you the best, sir, to get "it". Please, sir, soon. Then there's the liftman, the receptionist, the bus driver, the gateman, the dressing-room attendant. Then you, me, the boss, the rookie, mummy, daddy, uncle, auntie, grandparents, gym instructor, chaiwallah, all asking him to deliver the hundred as if it were a pizza that could reach your door in 30 minutes.

Now you know why he wears those giant headphones.

In 2005, it was about the 35th Test century. When it was done, he said he had been "glad and relieved . . . I could then start enjoying

---

This article was first published on ESPNcricinfo in November 2011

the game again". From No. 34, it took five Tests and seven innings to get to 35.

Only five Tests, you're thinking. Only seven innings. What about this excruciating torture now, which doesn't seem to end? It's been 14 innings, nine matches – ODIs, Tests, World Cup, England tour, Kotla, the whole fruit basket. Still we wait. And we will begin all over again in Kolkata. Best now to think of Master Shifu and find inner peace.

The 35th took a whole year. That is how they stretched out five Tests in the pre-IPL days. So zip it. It has only been eight months since No. 99. Be grateful that he can get this one in either of two formats. Remember, he was so spent after 35 that it took 17 months, 17 innings and ten Tests to get to No. 36, which doesn't seem like such a big deal now. It is the longest he's ever been without the reassurance of a century since he started playing for India. Once he got to No. 36, he raced away; between then and now, 15 centuries in Tests, seven in ODIs, 7500-plus runs in both forms, the world's first one-day 200, a World Cup finally won.

He knows how this hundred business is done, okay? He's just approaching middle age, you know, when we all begin to creak a little. Everything takes time these days. Now stop fretting, go study, pay attention to office mundanities, spend time with the family. Take the damn hundred off your mind. He's not thinking about you, anyway. Who knows, maybe he's even not thinking about his 90s. Twenty-seven in 743 innings for India, after just five in the first ten years of his career.

To closely study the effects of the 100th on crowd behaviour, psychologists should have gone out to all the grounds where he has played since March 13. They would have come across classic case studies in these key categories: worshippers, worriers, theoreticians, tall-poppy trimmers, poets even, sitting next to each other, hearts beating, minds racing.

Please, God, this time, this one. I promise you I won't ever call him God again. Please, please, please.

Suppose he gets out again? Suppose he can't do it? The sun won't rise, I won't able to live.

Cross-bat? On a wicket that kept low? Refusing a single? Farming strike? Clearly the sight of that hundred caused a brain-freeze.

Serves him right, let him stew; obsessing about records. He's old, he should retire. The team comes first.

Ninety nine, no more.
O, Bradman. Incomplete.
Yet rounded off.

The 100th isn't just about the score any more; ideally it must involve a suitable, noble occasion. Which is why the Oval innings of 2011 made some sweat; as if he would have gone around the ground for a lap of honour. Versus West Indies at the Kotla, it was said he had "missed" another chance – narrowly, by 93 runs. The second-innings 24-run "miss" had effectively controlled India's third-highest successful chase, before the 100th got in the way. Now, as if we control it, like a choice between margherita or quattro formaggi, we think, what would be better, Kolkata or Mumbai? Kolkata didn't get an India World Cup game; November 15 is the day his first Test began, 22 years ago. But surely, Mumbai, his home town?

To generate real suspense, Hitchcock believed, "you must let the audience have the information". What would he have made of this? The information here is available not only to the audience but to the central character as well. The suspense, all the same, is killing. Eden Gardens begins on Monday.

We'll let you in on a secret. When the moment comes – and it will, it will – everyone will stand up and applaud, dignified, teary, joyful. Including us journalists. We will not, though, be scrambling.

While you were chewing fingernails and hiding behind the sofa, the media, dear reader, was getting ready. Newspapers, magazines, erm, websites, television channels. Reams have already been written about the 100th, pages designed, programme packages prepared, footage edited, voiceovers recorded, even quotes obtained. Like everyone, they are waiting too, pulled in by the allure of the 100th. This is tribute, not deceit.

At the end of the day, what's marvellously monumental about a 100th international hundred, is equally so now, after 99. Qualitatively the difference of that one more is really, just a number.

Sharda Ugra is a senior editor at ESPNcricinfo

THE BRINGER OF INFINITE POSSIBILITY

SOUMYA BHATTACHARYA

I wonder how it is for other fans. Speaking for myself, I have two sorts of Tendulkar memories. They are discrete sets of memories, although, given that the one would not have existed without the other, the discreteness is a paradox. (But when on earth was fandom a rational thing?)

One set of memories involves innings. The debut hundred at Old Trafford in 1990 that helped India save the Test. The blitzkrieg of a century on a brutally quick Perth pitch in 1992 when Tendulkar was still only 19 years old. The two ODI innings in Sharjah against Australia in 1998. In the same year as the slayer of Shane Warne, the unbeaten 155 in Chennai that won the Test. The century in the Bloemfontein Test in South Africa in 2001, when he turned the spooned shot over third man into a potent, attacking stroke that is now commonly known as the upper cut. That plunder against Pakistan in the 2003 World Cup. The 241 not out against Australia in Sydney in 2004, the innings on the back of a lean run in which he left out the cover drive from his repertoire because he had been getting out playing it earlier in the series. The 175 against Australia in the Hyderabad ODI in 2009, in which the wary gatherer was subsumed into the savage hunter of old in a display of brilliant ferocity. The double-century against South Africa in Gwalior in a 2010 ODI.

Then there are the shots that would make us catch our breath, wonder how he did it, clap our hands to our foreheads as we realised why no one had quite been able to do it before him, and think of how, once his career was over, no one ever would.

The push drive, the ball meeting the sweet spot at just the perfect instant and racing away. Oh the sound of that contact, the precision of that timing. The textbook cover drive, full of poise, intent and beauty, which split the field no matter how many men the opposition had positioned on the off side. The canny improvisations that yielded runs behind the wicket. The flicks off his legs backward of square. The hoicks in the arc between mid-on and midwicket that were destined to be boundaries no sooner had they left his bat.

But when I think about Tendulkar now (and I think quite often and rather hard), more than either of these two sets of memories, the image that comes back to me most vividly and with most power is something else.

It is the image of a mid-career Tendulkar, say, from 1998, walking out to bat. Bat under his left arm as he slips on the gloves, left one first, then the right. Loosening his body as he walks towards the wicket. Then breaking into a little jog. A touch of shadow practice, often involving the push drive. And the roar all around loud enough to threaten to blow the roof off the stadium. The alertness in the crowd. The quickening of the pulse. The adrenaline pumping. A sequence of moments, repeated over and over, hundreds of times, and still unique every time it occurred. The thrill of it.

And most of all: the sense of infinite possibility that he brought to the crease. The sense that, while he was out there, anything, simply *anything*, was conceivable.

More than the runs and hundreds and records and longevity, I sometimes think that what I treasure most about Tendulkar – prodigious, peerless, generation-straddling poster boy of a sport that defines the world's most populous democracy – is that sense of infinite possibility that he embodied. How, with him, we knew everything had changed for ever.

The time at which Tendulkar burst upon our consciousness is vital. His career was entwined with contemporary India's story of growth, hope and change, and its desperate need for self-congratulation and chest-thumping.

When he appeared, India was beginning to give birth to a new, affluent, urban middle class. Tendulkar began to embody all the qualities that this new class treasured. He was a world-beater, a global citizen. He was smart. He dressed well. He drove sexy cars.

Allow me a little digression. When I interviewed him in 2012, I asked him what he enjoyed spending money on. "I love food, shoes, cars, perfumes," he said. Which one of his many cars was his favourite? "The BMW 5. It is a magnificent car. It is sporty and comfortable." The perfume he was wearing was Comme des Garçons. Thanks to Wikipedia, I found that it is a Japanese label that introduced in 1998 the "anti-perfume Odeur53, a blend of non-traditional notes to create a modern and striking scent". His shoes were a pair of Berlutis. Again, Wiki enlightened me that it is a French company "that manufactures and retails a very exclusive luxury brand of shoes and boots solely for men". His watch was an Audemars Piguet, a luxury brand for which he is a global ambassador.

He was, above all, a self-made man. And the money he earned: huge sums, unthinkable ones, more than anyone had ever made before him. He was Indian sport's first global brand. Without him, there would have been no MS Dhoni, no Virat Kohli. He was the epitome of the successful cricketer as a global superstar. When I met the legendary English novelist Martin Amis in 1993, one of the first things he asked me was: "How does Sachin Tendulkar pronounce his first name?" (Lots of Englishmen used to pronounce it "Sa-shin" at the time.)

Matthew Hayden once described the behaviour of a crowd in India as Tendulkar walked out to bat as "the frantic appeal of a nation to one man". And in his 2002 book, *A Corner of a Foreign Field*, Ramachandra Guha tells us that when Tendulkar batted against Pakistan, India's TV audience was larger than the population of Europe.

Fathers loved him. Sons loved him. Why, grandmothers loved him. I remember an Adidas ad in which a grandmother was seen praying for his success, her rosary beads clattering to the floor as Tendulkar smashed one out of the ground. He bridged the gender and generation divide.

Once upon a time, he was the son every mother wanted. Now he has become the father every daughter would like to have. The iconography has accordingly changed. As a teenager, he did ads for an energy-boosting drink for children. Towards the end of his playing days, he endorsed life insurance.

Not one of the young men and women who will be eligible to vote for the first time in the 2014 general elections has seen Indian cricket without Tendulkar. His career has spanned their lifetimes, and more.

Then there are those such as myself. He was the first sporting hero I had who was younger than me. When I first watched him play, he was 16, and I, 20. Having a hero younger than you is a bit of a life-altering moment. For fans of my generation, that was one of the ways in which he altered our lives.

"I believe that heroes," wrote the poet, critic and cricket fan Alan Ross, "are necessary to children and that as we grow up it becomes more difficult to establish them in the increasingly unresponsive soil of our individual mythology. Occasionally, the adult imagination is caught and sometimes it is held; but the image rarely takes root."

Tendulkar's magic has been that his image has taken root in the adult imagination. I was studying for a degree in English literature at Kolkata's Presidency College when Tendulkar toured Australia for the first time in 1992. In those days, the tagline for the ad of a filterless cigarette called Charminar ran – roughly translated from Bengali – something like this: "For us, there is only one cigarette." My friends and I, up in the early Kolkata winter mornings, huddled together with a blanket thrown across our knees, watched him come out to bat and riffed on that tagline. "For us, there is only one cricketer," we said in Bengali, over and over again.

He was the first Indian batsman who could score mountains of runs, and score them with a sense of murderous intent. What could we do but succumb to his allure? Here is Ross again. "Heroes die with one's youth. They are pinned like butterflies to the setting board of early memories." Tendulkar compelled us to revisit those early memories of sporting heroes (John McEnroe, Gundappa Viswanath, Viv Richards, Diego Maradona) and revise our pantheon.

I have watched Tendulkar bat in 2012 and 2013 with an odd feeling. It is not nostalgia on the rocks. Neither is it with the hope that anything might be possible while he was at the crease. There has been sadness at his dwindling. But there has been joy that his gifts were at their peak for so very many years. Long enough for the world to have changed beyond recognition.

I have watched Tendulkar bat in 2012 and 2013 to spot and celebrate the odd image that is a part of one set of my memories of him. The push drive; the flick off the legs; the hoick between mid-off and mid-on; the cover drive so redolent of balance, precision and grace.

I have done that because the end – the farewell, the retirement, the final, final match – was on its way. We all knew that the end was near. It seemed churlish not to celebrate the end-nearing moments.

In the statement he issued to announce his retirement, Tendulkar said that he would not know what to do without cricket. Indian cricket will find it just as hard to make an adjustment to life without him. As I watched him in his twilight years, I – along with millions of my fellow fans – was all too aware that we shall never see the likes of him again.

Soumya Bhattacharya *is the editor of* Hindustan Times, *Mumbai, and the author of the books* You Must Like Cricket?, All That You Can't Leave Behind, *and the novel* If I Could Tell You

SEVENTY-FOUR TO FINISH

SIDHARTH MONGA

At around 4pm on November 14, 2013, a flight from Chennai landed in Mumbai. Along with providing facts about the weather outside, the captain informed the passengers – who had boarded the plane two hours before – "God has come out for one last dance." On the radio with the control room, he had been following events at the Wankhede Stadium. This was possibly the last time Sachin Tendulkar was going to stop time.

About a half-hour before that flight landed, Tendulkar had indeed come out for what seemed like a last dance, because West Indies had been bowled out for 182 and had not inspired any real possibility of making India bat again in the second and final Test of the series.

This was a hurriedly organised series. Some felt it came about because Cricket South Africa had gone against the BCCI's wishes when choosing its new CEO, and thus the BCCI was making it pay by shortening the South Africa tour to the bare minimum and shoehorning a West Indies series in so that the players didn't sit idle at the height of the season. Some felt it was a means to ease Tendulkar out of the game: give him his 200th Test at home, make him retire so that a new young batsman could be taken to the bigger test in South Africa. Some felt the series, and the resultant mutation of the South Africa tour, came about because the host broadcaster, which had paid big money for the rights, wanted to relaunch its brand and needed a big event to do it with.

If there is one Indian who can make you overcome such cynical thoughts, it is Tendulkar. His bond with the average Indian is stronger than scepticism. It transcends every intermediary, as was the case during the two-match pushing around of West Indies that was called a series. Fans travelled from outside India without any assurance they would get tickets: Kolkata put 6500 on sale, Mumbai 5000. The rest went to members and clubs and anybody who needed to be appeased; some of these beneficiaries were seen scalping their tickets outside Eden Gardens on the eve of the match.

Tendulkar's fans, though, begged, borrowed and paid many times the marked price to get into the stadium to bid him farewell, never mind the lack of contest or context in the series. So at 3.31pm on this Thursday afternoon, about 25,000 cheered the fall of two Indian wickets in one Shane Shillingford over, which meant there was enough time before stumps for India to not entertain thoughts of sending out a nightwatchman.

As the ball lobbed off M Vijay's bat and pad, 25,000 necks turned towards the Indian dressing room. It took them about a minute to realise that Vijay had been asked to wait because the umpires were checking if Shillingford's front foot was fine.

Their attention didn't move from the dressing room, where Tendulkar now put an arm guard on, then the helmet, and lifted a bat with a green, white and saffron grip. He played some shadow pulls, flexed his arms by rotating the bat over his head and down, then looked up at the sky to adjust to the light, and when he looked back down he saw the West Indies players, the unbeaten batsman, Cheteshwar Pujara, and the umpires had formed a guard of honour.

He shook the captain Darren Sammy's hand, acknowledged the others with a nod, knocked gloves with Pujara, touched the soil and then took the same hand to his helmet and sort of crossed his heart, and then asked the umpire for his guard after patting the pitch all over. One leg.

Thus began his final international innings, facing Shillingford, who had dismissed him in the previous Test with a doosra. A slip, silly point, forward short leg and backward short leg in place. If he had a tear in his eye, like Donald Bradman supposedly did in his last Test, they were all ready to snap him first ball. It drifted in, dipped slightly, but was still too full, and was defended to leg, although short leg got a little excited. The next one was flatter, which meant he could retreat from his forward press and defend off the back foot.

In the next over, Pujara hit two fours, but the crowd chanted, "Sachiiiin, Sachin." They had come to watch Tendulkar bat. Today, nothing else mattered. For his part, Tendulkar had shed some of his restraint, which had become a trademark in the last few years of his career. He soon got off the mark, sweeping Shillingford from around off, a shot he managed to keep down, though he didn't get to the pitch of the ball. The foot movements were precise. He was either properly forward or right back. His next run came with a push wide of mid-off, against Shillingford's turn. This shot would be a major part of Tendulkar's final innings.

Soon the big screen at the stadium showed clips of his mother, Rajni Tendulkar, and his coach, Ramakant Achrekar, being wheeled into the Wankhede. Rajni had never been in a ground to watch him play before. Achrekar never said "well done" to him, lest he became complacent.

Also in attendance were a host of former players: apart from those commentating – Rahul Dravid, VVS Laxman, Ravi Shastri – there were Lalchand Rajput, who was run out on 99 when batting with Tendulkar on the latter's first-class debut; the other opener in that match, Shishir Hattangadi; India team-mate Kiran More; Balwinder Sandhu; Nilesh Kulkarni; and a number of former Mumbai cricketers. The noise overall was deafening, and it would have been awfully difficult to concentrate, what with all the emotions in his head.

Tendulkar seemed to have got the better of it all, though. Though the attack wasn't a stern test of batsmanship, he defended off the front foot well, left judiciously, and was quick to go back when needed. With the ninth ball he faced, he displayed his meat-and-drink shot: Shannon Gabriel bowled short of a length, angling into off, Tendulkar rose with the bounce, was on his toes to get on top of the bounce, and closed the face at the right time to help the ball along to long leg for a single. Perfect execution of this shot was usually a good indicator that Tendulkar was in good touch.

Just after, though, Tendulkar asked for a change of bat. Three with similar tricolour grips came out. The right bat selected, he proceeded to hit three fours. Cut against the offspinner, done. Extra-cover drive against the turn, done. Extra-cover drive against a quick, done. Tendulkar 16 off 15, India 99 for 2, roof off the stadium.

Fifteen overs remained in the day. We were sure to go into the extra half-hour, taking the game to around 5pm. People in offices started hoping Tendulkar didn't get out before stumps. People at the ground too, but they wanted him to take as much strike as he could. He would play 57 of the remaining 90 balls in the day without looking uncomfortable, except against Shillingford's bounce on occasion. During that spell, Laxman, who had retired earlier in the year without announcing it in advance, marvelled at Tendulkar's ability to shut everything out, playing one last match of what had been "his life".

It wasn't turning out to be a great innings. It couldn't have done. The attack and the opposition's score didn't allow for it. It is open to debate how Tendulkar would have fared against a better, more persistent, attack in the circumstances, but this knock was a last round of hellos to old friends before leaving. Next up was the leg glance, which was facilitated by Marlon Samuels firing one down the leg side. It took Tendulkar to 29 off 45. A little over seven overs remained in the day.

With the fast bowlers coming back on, it was time to visit a dearer friend, the drive down the ground to a ball not quite a half-volley. Sammy bowled length, Tendulkar moved forward, met the ball on the up, with the full face. The ball nipped in a little, and even though it hit the middle of the bat, it went to the on side a little, to the right of Sammy, to the left of mid-on.

Minutes later Tendulkar was right forward to defend a length ball, the last delivery of the day. Having negotiated it, he lingered on the pitch a little, taking in the moment. Surely this was the last time he was walking back unbeaten at stumps? Walking back with the promise of more tomorrow. He waited for Pujara, who had gladly reached an inconspicuous 34 off 49, and patted his back before walking off. He even allowed himself to raise the bat as he walked off, possibly for those who might not be able to make it to the ground on day two.

A huge queue welcomed you at the Wankhede an hour before the start time, 9.30am. It spilled well onto Marine Drive. The number inside the ground was above the ground's stated capacity, 30,000. It was more like 40,000. People sat in aisles, on stairs, or just stood. One final century was now a possibility, but Tendulkar needed to start well on a pitch that usually did something in the morning.

This morning there was a better cricketing test for Tendulkar. Tino Best – Darren Sammy reckoned he would be ready to bowl an 11th over if he had got a wicket to bring Tendulkar in in the tenth – was charged up. The first ball he bowled to Tendulkar was 143kph, on a length, angling in towards middle, and Tendulkar was right forward to defend. Good sign, then. More friends were to be visited. In the second over of the day, he pulled out the fine paddle sweep, his way of milking offspinners, from well outside off, reaching 47.

Best kept at it. As if to provide this final act the legitimacy it needed. Otherwise it was becoming a touch too easy. Now he bowled with a short leg, two slips and a gully. Short, fast, into the body. Next he bowled one that held its line and got a little big. Tendulkar, averse to hooking or pulling since the tennis elbow, tried to steer it over gully. Beaten. Best appealed. Not given. He had missed it. At the end of the over, Best got into Tendulkar's ear. Tendulkar, who is renowned for not reacting to such provocations, had a cheeky smile on his face after Best walked away.

Best was booed as he went to field at the boundary, but his over had been a timely reminder why Tendulkar was going. Among other things, you could trouble him with good quick, short bowling, because he wouldn't hook. His late-period counter to short bowling, the ramp over the slips, or even the keeper, pretty effective in its own right but not liked by those who knew Tendulkar's game well, nearly let him down on this day. Twice he tried it, twice he was beaten.

However, when Best pitched one up, he was ready to drive it to the right of mid-off to bring up one final half-century. Off drive. Check.

Best went back to the bouncer, Tendulkar ducked, Best implored him to hook, Tendulkar showed no interest. In the next over, though, he pulled out one final special. Best bowled short of a length, not too wide, Tendulkar went back, went tall, and punched it through cover for four, possibly the toughest shot in the book, to go on the back foot and drive the rising ball along the ground through cover.

That shot also marked the end of that contest between Best and Tendulkar: 18 balls in that five-over spell, 12 runs, bat beaten, bouncers bowled, looks exchanged, the odd word, a pat from Tendulkar on Best's shoulder, a gorgeous back-foot drive, but like he had done with many greater bowlers in his career, Tendulkar had seen Best off.

Now arrived the twist. Narsingh Deonarine's part-time offspin provided the dip in intensity, as did Gabriel. Smoothly, Tendulkar moved to 74, a century now a distinct possibility, with West Indies' early surge thwarted, but at 10.38am on November 15, three balls after having played a cheeky little lap sweep, Tendulkar made his last batting mistake.

Deonarine bowled short of a length, outside off, angling it in, and Tendulkar tried to guide it fine, ending up playing it too fine, straight to slip. He had previously cut two such deliveries from Shillingford in the traditional manner, but this time he tried this cute shot. He didn't hang about at the pitch but tucked his bat under his arm and walked off. The collective silence soon turned into a cheer as they saw him walk back for one last time. Best patted his back as he rushed in to celebrate with his team-mates. Tendulkar's face didn't give away much – was he disappointed, was he relieved, did he wish he had played the full-blooded cut or punch? – and, as he approached the steps, back he turned to raise his bat to the crowd, sending them into raptures.

Caught Sammy bowled Deonarine for 74 off 118 balls in 150 minutes with 12 fours. It wasn't the perfect result for Tendulkar's fans, but it was a fair one. No one went home complaining. While Tendulkar provided glimpses of almost all his trademark shots one last time, the hook was conspicuous by its absence. It was a friend Tendulkar had said goodbye to long ago. The innings provided glimpses of how he had become a lesser batsman than the one the country fell in love with. It was perhaps fitting that a cute shot against a part-time bowler ended it, a reminder of the evolution of Tendulkar the batsman.

Sidharth Monga is an assistant editor at ESPNcricinfo

A TOUCH OF VIV

SANJAY MANJREKAR

I was privileged to watch, from close quarters, a child prodigy go on to become a true legend of the game. A batsman who stunned the world with his voracious appetite for the game and for making hundreds.

Sachin Tendulkar only played a single international T20. His exploits in the format were all in the IPL and at the Champions League. You will agree that his impact on the shortest format of the game has been less than on the others.

T20 cricket came into Tendulkar's life a little too late and cricket is slightly poorer for that. Had the format been in the game when Tendulkar was in the youth of his batting career, he would have been one of the most dangerous T20 batsmen in the world. Sure, he would not have hit the ball as long as Chris Gayle does, but he would have given the bowlers the same kinds of nightmares.

A version of this article was first published on ESPNcricinfo in November 2013

Brian Lara once confessed in a TV chat that he would have struggled in T20 cricket because it just did not suit his temperament; for starters, he needed a bit of time to get going while batting. Not Tendulkar. The Tendulkar I saw early in his career was as much a master in the short formats of the game as he was in the longest.

In the early '90s we used to play lots of privately organised tournaments, among them various single-wicket, double-wicket and six-a-side affairs. These were typically two, three, or a maximum of five overs. Away from the glare of TV and the other media, Tendulkar produced some mind-boggling innings in these games. Whatever target was set, he would achieve it, single-handed. (Yes, even in a double-wicket match or a six-a-side tournament.)

I noticed that Tendulkar was at his best when he was pitted against someone one on one. This happened a lot in such tournaments, where it was a battle between one bowler and one batsman that decided the fate of a match.

The most memorable of these that I saw was in a double-wicket tournament played at Salt Lake Stadium in Kolkata, when he took Manoj Prabhakar and Kapil Dev apart to reach an almost impossible target to win. Vinod Kambli was the lucky beneficiary as Tendulkar's partner in that tournament.

During that contest I saw some well-aimed yorkers from two highly accomplished India bowlers disappear over the midwicket boundary for huge sixes. It was the first time I had seen yorkers being dismissed in that fashion. That innings was played away from the international arena but the bowling was international-quality and the intensity very high. The strokeplay that night from Tendulkar left us in a daze.

In the nets too, one-to-one combat brought the best out of him, and we would stop everything we were doing to watch. Sometimes Javagal Srinath, towards the end of one of Tendulkar's batting stints in the nets, would throw him a challenge: "Okay Sachin, last four balls from me, 12 runs to win." Tendulkar would come up with a counter offer: "No, eight runs in four balls." A number like 10 would be agreed upon. The stage was set: four balls from Srinath and Tendulkar had to get 10 runs to win the "match".

Srinath would then set an imaginary field, and after every ball bowled, this field would be adjusted. All this would happen while the other net bowlers continued to bowl normally at Tendulkar. But when Srinath ran in to bowl, you could see Tendulkar's demeanour change. It was not just net practice now.

I saw this little contest take place many times during my career, and I never saw Srinath win. The same went for the other bowlers who attempted it. Tendulkar was just too good for Srinath. He would play around with him and his "field". Often, to add salt to the wound, he would deliberately hit the ball into areas from where Srinath had just removed his "fielders". Tendulkar would walk off, pleased as punch, having won another bout with a bowler, and Srinath would be seen standing in his typical arms-crossed stance, having accepted defeat, but you could see his eyes were full of admiration for the little fellow.

During my formative years I was introduced to a variant of backyard cricket by my friend Shirish Godbole, who is now a successful investment banker. We used to play it as kids in the compound of our building. The bowler threw the ball at the batsman instead of bowling it, and from a much shorter distance than a normal pitch length.

The chucker would use his fingers to produce fast offcutters and legcutters. The batsman would face all this with a wall behind him. If he edged and the ball hit the wall on the full, he was out. So the wall was a like a slip cordon that never dropped a catch, a bit like the great West Indian team of the '80s.

It was almost impossible for a batsman to survive for more than a handful of deliveries. If the chucker could not get him with cutters then his main weapon, the yorker, would come into play, at a speed of about 110mph, and before the batsman could bring his bat down he was bowled.

It was a simulation of international bowling at its best with a rubber ball. It was like facing Dennis Lillee, Glenn McGrath or Richard Hadlee at their peak, only quicker and with more vicious variations.

When I went on to play for India, I sometimes put my fellow India batsmen to my chucking test with the rubber ball. Obviously, they had never seen this kind of cricket before. I had mastered the art of bowling those chuckers at the batsman from a short distance, with all kinds of variations. All the batsmen struggled against my "bowling", even Mohammad Azharuddin, who could not last beyond five or six balls. Some of them even refused to take part in the game, saying it was impossible to survive and that it was too unreal a game of cricket.

Yes, you guessed right, they all tried and failed, except Tendulkar. He not only withstood my first-six-balls test, he continued to bat comfortably well beyond that. I tried everything but just could not get him out. Tendulkar knew what was coming out of my hand – he knew when the legcutter was coming, and the offcutter, and much to my distress, even the yorker.

I suspected much later that when I first introduced the Indian team to this game, Tendulkar was watching quietly. Because he was usually among the first to take up such things, but in this case I remember he was not the first to have a go against my chucking. I assume he was closely analysing it all: the speed at which I was operating, and how I was using my fingers to get the ball to deviate. Only after he had worked out everything did he volunteer to bat against me.

Having known him for a while by then, I realised that for Tendulkar this was a challenge that all the others had failed at, and he could not be seen to fail at it too, like them – especially because there were people watching. He could not be seen to be coming out second-best in a contest. For me it was an early lesson that Tendulkar was different.

When Tendulkar was growing up, he idolised Sir Vivian Richards, and it was obvious to us that he also wanted to bat like him in his early days. Tendulkar was never a showman, like Viv could be, but that is not to say that he was less combative.

I remember another game that wasn't on TV. Mumbai were playing Baroda in a Ranji match at the RCF cricket ground. Tendulkar walked in at the fall of a Mumbai wicket, and we saw as he got up that he was not looking very motivated.

Baroda had this pace bowler called Mukesh Narula who had a bit of spirit. He liked to play hard, and in this particular innings he took that fighting spirit to the next level. Some bouncers were sent Tendulkar's way, and along with them some glares and words under the breath too. I suppose Narula wanted to show his team-mates that he was not overawed by the man, like they were. All of us in the Mumbai dressing room were thinking: "What are you doing, Mukesh?"

The inevitable happened. Bored till then, Tendulkar got charged up. The faster Narula bowled, the harder the ball bounced back from Tendulkar's bat to hit the sightscreen. I still vividly remember the force with which the ball thudded into the wall next to the sightscreen. This was not Tendulkar just scoring runs, it was him showing disdain for Narula without uttering a word.

This was the Tendulkar of the early days. Obviously, over his long 24-year batting career, he changed, but the one with the ghost of Viv in him was my favourite Tendulkar.

Indian middle-order batsman **Sanjay Manjrekar** *played 32 of his 37 Tests alongside Tendulkar*

GREATNESS IS A LONG-DISTANCE RACE

ANDY ZALTZMAN

How do you judge the greatness of cricketers? By their averages? By their totals of runs and wickets? By their victories? By their greatest performances in innings, matches and series? By their enduring quality over the span of their careers, and their importance to their team? Do you assess their brilliance during their peak years, or their record against their most formidable opponents, or their play in the most important matches? Do comparisons with their peers and team-mates count for more than those with their predecessors and successors? Is their standing outside the confines of the playing field of any importance?

Or do you judge them by their commercial value in a hypothetical Judgement Day IPL-style auction, by the quantity and quality of their advertising endorsements, by their volume of Twitter followers, by the wilful incomprehensibility of their tattoos, or by a cost−benefit analysis of their latest haircut? Or do you concoct some alchemic, fluctuating formula encompassing all of the above (with the possible exception of the final five) (or four)? Does it matter? (Please do not answer that last question. If a critical mass of people respond with a "no", I will have to reassess my priorities as a 39-year-old father of two.)

Sachin Tendulkar scores highly in most categories. Less well, most would agree, in the final three.

Taking the whole of his career, he is pre-eminent for his longevity and his unprecedented volume of international run-scoring and century-making, records that will almost certainly still stand when one or more of the following happen: (a) official Armageddon; (b) the reduction of all cricket to a five-minute thwack-out against a robot bowler modelled on Munaf Patel; (c) the reduction of all human life to one-syllable online grunting via social media, returning our species to its rightful cave-dwelling roots; (d) unofficial Armageddon; or (e) cricket being outlawed after an international conglomerate patents the concepts of spheres, bats and numbers.

However, ironically for a man who played 664 international matches spread over almost two and a half decades, assessing the whole of his career is neither the best nor the most flattering method for attempting to determine Tendulkar's place in the cricketing pantheon, particularly as a Test player.

In Tests since November 1989, when the 16-year-old Sachin made his debut, only Kumar Sangakkara (56.9) and Jacques Kallis (55.4), among cricketers who have played over 20 Tests, have exceeded his career average of 53.7. However, if you discount matches against the mostly sub-standard, average-boosting Bangladesh and Zimbabwe, Sachin's career average of 51.01 against top-eight Test nations puts him in the middle of a group of 22 players who have averaged over 48 (Sangakkara still leads the way on 53.2).

Conventional cricketing numbers – particularly career averages – are of limited value when viewed without context. Seymour Nurse played for West Indies from 17 February 1960 to 17 March 1969. On 18 February 1969, as he walked out to bat in the second innings of an SCG drubbing, his career average stood at a respectable 38.9 – fractionally ahead of Taufeeq Umar, fractionally behind Asanka Gurusinha, two useful players but unlikely to be included in too many Greatest Ever Cricketers lists. Nurse scored 137 as West Indies sank to defeat; followed by 558 runs in five innings in his final series, in New Zealand. He thus ended with a career average of 47.6 – precisely level with acknowledged all-time great Adam Gilchrist.

Gilchrist himself had begun the 2005 Ashes with a career average of 55.6 after 68 Tests, comfortably the highest of any wicketkeeper in Test history. In his final 28 Tests, he averaged only 30. In judging their statuses in the sport, do we ignore Nurse's extraordinary final month and Gilchrist's fading powers in his mid-30s? If Gilchrist had retired at 33, would he be viewed even more highly because his average was mid-50s rather than upper-40s? Conversely, if Gilchrist had played Test cricket through his early 20s, rather than arriving in the Test team as a mature, completed player, fired in a strong Australian domestic scene and honed to international level in 76 ODIs, would his overall career numbers have been significantly dented by the learning processes of youth, in a decade where great bowlers roamed the landscape like man-eating dinosaurs in a Raquel Welch film?

Such speculation is not restricted to cricket. Would Jimi Hendrix be less revered as a guitarist if he was still alive today, embarrassing himself by performing duets with Miley Cyrus in a desperate attempt to rebuild the credibility he lost during his commercially successful but artistically culpable early-1990s stint with the cock-rock supergroup Bon Jovdrix?

The comparison between Tendulkar and Gilchrist is instructive. The Bellingen Biffer is 17 months older than the Mumbai Maestro, but his Test career began ten years later and ended almost six years ago. His peak, from his November 1999 debut until his 2005 Ashes struggles, lasted five and a half years. Tendulkar is remembered for his teenage brilliance in scoring his first four Test hundreds away from home, from Manchester in 1990, via the MCG and Perth in 1991-92, to Johannesburg late in 1992. But these dazzling, auspicious innings were surrounded by failures, and at the end of that year, his Test average was 37.4 – decent for the time (about average for a top-six Test player from 1989 to 1992), good for a teenager.

From the start of 1993, however, he became a regular major run scorer in Tests, averaging close to 80 over the next two years, and over almost ten years between January 1993 and November 2002, he was consistently, world-leadingly effective. In 83 Tests, he averaged 63.5, well ahead of the next highest-averaging player in that period – Gilchrist (58.5), who, as noted above, was spared the bowler barrage of the mid-to-late 1990s by a combination of Ian Healy and the Australian selectors.

Even if you remove Tests against Zimbabwe and Bangladesh (Sachin scored heavily against the former), his average of 61.9 against the top eight nations keeps him well ahead of Gilchrist (still 58.5), from more than twice as many matches, with only Steve Waugh (54.9 in 104 Tests) and Navjot Sidhu (53.3 in 23) within ten runs.

Bear in mind the quality of bowlers confronting Tendulkar at this time – nine took 200 or more Test wickets at 25 or fewer, none of them Indian: Curtly Ambrose, Shaun Pollock, Glenn McGrath, Allan Donald, Muttiah Muralitharan, Wasim Akram, Waqar Younis, Courtney Walsh and Shane Warne. (By comparison, in the subsequent ten years from November 2002, only four took 200 wickets at under 30 – Murali, Dale Steyn, Warne and Makhaya Ntini.)

Tendulkar scored runs everywhere, and against everyone. His one minor blot was that in the three Tests he played against Pakistan, he averaged only 30 – but these included one of his greatest performances, the fourth-innings 136 in Chennai that took India to the brink of victory.

Pradeep Mandhani, India
I thought that an Indian teenager facing Pakistan's heavy-duty bowling on the tour of 1989 would make for a great photo. Sachin was shy, but in the middle he was emphatic. This was during the third Test, in Lahore. If I remember, Waqar Younis, also a debutant in that series, was stopped in his run-up, thanks to people walking in front of the sightscreen, intrigued by the sight of a boy playing amongst men. *Photograph © Pradeep Mandhani*

Jack Atley, Australia

I shot this at the MCG during the Boxing Day Test in 2000. Sachin was making his way back after scoring one of the best centuries I have seen. The MCG can seem a large and lonely place, especially for a batsman as he walks to the pavilion, and the picture conveys that. The seagulls outnumbering the batsman might seem symbolic of the might of the Australian team, but the picture becomes balanced when you realise who the batsman is, and that Sachin can virtually play any team on his own.

Photograph © Jack Atley

Santosh Bane, India

The thought of cricket always brought a smile to Sachin's face. He could hardly wait to get hold of his bat and get started. Here he was turning out in a college championship final at the Parsi Gymkhana ground in Mumbai in 1990. He had parked his car on the road that ran alongside the ground, and with a jump over the little boundary wall he was on the field. This picture has enthusiasm written all over it.

Photograph © BCCL/Source: The Times of India Group

Savita Kirloskar, India
This was taken during an exhibition match played on the outskirts of Mumbai in 1992. I had been tipped off that Tendulkar was going to be signed by Yorkshire there. I got my scoop, but this photograph stands the test of time better. There is a certain poignancy about it: Tendulkar was already a star, but there was still an adolescent innocence about him, which the picture captures.
Photograph © MiD-DAY

Mark Ray, Australia
Sachin Tendulkar and Shane
Warne are good friends
as well as rivals with a lot
of respect for each other.
This picture captures them
enjoying the experience
of being interviewed by Ian
Chappell before the start
of the first Test in Mumbai
in February 2001.
Photograph © Mark Ray

Subhendu Ghosh, India
I took this photo during
a Mumbai Indians practice
session in Vizag in 2012.
It was evening and the light
was insufficient for them to
bat in the nets, so Tendulkar
took to demonstrating some
strokes to Rohit Sharma.
So complete is his follow-
through that the bat doesn't
seem to be missing.
*Photograph © Hindustan
Times*

Philip Brown, England

I like this photo of Tendulkar that I took in Mumbai the day after India defeated Sri Lanka in the World Cup final. Some players were trotted out onto a hotel rooftop to pose with the heavy trophy for a select number of photographers. As Sachin held the trophy for a few seconds with the Gateway of India in the background some birds took off, making the background even more interesting.

He seemed quite serene and content at that moment.

Photograph © Philip Brown

Hamish Blair, Australia

This was from Tendulkar's first-innings century in the third Test, in Chennai, in 2001. At first it looks like a regular straight drive, until you notice that the wicketkeeper is standing in front of the batsman! Shane Warne was bowling at the time – mostly outside leg stump. Tendulkar came up with the perfect tactic, turning his back to the bowler, waiting for the ball and then playing what I think is best described as a straight drive behind the wicket.

Photograph © Getty Images

Thereafter, in Tests, beginning with India's disastrous two-Test loss in New Zealand late in 2002, Tendulkar's performances entered a significant fallow period, with occasional peaks. He played few Tests, unsuccessfully, in 2003. He began 2004 with an extraordinary 495 unbeaten runs in three innings in Sydney and Multan, but followed this with six single-figure scores in a row. From April 2004 to December 2007, against top-eight opposition, he made only one century in 27 Tests, and averaged 32. Then, he had his highest-scoring series – 493 runs in Australia in 2007-08. But more failures followed, four Tests in a row without exceeding 31.

In his mid-to-late 30s, almost two decades of constant cricket after his debut, a second staggering peak was built – from Australia's visit to India in October 2008 until the 2011 World Cup, Tendulkar was more productive than ever. Twelve centuries in 27 Tests, and an average of 72. It was a time of elephantine run-making – top-six batsmen from the top-eight nations collectively averaged 43, compared with 37 during Sachin's 1993-2002 zenith; and ten batsmen averaged 59 or more, as only Tendulkar had done in the earlier period. It was nevertheless an extraordinary late blooming, culminating in an influential, at times dazzling, contribution to India's World Cup success.

Ideally, the story would have ended there – with his greatest collective triumph, at the end of the final great flowering of his batting and run-making genius. Two and a half years and 23 Tests later, he has not added another century. He has worn his cricketing mortality obviously and sometimes awkwardly. His overall average has dwindled from almost 56.9 to 53.7.

Many (probably most) great players experience some kind of end-of-career decline, sometimes over several years, sometimes over a few harsh matches. Viv Richards' average drifted slowly downwards over ten years, from 62 in 1981 to 50 in 1991. Wally Hammond lost three runs off his career average by playing on for a year after the War (from

61.4 to 58.4). George Headley lost six (66.7 to 60.8) in the three Tests he played in 1948 and 1954. If he had politely said to the selectors, "No, I am too old for this", would we view him, standing alone with an average in the mid-60s, as clearly second only to Bradman? If Tendulkar had played from 19 to 37, instead of from 16 to 40, and averaged 58 instead of 53, would he be considered an even greater player? Would that not be a little ridiculous?

There are, as with almost all players, holes to be picked in Tendulkar's statistical record – his relative lack of dominant series; his significantly inferior ODI record outside Asia; his moderate fourth-innings numbers. Almost all players have such numerical imperfections. Even Garry Sobers was relatively moderate against Australia; Hammond was mostly pedestrian in home Ashes series; Clyde Walcott and Everton Weekes failed in Australia; Murali was ineffective in Australia and India; Warne struggled against India.

The greats of modern batsmanship have converged in that 48-53 average bracket against top-eight opposition, and all have blemishes of various types and sizes on their statistical CVs. Ricky Ponting had a 17-year Test career, but was a true champion for less than five of them. Up to March 2002, he averaged 43 in 54 Tests; from then until the Adelaide Test in December 2006, he averaged 75 in 53 matches, with 24 hundreds; in his final 61 Tests, he averaged 39. Kallis (who averaged just 30 in his first 22 Tests, then 62 in his next 131 over 13 years) became a truly great batsman in recent years, but for most of his career he was only sporadically effective against the very best. Both of these players also had the benefit of not playing against their own world-leading bowling attacks. Rahul Dravid averaged mid-30s, with four hundreds in 54 Tests, against Australia and South Africa combined; Shivnarine Chanderpaul has scored most of his runs in the relative comfort of the middle order; Sangakkara has been significantly less successful away from his home continent; Brian Lara had numerous series failures, and never mastered India. All of these minor glitches, of course, are dwarfed by the successes of these great cricketers.

Sachin's overall Test average against the non-minnows of modern Test cricket may look relatively unremarkable by the standards of the day. He never played an innings as great as VVS Laxman's 281, or constructed a series to match Lara's performances from the gods against Australia in 1999 and in Sri Lanka in 2001-02. But for me, two things set Tendulkar apart from and above his peers: firstly, his pre-eminence over a prolonged period at a time when bowling was brilliant and hundreds were hard to come by; and secondly, that, from his breakthrough year in 1994 until his World Cup triumph in 2011, he also scored vast quantities of runs, and hundreds, quickly, in ODI cricket.

How Sachin's peak compares with other players' greatest years, when compared against the standards of their times, is something for another article. Not for the first time, I need to leave Statsguru alone for a while and spend some time with human beings. But I would argue that the 1993-2002 peak of Tendulkar was the greatest sustained batsmanship since Sobers, another teenage prodigy maturing to become the greatest batsman of his era, averaged 70 over 56 Tests, from his 1958 breakthrough series against Pakistan, until February 1969.

Andy Zaltzman is a stand-up comic and writer

"TO SEE THE BALL RACE PAST THE BOWLER TO THE BOUNDARY WAS A GREAT FEELING"

INTERVIEW BY PRADEEP MAGAZINE

How would you define the art of batting and how do you approach your craft?

I have never gone so deep thinking about it. I have just gone out to bat in the nets, and whichever areas, looking at the opposition, I feel I need to work on, I have tried to replicate those situations, getting the bowlers to bowl to me in those areas.

For example, I prepared for Shane Warne when I was going to play him in 1998 in India. Till then, no one had bowled round-the-wicket legspin to me in the rough. But I knew before the series that he was going to do exactly that to us. I got all the local bowlers, left-arm

_____

This interview was first published in *Hindustan Times* in July 2012 spinners and legspinners, to bowl round the wicket in the rough to me. In fact, when I went to Chennai, I got [Laxman] Sivaramakrishnan to bowl to me.

We played a practice game against the Australians in Mumbai and in the entire match Warne did not bowl round the wicket to me. I got a double-hundred, everyone said well played, but I knew for the Test match he was going to come round the wicket. And it did happen like that in the second innings, when the match could have gone either way. I took him on. Not that I had planned the attack, because there was also an element of risk involved. The wicket had uneven bounce from the rough, so one had to be selective and also figure out what were the areas to attack. I had practised that in the nets, so it worked. This could be one of the examples of how I approach the game.

What about the earlier part of your career?

When I began and was learning from Achrekar Sir, I would focus on technique, but I was too young to know what was happening. I would listen to him and my brother Ajit, who would be watching me. Then we would discuss the areas I needed to improve on.

What were those areas?

Many. It could be to step out to cover-drive or on-drive. I practised a lot, and we batted on worn-out wickets. They were turning tracks and even fast bowlers got a lot of uneven bounce. The odd ball took off and we got hit so many times. When I look back, I realise that it also taught us how to take blows and get on with the game.

Who in your view is a perfect batsman, and what does he need to qualify?

If you talk about batsmen getting perfect, then you have to get into technique and all those things, but eventually I think it has also got to do with how to score runs. There may be certain areas where a batsman may not be perfect but as long as he knows how to score runs . . .

How would you describe knowing how to score runs?

You see, if you take ten match situations, you would get 20 different situations. The same bowler would be at his best and not at his best, whatever. Eventually what matters is your contribution to the team, how you have managed to get runs. To me, that is important and to do that on a consistent basis you need to be technically correct or close to being correct.

Has technical perfection been your strength right from the beginning?

Well, at the start of my career, the one thing I really needed to work on was shot selection. The shift from first-class cricket to playing the best in the world is huge. I played my first series against the likes of Imran, Wasim, Qadir, Waqar and Aaqib and the next against Hadlee and Morrison. They were all top-class bowlers, and against them shot selection becomes really important, which as a 16-year-old I lacked. I spoke to a lot of guys and they said it comes with maturity, it is not going to happen overnight, as you are used to reacting to a particular bowler in a certain manner. But that will change as the standard of bowling is going to get higher, and you have got to start playing differently. I felt that as time went by, my shot selection became better.

Is shot selection about being able to read the bowler well and respond?

I would say it is about knowing when to attack and be successful and also knowing when not to attack.

Do you have examples of times you failed and succeeded because of shot selection?

At the start of my career, I would look to punch off the back foot anything short of length outside the off stump. But I realised you can't keep doing that every ball. There are certain deliveries you need to let go. They may not be the best of deliveries but you need to leave them alone sometimes. And when you are set, it is all about knowing when you can attack and when you can let it go.

I thought that came to me with experience. I felt in Australia, where I went in 1991-92, which was a big tour for me, and before that in England, scoring my first Test hundred in the second match, was a big boost. I realised I was good enough to score big runs at this level. That hundred I scored kept the series alive, as we had lost the first Test and were about to lose the second as well. That confidence, having scored big and kept the series alive, was a perfect dose for my confidence.

Confidence you had lacked until then?

No, I was confident, only that I wanted to contribute more. After the second innings of my Test career, where I scored 59, I was confident I could score, something which was not there after the first innings of my Test career. There was a question mark. Am I good enough? But the moment I decided to hang around, get the feel, things became better.

You were referring to Australia 1992?

Well, England gave me the solid foundation that I could score a hundred, and I wanted to repeat this. In Australia I scored two hundreds. I played consistently well in the tri-series, where West

Indies was the third team, and both of them had some big names. And it was on those wickets that I picked when to play my back-foot punches and when not to. It is here that I felt my game had changed. On wickets like those you had to let a few balls go, you could not possibly attack every short-of-length ball and punch it. I figured out my shot selection on that tour and from there onwards it started changing.

Are your great strengths, the back-foot punches, the off-side play, god-gifted or are they the result of a lot of hard work?

I liked playing drives, straight drives, and I used to practise them quite a bit in the nets, make bowlers bowl at me, and even after nets, get them to chuck the ball at me, and hit the ball straight. Just to see the ball going past the bowler and racing towards the boundary was a great feeling.

Also, while doing that I figured out that this is possibly the safest shot to play because you are showing the full face of your bat, you are playing straight, and if you punch well enough and beat mid-on or the bowler, it is a sure-shot boundary.

The drive is supposed to be a top-hand shot. Didn't your bottom-handed grip become a hindrance?

When I started, Achrekar Sir did try to correct it. Then he realised the moment he changed my grip, my whole game was falling apart. He also called my brother and they discussed it and the final outcome was: we won't change the grip because when it comes to adjustments he is able to do it well. They felt, it really does not matter even if he looks like a bottom-handed player; as long as he is hitting the ball along the ground, it is fine. Let us wait for a while and see what happens and then we can think of changing his grip. Fortunately they decided to stick with my grip. I scored a lot of runs in school matches and after that there was no discussion about it.

On shot selection, in the 2004 Sydney Test you scored a double-hundred without hitting a single boundary on the off side. To do this for such a long time, especially when that happens to be your strength, must have been very difficult. How did you pull it off?

I was batting really well on that tour. I felt terrific when I landed in Australia, as I was in very good form. In the first three Tests I was moving well and batting well but I did not score the amount of runs I was expecting to. When I reflected on it, I felt I was shifting from fourth gear to overdrive, wanting to destroy the opposition. I decided that I would shift to fourth gear but not beyond that, however comfortable I felt against any bowler. No shifting of gears. And in doing that there were certain areas I decided to avoid. Not that there was a flaw, it was about controlling my aggression, and not about technique. I went out there with a challenge: if you are going to test me with your patience, I am going to test you with my patience.

Why didn't you implement the same plan on your recent tour of England and Australia, where you got out a number of times playing outside the off stump?

You can't go with the same approach every time. You have to trust your instinct, see how you are feeling, got to see your mental set-up. That was a different stage. This was also when I was on my 99th hundred and everyone focused on things I was not able to do, forgetting that in the last 21 years I had achieved things which were 100 times bigger.

I felt the focus was only on the hundred and if it did not come, no one, very few, focused on what I was able to do than what I was not able to do. It had also to do with how people were looking at that season.

As for my batting, I played some important innings. My 76 against the West Indies in the Delhi Test was crucial as we had lost Rahul [Dravid] early and my partnership with Laxman was important for winning. But all those things were . . . well, people were focusing only on the hundred. Normally, if you score 76 in a match-winning situation, it gives great satisfaction.

Did the pressure affect your game?

Yes, in a way it did. In those ten months, all that everyone spoke about was my 100 hundreds. It got to a point where I got thinking, why is it happening? It was not that I was not batting well and it would happen when it will.

I felt in the first part of the Australia tour, I was batting the best I had in the recent past. I was moving well, I was very aggressive, when there was time to leave, I left. I played five or six maiden overs, depending on the situation. But there were other opinions. "Why is he not playing his natural game?" It is easy for people to give opinions from outside. I can't be looking to keep everyone happy. I need to trust my instinct and play according to what I think is needed at that moment and approach the game accordingly.

In Sydney, when I was batting in the second innings, [James] Pattinson and [Ben] Hilfenhaus bowled a very good spell at the end of the third day's play, and we had to just respect that spell and let the ball go. That is what I did, with Gautam [Gambhir], who was batting at the other end. Even though I was leaving the ball, I knew I was in total control. It is all about knowing when to strike and when to defend. The next day, to the same line and length, I kept attacking the bowlers and they had to keep a deep point. You know, it has also to do with how people get it.

Over a period of time, how has your batting evolved? Changes in strokemaking – like, you were a terrific hooker earlier . . .

I don't think I was ever a natural hooker. It all depends on the feel, when you think you can play that shot and when you can't. I got my 51st Test hundred by hooking [Morne] Morkel for a six. In the World Cup match at Nagpur, [Dale] Steyn bounced and I hit him for a six.

How did the shot you hit over the slips to fast bowlers evolve? You don't normally play risky shots.

To me, it is not a risky shot, though it may look like one. I only look to play that shot when I feel confident enough. I started playing that in Bloemfontein in South Africa in 2001-02 a lot to [Makhaya] Ntini and a couple of shots to Nantie Hayward, and then I think I played one to [Jacques] Kallis as well. I played that shot when I knew I had time to guide the ball, and I did that in Australia and even against the West Indies at Mumbai, so yeah, I have played this shot.

Which is the stroke that gives you the most pleasure?

It has to be the straight drive. Then you know everything is correct, the balance is right, your head is right, the weight is transferring well.

Does the world's highest run-getter, century-maker, think he has a weakness?

I don't think there is a weakness, but as long as it does not make me overconfident, it is my strength. But the moment you cross the line and become complacent, then that becomes your weakness. Because you have worked on so many aspects of the game – over the years I have played so many deliveries and practised so many hours – you have rectified most of the things. But you face just that one moment when there is a lapse in concentration and it all collapses.

I spoke about aggression. Sometimes you become too aggressive and sometimes too defensive, but that is part and parcel of the game. I mean, you are not a robot where you push buttons and everything is going to fall right, that whatever you have imagined will happen exactly that way.

Are you still working on correcting something in your batting?

Not really. I only work a lot on my feel. I think that feel has to be there, good feel while you are practising in the nets. Just to be in that space is important. If you are in a good space, the rest follows because you know, having played for so many years, the subconscious mind has stored most of the things. But to be able to bring that out when it is needed, you've got to be in a good space and that is important.

You still feel you are in that good space?

I keep working on that because it is not something that you sit back and it will happen by itself. You need to look at the good things you have done to be able to do that. That is what keeps me positive. If you look to find problems, there are always going to be problems, so to be in a good space you have to understand what your problems are, work on them but focus on the good things you have done.

How far ahead are you looking at your future? That is what the world wants to know.

(*Laughs*) It is simple. As long as I am enjoying cricket there is no need to think otherwise. If I wake up one morning and feel I am not enjoying cricket and I start questioning myself, "Why am I here?", then I know there is a big question mark. When that day comes, we will deal with it. But right now I am looking forward to the season. I still have that enthusiasm for checking various bats, trying to figure which is the right one and what is the pick-up – they still excite me. As long as all these things are keeping me excited, it means the passion is alive.

People say the Rajya Sabha membership is an acceptance of the fact that you won't play on too long.

(*Laughs*) No. When the president nominates you, it is an honour. And I clearly said even at that stage that my focus is on cricket. All those sessions I have put in, the number of years of hard work, do not change at all. As long as my focus does not shift from cricket. I was nominated because of my contribution to cricket and I don't want to ignore my practice sessions, my preparation. It may not be a net session; it could be just gym sessions or mental preparation. I don't want to change all those things. I am sure about that. And as and when I stop playing cricket – I don't know when – that time we will think about it. Right now, I am not thinking about it, I am just thinking about the coming season and how best I can contribute.

Your fans want you to play the next World Cup. Any message for them?

Yeah, it is nice. All I can say is that I was honoured by the Indian Air Force and they made me Group Captain two years ago, but I still don't know how to fly. So the message is clear. What I am trying to say is, you know I am a sportsman and this is a nomination I have accepted with full respect, and my focus shifts immediately back to cricket.

Pradeep Magazine *is a veteran cricket writer, and sports adviser for* Hindustan Times

THE SMALL ENFORCER

MUKUL KESAVAN

Batsmen aren't remembered only for their shots; you remember them for their mannerisms, their stance, their physical presence. I remember Sunil Gavaskar for the military snap with which he shouldered arms, both pads together, bat raised high. I can't recall him shaping to play and then withdrawing the bat: there was a clean, lucid certainty to everything he did, which made him the great classical batsman of our time. I remember him for the compact grace that informed his presence at the crease, from taking guard to settling into his stance.

Sachin Tendulkar is different. He's about as tall as Gavaskar; they're both Bombay batsmen, and compared to someone like Brian Lara, Tendulkar seems correct, even orthodox, but he and Gavaskar are chalk and cheese. Tendulkar can produce the most wonderful shots but you wouldn't call him a beautiful batsman. Graceful he is

This article was first published in *Wisden Asia Cricket* magazine in September 2002 not, in any conventional reading of the term. His most repetitive tic at the crease has been described by the writer Ruchir Joshi as his "signature crotch-yank as he adjusts his abdomen guard". He can look oddly clumsy for a great batsman: when the ball keeps low, Tendulkar will jack-knife into an exaggerated half-squat, like someone who has just discovered that he urgently needs to go. When he plays forward, he is correct but always in a slightly over-produced way: his defensive play just lacks the clockwork economy of Gavaskar's technique. In any case, with Tendulkar the ratio of bat to body makes it hard for him to look pretty: he's so small and the bat's so big that it looks more like an accomplice than an instrument. VVS Laxman, long and languid, pulls and hooks in his easy upright way; when Tendulkar pulls, he looks like a small enforcer with a big cosh.

Tendulkar has a claim to being the greatest batsman in the world because he is that rare thing: an original. Gavaskar at his best used to make the classical prescriptions come to life; Tendulkar's genius lies in the impossible shots he hits off perfectly good balls. Not impossible in the sense of outrageous and chancy: men like Sanath Jayasuriya own that corner of the market; no, impossible because he hits shots mortal cricketers wouldn't attempt, and because he makes those shots look safe, even plausible, when they are not.

I have in mind the range of off drives he plays to balls pitched on a good length or short of a good length without much width on offer. He seems to stand up straight without doing much with his front foot. The bat comes down in a little arc and then stops well short of a follow-through. The scene ends with incredulous bowler staring at Tendulkar and cover fielder trotting off on peon duty, resigned to this game of fetch. Something similar happens with that attenuated straight drive that shaves the stumps at the bowler's end on the way to the boundary. It's not the straightness of it (straight drives, after all, are meant to be hit straight) but the lack of obvious effort or risk that makes the shot a bowler-killer. When Lara hits you straight, the bat describes such a flamboyant arc that it's like being lashed with a whip; Tendulkar's down-the-wicket shot is more like being heavily nudged by a barn door. When he hits that straight drive, his bat is at once shield and bludgeon, and as the ball speeds past the blameless bowler, Tendulkar must seem both irresistible force and immovable object.

And then there are those other shots: the upper-cuff over slips and gully, the inside-out shot driven through, or over, cover; the paddle sweep hit so perpendicularly that it finishes as a reverse straight drive completed on one knee; the pull off the front foot hit brutally over midwicket; the trajectory-defying flick that turns the ball on the off stump or outside, through midwicket. What these strokes have in common is that they are difficult and dangerous shots, methodically and safely played. That's why bowlers in their follow-through sometimes stare at Tendulkar as if he had grown another head: he makes unlikely shots look reasonable. It's this straight-bat magic that got Graeme Hick to turn out to captain his county, Worcestershire, against India in an unimportant tour match once: he said he just wanted to stand at slip and watch Tendulkar play.

Tendulkar's remarkable repertoire of shots, his style of play, grows out of a particular temperament and a peculiar talent. Tendulkar himself has often said that he is by nature an attacking batsman. This is true, but in itself it tells us little about what makes him special. Jayasuriya is an attacking batsman by instinct, as are Ricky Ponting and that cheerful murderer Adam Gilchrist; and they're very different from Tendulkar. Gilchrist, on present form, is the best batsman in the world. With a batting average over 60 and a strike rate that makes bowlers feel they're bowling in the highlights segment of the evening news, Gilchrist on form can make Tendulkar look low-key. The difference between the two isn't one of talent – indeed, if Gilchrist can bat like this and stay at 60-plus, he and not Tendulkar will be remembered as the great turn-of-the-century batsman. The difference is temperamental. Gilchrist bats in a wholly carefree way; coming in at six or seven in Test matches, he subjects all bowlers, in every situation, to his brand of assault and battery. Perhaps it has to do with the confidence of coming in low in the batting order of a great team; perhaps being a wicketkeeper-batsman with more than one string to his bow frees him from the fear of failure. Whatever it is, it makes his demeanour at the crease very different from Tendulkar's.

No Indian cricketer, not Tendulkar, not even the inimitable Kapil Dev, has survived cricketing glory in this country over a whole career without becoming careworn, and Tendulkar isn't a product of the Bombay school of batsmanship for nothing. However different they may be from each other, the great Bombay batsmen have distrusted extravagance or flourish. Like Gilchrist, Tendulkar will, most times, try to impose himself on the bowling; unlike him, he will discriminate between bowlers, change his game to suit the moment, come up with novelties, like a grandmaster discovering a new wrinkle in an old gambit.

In the first Test of India's 2001 tour to South Africa, Tendulkar hit one of the great hundreds of recent years. At the start of that innings, he hit Makhaya Ntini for 16 runs in an over, with three boundaries. One of these was tipped over slips simply because there was no third man. It seemed a zero-percentage play given how many slips there were, but it became the trademark shot of that particular innings. They kept bowling short outside the off stump to him, and he kept cuffing the ball in the air down to third man for four. And he did this, as he does everything, in a calculated, methodical way, and in so doing he made a bizarre shot seem like business as usual. Right through this masterful knock, Tendulkar continuously showed intent, an aggression unalloyed by doggedness or care. It was a rare moment in his recent career where we were allowed to see genius expressing itself unburdened by responsibility.

Tendulkar padded-up is usually a mass of inhibitions. His face is carefully inexpressive, but through the visor you can see his eyeballs virtually disappearing into his skull, so massively concentrated is he through an innings. In the course of every long innings he plays, you can see the tension build and then find release in shot-making. The weight of responsibility, the fear of letting his side and his country down, will sometimes have him leaving every ball bowled an inch outside the off stump alone, as he did against Glenn McGrath in Australia in 1999 before exploding into a flurry of shots once he was set. That innings was cruelly terminated by an umpire (this happens to Tendulkar a lot – not many umpires want to give genius the benefit of doubt) but most innings he plays are a bit like that one – his runs come in clusters, not in a steady stream; his innings are made up of explosive episodes.

Unlike Gavaskar, inevitability isn't the hallmark of a long innings by Tendulkar. A century by him is an odd mixture of calm and storm. His greatest innings, of course, specially his hundreds in one-day matches, are simply single, long, violent spasms. They have become rarer, those extended bursts of berserker brilliance, because he is too much the Bombay batsman to be recklessly prodigal. So sometimes you'll see him curb his shot-making, mainly in the interest of the team but also because he wants to prove to himself and to his audience that he can play with puritanical self-denial. The perfect example of a knock like this was his century in Chennai during the third Test against the Australians when they toured India in 2001. It was a dour, unlovely innings, all Bombay solidity, but it won India the match.

So much for temperament; what is Tendulkar's special talent? Every bowler who has ever sent down an over to him says the same thing when asked for a sound bite on what makes Tendulkar arguably the best batsman in the contemporary game. To a man, they say this: "He picks up the length of the ball earlier than anyone in the modern game, so he has more time than his peers to make the shot." There is such unanimity on this that it must be true. Till a year and a half ago, Tendulkar used the time that his eye bought him in the cause of aggression. He would get into position early for that perpendicular paddle sweep, skip down the wicket for the lofted drive over straight mid-on, or advance while making room to drive a spinner inside-out over extra cover. His batting average soared, and it took the combined efforts of McGrath, Australian umpiring, and some wretched luck (the miraculous catch that Ponting took at the Wankhede Stadium off Tendulkar's pull after it ricocheted off short leg's back is a prime example) to bring him down to earth.

Even so, his career Test average had risen to 58 and was threatening to touch 60 when Nasser Hussain came to town. Hussain had a plan for Tendulkar, a plan of great simplicity. The way to keep Tendulkar from scoring runs was to bowl wide of him. Karl Marx memorably said that everything in history happened twice: first as tragedy and the second time as farce. Well, in this replay of leg theory, a boy born in Madras played Douglas Jardine, a left-arm spinner stood in for Harold Larwood, and Tendulkar, against his will, was cast as Don Bradman. Amazingly, the ploy sort of worked: it frustrated Tendulkar to the extent of getting him stumped for the first time in his Test career. And the reason it worked was this: Tendulkar tried to wait the bowlers out as Gavaskar might have done, but this game of patience and attrition didn't come naturally to him. At the same time, being a Bombay batsman and not being Gilchrist, he hated the thought of being forced into unorthodoxy and extravagance. It was the same story in the first Test of the current tour to England, when run-saving sweeper fielders and cynically wide bowling goaded him into error. In between these two contests with England was a run of single-digit scores during the tour of the West Indies. No permanent damage was done, as the fine 92 in the Trent Bridge Test showed, but his dismissal in the 90s will have dimmed his aura a watt or two.

Right now, Tendulkar is a great batsman who doesn't scare the opposition. It's as if the fact that he sees the ball so early has begun to work against him: he has almost too much time to play the ball and he uses it to think and fret instead of using it to attack the bowling. There is a tense premeditation to his play these days, which is different from the calculated aggression we used to see earlier. Viv Richards said after Tendulkar's failures on the tour of the Caribbean that Tendulkar didn't seem to be enjoying his cricket. Perhaps he is right. Perhaps the master should learn from his protégé: perhaps Tendulkar could take a leaf out of Virender Sehwag's carefree book. He could stop being Atlas and just go with the flow.

Mukul Kesavan *is a novelist, essayist and historian based in New Delhi*

A GENERATION'S MODEL T

SIDDHARTHA VAIDYANATHAN

Sachin Tendulkar has retired from one-dayers.

Does this mean anything to you? Did you feel numb when he made the announcement on that Sunday morning? Or maybe it was Saturday night in your part of the world. Did the various stages of your life flash in your head, as they are supposed to in the instant before you die?

Do you remember one-day cricket in the 1980s? Travel back in time. What do you see? Red leather balls, players in whites, and some one-dayers in England where umpires stopped play for tea.

What else do you see? Doordarshan. The feed sputtering this moment, back live the next, your grainy screen filled with men who sport stubbles and bushy moustaches, the camera facing the batsman one over and the bowler the next, commentators screaming, "That's hit up in the air."

This article was first published on ESPNcricinfo in December 2012

Gradually, the texture changes. Coloured clothing and floodlit games become commonplace, fielding restrictions alter the definitions of a "safe total", Duckworth and Lewis appear, so do Powerplays, Supersubs and Super Overs. Pinch-hitters, a novelty for a few years, lose their sheen. Now everyone must pinch, everyone must hit.

Tendulkar has seen it all. Sometimes he has initiated the change, other times he has adapted. A master of the game in the mid-1990s, a master in 2011. The one constant in a wildly changing format. He was around when one-dayers were blooming, he was also around when they were allegedly dying.

You have been around too. Are you a kid from the '80s? Or the '90s? Or are you a straddler, part of the Tendulkar generation that has a foot in each decade?

Ah, you stand on the threshold. You have experienced Doordarshan before leaping to the riches of satellite, you have seen Shah Rukh Khan as a soldier on TV before he soared on to the silver screen. You know of life before the Internet but are quick to embrace the wonders of technology; you have watched monochrome but are a child of the colour-TV age.

What else do you see?

Tendulkar in a white helmet, his white shirt unbuttoned to the chest, blitzing Abdul Qadir in an exhibition game in Peshawar. A six, a dot, a four, then three more sixes, the ball traversing magnificent parabolas. Such audacity. Such *khunnas*.

Until that point cricket is merely a fuzzy idea. Tendulkar gives it shape, adds meaning, wraps it in colourful paper and winds a ribbon around the packaging. He makes you understand the game's place in your life, teaches you its significance.

Over the next few years you grapple, trying to swerve banana outswingers with a tennis ball. Standing in front of a mirror you imagine the opposition needing six off the last over. Eden Gardens is a cauldron. A hundred thousand fill the stands. Can you restrict the batsmen?

One morning in 1994, when large parts of India sleep, you awake to life and freedom. What a rebellion in Auckland. Eighty-two off 49 balls. A cameo that unshackles the mind. The greatest one-day innings you have seen. Can anyone better this?

You are carried along in the Tendulkar slipstream. During the 1996 World Cup, when he is stumped off Mark Waugh after illuminating the Mumbai sky, you sense the game will slip away. It does. A few days later his hundred against Sri Lanka in Delhi ends in defeat – the first Tendulkar ton in vain. You hope it's an aberration. You wish.

You observe his every move. In 1996, when he fires a swinging yorker to dismiss Saqlain in Sharjah and sends him off with an emphatic "f**k off", you blush. Four years later your vocabulary has expanded. When he mouths off against Glenn McGrath in the Champions Trophy in Nairobi, you puff your chest out, as if vindicated.

It's 1998, a time for decisions. Academics or sports? Arts or science? Biology or computers? Meet her or continue chatting on the phone? Buy a copy of *Debonair* or take a sneak peek? These are the burning questions that occupy you.

Do they matter? Tendulkar is dismantling Damien Fleming, Shane Warne and Michael Kasprowicz in Sharjah. A desert storm, a birthday hundred and a ballistic Tony Greig. A straight six off Warne when he starts around the wicket. Another straight six off Kasprowicz. "Whaddaplayaa," screeches Greig. It imprints itself in your head.

In your inconsequential gully matches you bat with an amped-up ferocity. You nod to tell the bowler you are ready, you hold your pose during the follow-through, you reverse-sweep and attempt straight-bat paddles. You pump your fist when Tendulkar manhandles Henry Olonga in Sharjah.

You spend your summer holidays glued to the TV set. India have lost their first two matches of the 1999 World Cup and are 92 for 2 against Kenya in Bristol. Tendulkar has endured a terrible loss of his own but returns just in time to reignite the campaign.

You remember the emotionally charged hundred not so much for its clinical construction as much for his gaze up to the heavens on reaching the landmark.

You start college. You are ragged, often with little imagination. You are confused about whether you made the right choices. Some of the courses don't interest you. Many of your classmates speak about things you have never heard of, in languages you are not fluent in. You're beginning to feel despondent.

One gloomy evening, as you sip tea in the college canteen, someone switches on a television set. India are playing Namibia in the 2003 World Cup. You find your bearings. This is a familiar world. Tendulkar is nearing a century. This is your comfort zone. The next ten days are some of the most joyous of your life. That six off Andy Caddick, those fours off Wasim Akram and Shoaib Akhtar. You feel you have turned a corner.

You hate your job. Your manager is a pain in the backside. Your assigned role is boring. You begin to care for little other than your pay cheque. This is not what you expected when you graduated. You assumed you would produce some thrilling work. You dreamt of a meteoric rise. How wrong you were.

Tendulkar is still at it, obsessed with his craft. He plays a blinder in Rawalpindi in 2004. India lose. Then he endures a lean patch but says he must go on. He knows no other way.

You are engaged, then married. Life gets busier: an apartment, a car, daily chores. Tendulkar is brutalising Brett Lee in Brisbane. An uppish cover drive, then a bullet past the bowler. Lee offers an angelic smile, Tendulkar stands still, zen-like, unconcerned about the past or the future, immersed in the present.

You switch jobs. You like your new role but your boss is a slave-driver. You take sly peeks at a live-scorecard tab that is open on your desktop as India chase Australia's 351 in Hyderabad. Tendulkar is flying but you are not near a TV set. You wish you could get back home, but what if he gets out when you are on your way? Would you be able to forgive yourself? India lose. You call in sick the next day.

You relocate abroad. Cricket matches are in a different time zone. You scavenge illegal Internet streams, slap your head when the feed hangs. You are reminded of your days of watching Doordarshan. The sun is yet to rise outside your apartment, and Tendulkar is batting in the 190s against South Africa in Gwalior. ESPNcricinfo is hanging. ESPNcricinfo didn't even exist when Tendulkar and you started this journey. Your Twitter feed is on steroids. He has reached 200.

You watch every ball of India's World Cup campaign in 2011. How could you not? A hundred in Bangalore, a hundred in Nagpur. You suffer palpitations during Mohali. Then the eruption in Mumbai. Virat Kohli raises him aloft and talks of Tendulkar's burden. He speaks for you. He understands how you feel. There are tears everywhere, including on your cheeks.

Here's John Steinbeck in *Cannery Row*:

> Someone should write an erudite essay on the moral, physical and aesthetic effect of the Model T Ford on the American Nation. Two generations of Americans knew more about the Ford coil than the clitoris, about the planetary system of gears than solar system of stars . . . Most of the babies of the period were conceived in Model T Fords and not a few of them were born in them.

You can apply the same to your generation. To understand us is to take into account the moral, physical and aesthetic effect of Tendulkar. To feel your pain, when he retires from a format he made his own, is to know what it means to grow up with him.

You are the lucky ones. Cherish the memories. He was, and will remain, your Model T.

Siddhartha Vaidyanathan *is a writer based in Seattle*

GIFTS, APPETITE, GAME SENSE, AND VERY LITTLE BENGALI

SOURAV GANGULY

Very often in Indian cricket, when you add two and two, what comes out, at least in the public eye, is 22. Or 222. Certainly when it comes to what is happening inside the Indian team. When people ask me about Sachin Tendulkar, I tell them he has been my team-mate since he was 15. And though that may sound like a 222 story, it is true.

Sachin and I first met properly as teenagers, on Kailash Gattani's Star Cricket Club tour in 1988. He was 15 and I was 16.

The Star Cricket Club was a collection of under-19 players gathered from around the country by Kailash, one of Rajasthan's foremost first-class cricketers. Star CC would tour England in the summer and play against schools, colleges and clubs. These tours ran from 1987 to 2004. Kailash reckons, and I don't doubt him, that 97% of the teenagers who played for Star CC went on to play first-class cricket. Many played for India. Sachin and I were part of that Star CC Class of '88, like Sachin's great buddy Vinod Kambli.

On the field you saw Sachin's talent; off the field you saw his intensity. When you're a teenager, you judge other teenagers by what you see. Who could have predicted he would play for India? About 18 months after that tour, Sachin made his debut against Pakistan. It was astounding.

On that tour we lived in some fabulous old schools: Hurstpierpoint College in Sussex, Ardingly College, and Westminster School, next to the famous Westminster Abbey in central London, where a bunch of us boys found ourselves housed in cells in which monks had slept hundreds of years ago. Switch off the lights and it was pitch darkness.

There were more reminders of medieval times on the ground. Like the bowling machine. It was completely out of whack. Set it to 30mph, there was a good chance it would spit out a 100mph beast. Sachin and Vinod faced this machine with no pads, no helmets, just their bats. They would bowl bouncers at each other and not back off. I remember Mike Brearley came to watch. Who knows, maybe he came to see Sachin because he'd heard about him through the grapevine.

In India, that grapevine had started buzzing many months before the Star CC tour. We'd begun to hear that Bombay cricket people were saying this boy would play for India. In the '80s, Indian cricket was only Bombay, so when Bombay people said that, the boy was already a star.

I first met him at a national camp for juniors in Indore in 1987, where the board had pulled in what they thought were the 25 best juniors in the country. The camp was run by Vasu Paranjpe, a great figure in Mumbai cricket and a name synonymous with tough coaching.

At the camp Sachin would just keep batting in the nets. If you didn't actually stop him, he wouldn't leave and it could be hours. Once, Vasu had to pull him out, saying, "This is a camp for everyone." Sachin stopped immediately, because he is a fair guy – but until you told him, he wouldn't. He had a massive hunger to bat.

At an under-17 Vijay Hazare Trophy match in Kanpur once, he was using a Pakistani bat, called Ihsan, which was probably heavier than him. West Zone had crossed 450, I think, and he was the not-out batsman overnight, and it was obvious they were going to declare soon and he was going to field all day. When I went out on to the ground in the morning, he was in the nets for an hour. Knocking, hitting, engaging with the bowler. He made 175 in that game, and at the time I thought he was just a cricket-crazy boy. It was his enormous appetite for cricket, for batting, on display.

He was quick on his feet, reedy, with a voice not yet broken – like all of us – and he was dead serious about his game. "Sincere" is the word that comes to mind now. Earnest. His way of working hard was to bat. No running, no gym, just batting.

There was a tour to India by a Pakistani junior team in 1989, led by Moin Khan, and Sachin would have been an obvious pick for the Indian side had he been any other talented under-19 batsman. But you could see that everyone sensed he was different. He got pulled out of that series, and while the Indian under-19 team played Naeem Khan, Athar Laeeq, and an Afridi called Mushahid, Sachin was batting against Wasim, Waqar and Imran in Karachi.

Our paths had diverged. After Star CC, the next time I shared a dressing room with him was in Australia, on my first tour, in 1992.

Everyone was struggling and the nets were quite comical. On that tour, I became a full-time bowler. Optimistically, I carried my bat to the nets for the first few days and by the time it was my turn, I was facing the lethal bowling pair of Chandrakant Pandit and Kiran More. There was what seemed like a line of 17 batsmen ahead of me. The younger bowlers were being run into the ground. Sachin, my room-mate on that tour, kidded me that I should bowl start to finish, like Vivek Razdan had done on the tour of Pakistan. "Boss," I said firmly, "I am a batsman-allrounder, Razdan was a front-line bowler." The bargain I tried to strike became our joke: *Give me batting one day in a week and I will bowl to you all day.*

Each time I saw him after that tour, I realised he had got better. Mentally, technique-wise, one notch at a time.

Sachin's other plus was how well he read the game as a batsman. He picked up length quicker than anyone else, and that was inborn. He just made the most of that gift; I would say he "maxed" it. To have both gift and appetite is rare. That's what true champions are made of.

By the time I returned to the Indian team, he had become this very big star and for good reason. He was my second captain, and in the West Indies I was the recipient of some terrific bollocking from him.

My fault, actually. After the 1997 Barbados defeat, when we were all out for 81 chasing 120, Sachin was utterly dejected and very angry with us. To get him to think positive and stop beating himself and us up so much, I asked him to tell me what to do. "Go for a run tomorrow morning," he said.

It's a story to tell now, but when he found out that I had missed the morning run the next day, his face was almost purple with anger. He told me, in language that cannot be printed, that he was going to send me home and that I should sort myself out because my career could be ending. The thought of being sent home was enough to light a fire under my shoes. I wouldn't have broken any records, never have, never will, but from the next morning, I was up and running.

Sachin was a better captain than his results show and better than people make him out to be. He led on some very tough tours – South Africa, West Indies, Sri Lanka, Australia – and it must be said he didn't lose eight in a row. This when he didn't have a very good team around him. The older players were fading and the newcomers were too raw.

Sachin demanded performance from his players; he wanted us to raise our game. He could be both good cop and bad cop, and yes, he did love talking to the bowlers non-stop. (And he got teased about it non-stop.) Sachin knew he needed batsmen like Rahul, Laxman and me to fire for the team to do well, which is why he was tougher on us. He believed in us and wanted us to do well. We were all around the same age but were at different stages in our career.

Towards the end of 1996, we also began to open the batting together in ODIs and it marked another step in our friendship. We opened together in 136 games, and it amuses me no end that the two of us, neither a conventional opener, went on to form the best opening partnership in ODI cricket.

Being at the other end as we scored those 6600 runs helped me understand and read his game well. It sounds fanciful, but I would say that when we were batting well, we read each other's footwork before the other guy had moved. I could tell when he was predetermining his strokes and working out in his head which bowler would go where. Our equation was such that I could warn him if I thought he was trying to be too adventurous.

He tried to keep things light when we were batting, and cracked jokes. I was the fidgety, wound-up one and would tell him: this is not the time to fool around, we must be serious. But I knew he loved being there in the middle of the fight, taking the world on.

For all his great talent, I must let you know Sachin is not a natural linguist. He tried to speak to me in Bengali for years. He would listen to me chat to the Eden Gardens attendants and try to repeat that kind of conversation. What came out was Hindi and *"bhalo, bhalo"*. More than ten years of nonsense sounds trying to disguise themselves as Bengali. I kept saying, please stop, give up.

Now to the captaincy business. Sachin and I had to work together as captain and vice-captain for a while, and again that added to our understanding of each other. It was very important that we were one team, so we talked, shared, agreed. And disagreed. Lots.

Sachin didn't like the business of negotiating with selectors about players, so I often ended up being the one who made the request to them. He had a tough time as captain with the selectors because the team wasn't doing well, and I would step in to do the talking. Not because I am a diplomat or anything. I thought of myself as the postman.

Maybe because of what we had shared – at the crease and in the dressing room – being his captain wasn't as daunting a prospect as people made it out to be. Certainly those who think all great players must be prima donnas and hard to deal with. My captaincy came from nowhere in 2000. I didn't expect it and it came at a difficult time for the team.

When it came to being Sachin's captain – and I was his third – it was about giving him due respect: treating him like a team-mate, but also as the special player he was. He was central to the side doing well. He had to feel relaxed and comfortable. Batting when you are nervy and unsettled can be hell.

With all these guys – Anil, Rahul, Srinath, Laxman, Sachin – it made a big difference that they were good human beings. You let them get angry and let out steam; you gave them what they wanted. Like, for example, Sachin was not really happy about having to bat at No. 4 in ODIs in 2002-03. You have to communicate about this new role. You say, please, do it for a short while; of course you'll be back up, let's see how long it goes.

Once he settled down to the idea and saw it work – I am performing, the team is doing well – it was fine. When things went a bit wobbly at the 2003 World Cup, he was back up straight away. No issues.

In teams, like in friendships, give and take has to be mutual; there can't be grudges or the business of accounting. On the 2003-04 tour of Australia, Sachin hadn't got big runs by the time we got to the third Test in Melbourne. On day three we had to open our second innings late in the day, with about 40-45 minutes left. Sachin came over and said to me that he really didn't want to bat that evening if it came to it. It was fine with me and I said, yeah, not to worry, I'll go.

I didn't think we'd lose two in about 20 minutes but the openers were gone inside the first half hour. Rahul and I batted it out, and everyone made a big deal of it because I had come out to bat instead of Sachin. To my mind, it wasn't a big deal, and I remember saying that great players need looking after.

I do believe that great players need to be looked after and need special treatment because they are special. Without them, you don't win as much as you can otherwise. They are vital to your team's success, and in our case, growing stature. I was clear in my mind about that, which is why captaining Sachin was far more simple than people imagine.

Sachin and I trusted each other, as batting partners and as teammates. I could say things to him that few others would, tease him about his skyrocketing endorsement contracts, and cajole him to do stuff we needed. He could nag me about my fairly predictable eating habits, joke about how I didn't believe in the single and about my dress sense. Once, in Pakistan, when I stepped into the team bus wearing leather pants, he announced that the rock star had arrived and photos must be taken.

Sachin is who he is because of his want to play the sport. Not many have the ability he was gifted with, but people can learn from his hunger and his want to play cricket. Irrespective of success, failure, money, that never changed.

He is, and has remained, a normal Indian boy – he wants to go out and eat, he wants to wear good clothes, he likes cars. What others find more surprising than this idea is that even Sachin has his fears, his anxieties and his worries. During the 1992 Sydney Test, maybe the second or third night, I found my roomie awake at around 2am. He was anxious. "My adrenaline is pumping, I can't sleep. I've got to play, I want to get runs, this is a very important Test for me."

India had not crossed 229 in four Test innings and he had scored 16, 7, 15 and 40 in his four innings in Brisbane and Melbourne. I kept telling him to go to sleep. India's innings was on and he would have to bat in the morning. But he was too wired up. The next day he was very sleepy during play and, just before passing out on the table in the dressing room, he asked me to wake him up when the wickets fell. He didn't get to sleep for too long: Dilip Vengsarkar fell early, Azhar was out flicking to square leg, and out went Sachin. He scored 148 while partnering Ravi Shastri and it totally opened up his batting after that.

In the next Test, in Perth, he played what I think was the most dazzling innings of his life. The Sydney century had pushed him up to No. 4, and as wickets kept falling around him – all the big players, Sanjay Manjrekar, Azhar, Vengsarkar, Kapil, Manoj Prabhakar – he batted as if it was against a normal first-class attack. Craig McDermott with his green zinc paint, Mike Whitney who was having a good day, and Merv Hughes with all his bluster and aggro. My jaw dropped at his strokes, at his aggression, how he punched off the back foot, cut, and drove square. He has played many more important innings after that, but to me Perth was Tendulkar in full flight. It was sheer beauty.

And to think that the ground wasn't even half-full. Richie Benaud said it was an innings that deserved a crowd of a hundred thousand. This is Indian cricket, so I am very tempted to make that 222,000.

Sourav Ganguly played 341 of his 424 international matches in the same side as Tendulkar, and captained him in 143 of those

HERE AT THE END OF ALL THINGS

RAHUL BHATTACHARYA

To Lahli we went like pilgrims to a *mela*. Outside a village of exposed brick, beside a highway flanked by eucalyptus and an unelectrified railway line, a sparkling stadium grew out of cane and paddy fields. This was a single-deity mela – the hoarding welcoming "Cricket *ke bhagwan* Sachin Tendulkar" told us so – but the routes to him were various. There were no tickets for *darshan*. Pilgrims could approach the *sarpanch*, or the DC or SP or DSP or a cricket administrator, or one Mr Malhotra who had sold his farmland to the stadium, or leave one's name and phone number at a stall outside the stadium and hope that somewhere a greater god was watching.

We were diverse pilgrims: diehard pilgrims, timepass pilgrims, cheap-thrills pilgrims, connoisseur pilgrims, sceptical pilgrims, unbeliever pilgrims, we were youth from Lahli and Rohtak, wrestlers from Bhiwani, the mother of a Haryana women's cricketer, press from

---

This article was first published in *India Today* magazine in November 2013

Chandigarh, Kolkata, Mumbai, 300 private security men from Delhi, and at least 1400 policemen ("*Congressi hai woh ab, aap samajh liyo,* he is an MP after all.")

The leading devotee among us was 33 years old. He had committed every Sachin Tendulkar innings to memory. Throw him a Test number and he returned, within the second, the venue, opposition and his god's scores. Ajeet Singh Tanwar was a daily-wage labourer, a *mistry*. He had travelled from Dabla village, Sikar district, Rajasthan. He had brought with him a letter telling Sachin Tendulkar about himself and his life, and included in it a poem of appreciation. He wished to hand this over.

I would go to Lahli not Mumbai, I thought, because that overblown *shaadi* feeling, the custom-made finale, the *netas* and the celebs, the ticket-quota farce, the spectacle of a visiting Test team received like a troupe of extras, would be cringe-worthy. And to report on Sachin Tendulkar one last time, I was finding, was not very different from the very first time.

I'm thinking of an early morning net 12 years ago at the Middle Income Group Club in Bandra East. I had gone because I wished to see how genius works in the shadows. Can genius hope to evade company?

"Aala ka? [He's come?]," MIG members conspiratorially asked the guard as they made their way in, and then delayed their visit to the pool or the gym to watch him from the verandah. Tendulkar batted an hour against five bowlers, he rehearsed his cover drive for 20 minutes against the back of the net, filling the morning with beautiful bassy sounds. Occasionally he consulted his pal Atul Ranade and his brother Ajit. From the gate we watched: photographers, autograph seekers, kids. Among us was a little boy with the brightest eyes and a buzzing excitement.

"Does he play cricket?" I asked his guardian.

"It's the only thing he loves," he smiled. "Actually he is from Latur. He has come to Mumbai for a brain tumour surgery. He stays in a nearby hospital and watches cricket all day. He brought me when someone told him that Sachin practises here."

Sportswriters and their editors are partial to overreaching. They like to assess *significance*, no, not enough: they like to see *meaning*. When CLR James wrote that "West Indians crowding to Tests bring with them the whole past history and future hopes of the islands", he instructed generations of writers. Other sportswriters are superiorly concerned with the craft of the thing, constructing with similar diligence their own cocoon. But to go watch Tendulkar bat is, fortunately for us all, to invariably see what Tendulkar means. This too is what Tendulkar means.

—∞∞—

In his final domestic match, Tendulkar emerges to bat with 12 wickets gone in the first four hours. He walks out to the customary roar and hoots, to a scramble of photographers and crowds, to that old anticipation that has never faded and never will, and with one unimpressed Haryanvi telling another, *"Dhai* foot *dikhta hai yeh* [He looks two-and-a-half feet tall]," because height too is something Sachin owed them. He has become broader if not shorter, that much may be said. In his silhouette there is a faint suggestion of love handles.

The pitch is magnificent. The water table at Lahli is so high, we are told, that the grass on the pitch doesn't die, it gets greener with the match. Cars sink in their makeshift parking lots in the fields, fields bloom, seamers prosper, and the TV crew have had to construct a cement platform to reliably hold their scaffolding lest a cameraman crash into Tendulkar's head from 40 ft above.

Sachin Tendulkar plays a broad old-school punch down the ground, defeating the thick outfield. The ball rolls into a sightscreen so immense that even Tendulkar cannot fault it. Not long after, he is out. He is bowled, by a ball nipping back, as he has been for the last two years. Within 20 minutes the *chhole-kulche* and *ganne ka ras* vendors clear out of the *khets*, the 6000 people ringing the ground are gone, and only the ghost of a Ranji Trophy match remains. This too is what Tendulkar means. He is in the pavilion, and everybody wonders what he must be thinking.

"If my batting is having a good day, I'm having a good day," I once heard him tell a companion. But there is no question of good or bad days, really. Every day is a Tendulkar day in a Tendulkar life.

After play he travels back in a white 5 series BMW sent from Delhi, because contractually he must not be seen in another brand of automobile on public occasions, and as he does, boys on bikes race beside the car and photograph him through the windows. Tendulkar does not want blood spilt; he requests the driver to slow down. Slow down, be calm. Too much riding on you. Blunted into caution, as ever, by the manias of his people.

At the gates of the Canal Rest House, where he along with four Mumbai "seniors" is put up, a huge throng awaits him. Those with connections have already penetrated the security and wait inside in ambush. These number about a hundred. They want to shake Tendulkar's hand, take photos, have something signed, seek a blessing, show off their child, simply stare. He has been obliging. I'm told this by the makers of his farewell-tour documentary, who as a consequence cannot get enough filming time with him. Tendulkar has commissioned the film.

A team of six, imported from ITC Maurya, Delhi, caters to him at the rest house: food-poisoning would be no less careless than allowing a cameraman to fly into him. Once in the morning and once in the evening he drinks a *meethi lassi*. The dietary development is of extraordinary interest to press pilgrims. Sachin Tendulkar likes the *meethi lassi* of Rohtak.

Among the successful petitioners on the second evening is Ajeet

Singh Tanwar. He presented his letter. In return he received warm encouragement and a signed training vest. In the innings-game, Tendulkar tried him with Test nos. 130, 80, and 155, and Ajeet Singh nailed them all. (Test no. 130 was the 103 not out v England in the shadow of 26/11.)

"Dravid *nahin barabar* Sachin *ka?* [Isn't Dravid the equal of Sachin?]," I ask Ajeet Singh afterwards. This is a proper provocation, I had learnt from the enjoyably combative book *If Cricket is a Religion, Sachin is God.*

"Bradman *bhi nahi muqabla kar sakte* Sachin *ka.* West Indies *ke khilaf* Bradman *ka* average *dekho: 74.5.* [Even Bradman cannot match him. Bradman's average against West Indies was 74.5.]"

"Sachin *ka itna kisi ke bhi khilaf nahin.* [Sachin doesn't average that many against anyone.]"

The pilgrim from Sikar has set me up.

"Bangladesh *ke khilaf* Sachin *ka* average *hai* 136.66. [Against Bangladesh he averages 136.66.]"

Soon Ajeet Singh causes a fight between television journalists: he had been signed up by a channel for Rs 50,000, exclusively, and this too is what Tendulkar means.

There is no telling how a cricketer goes because sport takes note of neither spontaneity nor stage-management. Bradman left Test cricket with a famous duck at The Oval. Five months later Australians waved him off at a first-class testimonial, 94,000 people streaming into the MCG in tribute, 52,000 on the Saturday alone to watch the hero amass another century. A few months on, to boost attendance, he played a couple of testimonials for friends. In a dead Shield game in Adelaide the toss was fixed so Bradman could come in on the Saturday, a participant would reveal decades later. As it happened, he was in on Friday evening, out for 30 early next morning, tweaked an ankle afterwards and left the field. And that was Bradman's final first-class match.

Sunil Gavaskar's last Test innings was a classic 96 against Pakistan on a flaking pitch. India lost. In his last first-class match he compiled a colossal 188 for Rest of the World against MCC at Lord's; in the second innings he was bowled by Malcolm Marshall for duck. His last international innings was against England in the semi-final of the 1987 World Cup. Bowled through the gate for 4, India knocked out.

In his final Test, at The Oval, like Bradman, Viv Richards, despite a 60, failed to lead West Indies to a series win against England for the first time in 17 years. Two seasons on he played his final game for Glamorgan in Canterbury, for the Sunday League title. He was harassed by a young Kent quick: Viv Richards, of all people, hurried by pace, Viv Richards hit on the chest, Viv Richards too late on a hook and caught. No-ball! Resuming, on a stage smaller than he strode, he took Glamorgan to a precious, hard-earned trophy.

In Lahli, diminished, depleted Tendulkar is not unlike Richards. He is fighting below his weight and still only coping. His tics have become more muscular with time, the two crotch adjustments more pronounced (the first at the edge of the crease, the second subtler one before taking stance), the nod more strident (so that one worries his helmet will tumble off), the gardening more obsessive. His running between the wickets is half hound, half Ranatunga: off the blocks in that familiar low-centre-of-gravity flash, but determinedly down to a walk once he has assessed the fielder's chances. There are no signs of levity in his body language, not a whit of carefreeness in his strokeplay, and although this is not surprising it is remarkable. The one moment he lets himself loose is when he sways too early to a sluggish bouncer, then belatedly attempts an upper cut. And misses. He looks sheepish. He is reluctant to play the spinner on the front foot. He is careful not to drive the seamers on the rise. This is sound strategy for the pitch;

but Tendulkar also knows, perhaps, what observers have suspected for longer, that his reflexes, his instincts, call it what you like, are in terminal decline. But he is there, all there. Mumbai's coach, Sulakshan Kulkarni, who played with Tendulkar in his first Ranji game, would tell me afterwards that he'd seen players relax after announcing their retirement, but Sachin turned up for all five net sessions and with the intensity of a debutant. "Be honest with cricket," he told his young Mumbai team-mates in the time they spent with him. It is what Achrekar Sir had told him and he always remembered. Tendulkar is still at the crease, batting like it is his dharma. Scrapping, leaving, pushing, glancing, middling, prising out victory in a superb cricket match. On winning he holds his arms aloft, with feeling.

Soon he is thrust into a thousand photos: with the teams, the administrators, the groundsmen, the maintenance staff, the police, eventually the photographers themselves. (In the stands, Sachin not at hand, the ubiquitous body-painted Sudhir Gautam of Muzaffarpur fills in.)

In the dressing room, Mumbai have a brief celebration. "I had told the boys 'let us give Sachin a farewell gift' by winning the match for him," Kulkarni said, "but Sachin gave us a bigger return gift with his innings." Then Tendulkar spends an hour in the Haryana change room, talking to the young team. One of them, Rana, had changed his name as a teen from Pramod to Sachin. Elsewhere in India, a player with the one-day team has been wearing a Tendulkar T-shirt beneath his jersey. Another Test cricketer recently set an imprint of Sachin *paaji*'s right palm in plaster of Paris to hang in his new home. These are cricketer pilgrims and this is their form of *Vishwakarma puja*, craftsmen worshipping their craftgod, and no matter how cloying, it is genuine. To them the meaning of Tendulkar is so obvious it needs no elaboration.

Pressmen are contemplating his great innings for Mumbai: the child-genius century on Ranji debut in 1988, the galloping 96 in the classic final of 1991, the phenomenal 233 not out in the semi-final of 2000. Personally I'm thinking of the 204 not out, Mumbai v the Australians, made in two sessions more or less, the compressed synchronicity of his batwork, footwork, handwork, madwork, stroke after stroke, inevitable and exhilarating and rejuvenating as waves; we surfed them and we were happy a long time. North Stand, Brabourne '98.

To watch Tendulkar amid wagtails and ibises and the grey stretch of northern winter was rewarding, it was intimate and it was instructive. And yet who wouldn't want to feel the moment it finishes? When the final applause and the double-Sachin chant falls torrentially upon him, it will be the longest and loudest of his career or anyone else's. There will be tears, in the stands and in homes across the country, perhaps in his own eyes, as one last time that mad potion of adulation and ownership ignites a stadium and every watcher will pulse with the power of a common purpose, no matter that the purpose was symbolic or stale or delusional, because they had all known some time or another when the Tendulkar feeling was as good as things got.

Rahul Bhattacharya is *the author of* Pundits From Pakistan *and the novel* The Sly Company of People Who Care

THE SAINT

GREG BAUM

The two keenest appreciations of Sachin Tendulkar were made from vantage points that could not have been more opposite to each other, and together serve as an incontrovertible cross-reference to his greatness. The first was Sir Donald Bradman's famous remark to his wife during the 1996 World Cup that Tendulkar put him in mind of how he himself batted.

The second is the widespread understanding in the cricket community that match-fixers will not successfully get on with their crooked business until Tendulkar is out, and an anecdotal account of how Tendulkar once unwittingly ruined a fix by batting too blissfully well.

It must be understood that neither reflection would have been made lightly. Sir Donald was not given to hyperbole or glibness but rather was precise in everything he did and said. Nor would the fixers

This article was first published in *Wisden Asia Cricket* magazine in November 2003 have bothered with throwaway lines.

Together, these tributes convey immutable impressions of Tendulkar that accord with less quantifiable, more aesthetic, understandings of the glory of his batsmanship. Here is a man capable of changing the course of any game. Here is a man incorruptible in the face of the venal temptations that so many of his peers could not resist. Outside the laws or outside the off stump, he could not be lured. Here is a man not susceptible to human failing in any endeavour, a man not so much invincible as invulnerable.

Here is a man whose name is synonymous with purity, of technique, philosophy and image. If Ian Botham can be seen as the Errol Flynn of cricket, or Viv Richards as the Martin Luther King, or Shane Warne as the Marilyn Monroe, or Muttiah Muralitharan as the hobbit, Tendulkar is surely the game's secular saint.

Right from the beginning, he appeared to be touched by divinity. He came among us as a boy-god, unannounced. He was 16 and was hit in the face in his first appearance but neither flinched nor retreated a step. Nothing thenceforth could harm him, temporal or otherwise. He was short and stocky – like all the best – and mop-topped and guileless to behold. He has scarcely changed since.

Tendulkar was born with extravagant natural talent, but he was also driven and indefatigable. When a boy, he would bat from dawn to dusk, and even a little beyond. As with all the greats, he came not from another dimension nor the mystical east but from the nets. By such dedication he came to understand intimately his own gift, and at length to lavish it upon others.

His movements at the crease are small but exact. He said once that he did not believe in footwork for its conventional purpose, because the tempo of Test cricket did not permit a batsman the textbook indulgence of getting to the pitch of the ball. Rather, he thought of footwork as a means of balancing himself up at the crease so that each shot was hit just as he meant it. He scores predominantly through the off side, an unusual characteristic for such a heavy run-maker, but of course he can play every shot.

Tendulkar's method promotes an air of calm, reassurance and poise at the crease. Brian Lara's batting is characterised by explosion and violence, and Steve Waugh's by grim resolve, but Tendulkar's ways are timeless. His battles with Shane Warne, genius versus genius, have been for the ages. It is said that the common element to concepts of beauty among all peoples is symmetry, a balance between all the parts. So it is with Tendulkar's batting.

How easily he carries the hopes and takes responsibility for the well-being of untold millions on that impossible subcontinent; in this, he is also divine. All eyes are upon him, day and night, but no scandal has attached itself, not in his private life nor in his cricket endeavours. Across the land, he is the little man on the big posters and hoardings, creating a kind of reverse Big Brother effect; he is not watching them but they are watching him. Still he stands tall.

Sometimes petty criticism is made that he fails India in its hours of need, but it is not borne out by the figures, and besides, no one man could take upon his shoulders all of India's needy hours. Just 30, he has already made more than 50 international centuries.

When called upon, he also bowls intelligently, if sparingly. He is sure in the field. There is even about him, as there was about many saints, something of the ingenue. He is not a natural captain for the modern era, because he can lead only by example. He does not have a charismatic presence in a cricket stadium but rather fills it in a different way, as the one certainty in a sea of doubt. Batting is the most fraught of sporting pursuits because even for the best the end is only ever one ball away. Tendulkar seems to turn that verity upon itself.

As Tendulkar put Bradman in mind of himself, so he puts others in mind of Bradman. Once I was on a night train winding down from Shimla to Kalka that stopped halfway for refreshments at a station lit by flaming torches. On a small television screen wreathed in cigarette smoke in the corner of the dining room Tendulkar was batting in a match in Mumbai. No one moved or spoke or looked away. The train was delayed by 20 minutes. Not until Tendulkar was out could the world resume its normal timetables and rhythms.

Greg Baum *is the chief sports columnist at the* Age, *in Melbourne*

A HERO FOR HIS TIME

OSMAN SAMIUDDIN

Generally speaking, the Pakistani experience of heroes is that they are a luxury – if not entirely a figment of the human imagination. It is not that there are not people fit to be heroes. It is that nobody quite believes in the possibility that a hero can really be a hero; and heroes are as much the construct of the faith of their people as they are of their own heroics. It is one of the things I love most about Pakistan: that it maintains this deep-rooted scepticism about the very idea of the hero. I like to think we find it absurd that heroes can exist in the real world, of which we have had a very real, and so extremely bitter, experience thus far.

Cynicism is a necessary human and societal foible. We cannot ever take ourselves too seriously. Cynicism is vigour and rigour. But sustained over a period as long as a young country's existence that weight of cynicism can become tiresome and deleterious, nibbling away at hope, unity and energy, those layers that, when stitched together, make a national quilt of progress. There is a reason after all that Pakistanis are familiar with so many variations on the parable of humans preventing each other from succeeding. The easiest to recall right now is the joke about how Pakistanis are unable to climb out of the dungeons of hell when given an opportunity, because someone below them keeps pulling them down by the leg.

Can there be clearer, more distilled, proof of how incapable Pakistan is of creating, accepting and responding to heroes than Malala Yousufzai, a 16-year-old girl who simply wants an education and wants the same for women in her country? Doubting her, her shooting, her motives, her allegiances, her actuality, her father's intentions, is a genuine constituency of people across the country, from that cave in Waziristan to that lounge in upscale Karachi and most places in between.

Which is why 24 years of Sachin Tendulkar next door have been, in a subterranean way, both an unsettling and educative experience. Pakistanis don't have a homogenous opinion of Tendulkar, but very broadly it would not be difficult to detect a degree of cynicism about his batsmanship. Not enough match-winning hundreds, an ordinary record against Pakistan, that Chennai hundred; multitudinous tiny deaths by comparison: Inzi won games, Brian Lara and Ricky Ponting did; Sehwag is more destructive, Dravid more dependable, etc. But over time, personally at least, Tendulkar the Batsman ceased to fascinate, overtaken by Tendulkar the Hero.

I'll admit there was a little envy, but more than that was curiosity that India was capable not only of creating a hero but of dealing with one in the way heroes ought to be dealt with. Sure, it wasn't a smooth ride. Twenty-four years and more in the public eye, from which has emanated greater and greater heat each passing year, will curdle anyone. Tendulkar was booed in his home town. There was that whole Ferrari mess. As a voice on a game that underwent such tumult during his career, his was no voice, its literal thinness matched by a figurative one. Even within India, as might be expected of any normally functioning and long-established democracy, there are those who aren't fans, and cynics armed with revealing stats of Tendulkar's real, less-than-overwhelming impact on India's performances.

But the tsunami force of perceived wisdom is that Tendulkar is a hero, and nowhere was that more apparent than in the glow of the extended farewell he received, not just in Mumbai but across India. It was a glow so vivid it penetrated borders around the world, even taming that new monster, the ultra-jingoism of the virtual world. It is unimaginable that any person could receive something like that farewell in Pakistan, not just right now but almost at any point in its history.

Mohammad Ali Jinnah, father of the nation, could have been a first hero, but the cut of his jib was altogether wrong. Jinnah was too stern and distant, and too pragmatic a figure to be a hero. Moreover, the cause for which he fought and which he achieved remains too knotted for easy, definable narratives. No military dictators or politicians qualify, obviously: for them, non-heroism is an occupational hazard. A strong case could be made for Abdul Sattar Edhi, the legendary philanthropist and social worker who has achieved a kind of immortality by instituting an informal welfare-state net through the country. But his work is too unsexy and too real; activism is necessary, not primarily heroic.

Sport has compelling nominees but no decisive candidate. Even before Imran Khan effectively forwent his claim by becoming a politician, he was too divisive a figure. Even during his peak as the greatest cricketer of his country, as a World Cup-winning captain, as a male single-handedly responsible for boosting the desirability of the Pakistani man, he was too divisive a figure. Crucially, Imran also lacked one central attribute of the hero: one may be distant from the masses who adore him, but one cannot be cold and arrogant. A little warmth must emanate, a little humility must be maintained. The rest, after him, were too tainted; the ones before of too different an age.

It is a stretch, but it is still tempting to wonder whether Jahangir Khan could have been a parallel to Tendulkar. He had the sporting pedigree and greater success in his sport. His backstory of general strife and hardship had some romance to it as well, and he was prolonging a lineage. Scandal ignored him and he had the humbleness that Imran didn't. But squash, despite a greater international traverse, never had the *nasha* that cricket had. And not only was Jahangir in the wrong sport, he was around at the wrong time, when Pakistan had one TV channel, one Zia, and the world no Internet.

Which leads us to the overriding conclusion that heroes can be many things later but they are accidents first, in the way that an immaculate conception might be seen as an accident. Tendulkar was as much because of himself as he was because of the time he emerged in: India rewiring itself economically and sociologically, a weakish side in need of an Atlas figure. India didn't necessarily need a hero but it was as good a time as any to happen upon one. Had he been born a decade earlier, had he been born a decade later, who knows? He would have been as great a bat arguably, but as significant a figure? Had *Zanjeer* been released in a different India, and not the India of 1973, politically and economically frustrated and on its way to Emergency, would Amitabh Bachchan be what he is today?

Maybe I've been harsh in singling out Pakistan as no country for heroes. Where and when else could a figure like Tendulkar emerge? In the US probably, whose soft power spills out like cold, addictive lava so freely upon the world that it doesn't matter that nobody else plays or really cares about the sports they play.

Are heroes then merely the delusions of superpowers or superpower wannabes? They don't necessarily need democracy. Had they greater success – and China been more accessible – it is easy to imagine that a typhoon of controlled and uncontrolled forces around Li Na and Yao Ming could have created something similar. The Philippines has Manny Pacquiao, and a whole breed of footballers across Africa could fit the bill: George Weah, Didier Drogba, Samuel Eto'o all mean far more to their people than just the football they played.

But if Tendulkar is not unique, he may well be the last hero of his kind, because the nature of the hero is changing. For one, the rest of the world has a voice now and it cannot help but be heard. Heroes have to listen; they need to be accessible, to interact, respond, assure, clarify and pacify. Heroism is also much lighter apparel these days; it can be taken down by not only cynicism but humour. Through much of Tendulkar's career, if it felt like questioning his batting was something you could just about get away with, making fun of him was definitely not. (Humour, but especially a sharp line in self-deprecation, is why the English will also never really have a hero.)

So where you may think heroism needs to be more robust, to withstand greater scrutiny of its substance, it actually has to be light enough not just to be taken down, but so that it can just as easily be resurrected. Redemption is a prerequisite of the hero's tale now. Tendulkar never really needed redeeming. If he had left during any of his lowest phases, he still would have remained a hero; indeed, he did retire at the end of one of his worst, and look at how he went. In that sense, Shane Warne is much more a modern-day hero – he can, when required, also become a bit of a national joke. He is, though, an altogether more deliberate hero. The difference between him and Tendulkar is that between fame and celebrity: fame is not exclusively a choice; celebrity is.

The one thing that hasn't changed in the idea of a hero is the intimacy implicit at its core. What a hero means remains clearest between the hero and the hero-worshipper. What Tendulkar, and heroes of his kind, do so well, so uniquely even, is to retain and recreate a billion different intimacies. The hero endures, though, because, ultimately, any one of us can be a hero to any one of us.

Osman Samiuddin *is a Pakistani writer based in the UAE*

THE MASTER MORALE-BOOSTER

VVS LAXMAN

We had already heard a lot about Sachin Tendulkar when we first saw him. He had come to Hyderabad to play a Ranji Trophy match for Mumbai, and I was practising with Hyderabad Under-15. I had seen him on *Cricket with Mohinder Amarnath*, a television show in which Amarnath would explain technique and interview players. He had interviewed Sachin at Shivaji Park.

In Hyderabad, Sachin scored 59 at Ensconce Cricket Club, where I played. The club belonged to Arshad Ayub, the India offspinner, who had told me about this 15-year-old kid who was playing against world-class bowlers, to motivate me. With every innings, Sachin was becoming more and more popular. He was an inspiration for all of us growing up in that era.

In 1994, I had a very good series against the Australia and England U-19 sides. Some months later I met Sachin for the first time when

This article was first published on ESPNcricinfo in October 2013

I was playing for Hyderabad and he was playing for Wills XI in the Wills Trophy. I was surprised when he congratulated me on my performances against the youth teams, surprised to know he had an eye on domestic cricket. It turned out that he kept up with domestic cricket through his friend and Mumbai team-mate Amol Muzumdar.

Amol and I used to talk about Sachin. I spent one night at his house, and saw that behind his bedroom door was a big poster of Sachin. Amol used to admire and adore him. You expect that from a fan or a younger cricketer, but this was a colleague and a contemporary. In time, I understood why he felt that way.

Sachin and I had many memorable partnerships, but one that is not mentioned a lot is our stand in Sharjah, when he single-handedly took us to the tri-series final. I came in to bat at 138 for 4, and out of the 112 runs that were scored after my arrival, I made only 23. His 143 was one of the most dominating knocks I have seen by an Indian batsman. That was the first time I saw someone in the zone. I was talking to him between overs, but I know he wasn't listening to me.

Another memorable partnership between us that I remember, apart from an obvious candidate like the 300-plus stand in Sydney in 2004, would be the 91 we added in Mumbai later that year, on probably the worst pitch I have ever played on.

Whenever we were in a tough situation, Sachin would say, "Just go out and enjoy and play your free game." In Mumbai, I had been promoted to No. 3, and we were trailing in the first innings. We decided we would play freely, because we could be dismissed any moment on that pitch. We played our strokes and everything fell into place. We began to get boundaries and the pressure shifted to Australia.

More than in actual matches, it was in the nets that I learnt a lot from watching Sachin trying to get ready for the challenge of facing a particular bowler or a particular team or a particular surface.

In my third Test, Cape Town in 1996-97, we were facing a quick pitch, trailing in the series, and up against Allan Donald, Shaun Pollock and Brian McMillan. Those days we didn't do much in the nets. During throwdowns just before the start of the match, Sachin changed his stance to a more open one, and instead of keeping the bat behind the right toes at the crease, like we normally do, he placed it between his feet. He batted with that stance in the match and got one of the best hundreds I have seen.

I have told him many times that for the rest of us mortals, if we want to change something, we have to first do it in the throwdowns, then in the nets, and then carry it into a match. Here he was, against the best bowling attack of the time, trying something new in the throwdowns and then using it to get a brilliant Test hundred. That shows the kind of mental control and ability he had. There was no indication that he had tried something new, or was anxious about whether it would work. He had just tried it moments before the match and it worked.

Everybody knows how he cut out the cover drive in Sydney 2004 because it was getting him out early in the innings. The discipline it takes to do something like that is incredible. We had a chat about it in Melbourne, before the Sydney Test. He told me he wasn't going to play the cover drive. We have all, at certain times in our career, tried to avoid shots that have been letting us down, but usually once you get your eye in, once your game starts to flow, you start to play all the shots. Sachin, from his first fifty in that Sydney Test to the double-hundred, never once played a single cover drive. Not only against the top bowlers but also against part-timers like Simon Katich and Damien Martyn.

Not everyone was happy with the change in Sachin's game, though. He was the most scrutinised cricketer of our era. There was criticism when he toned down his aggressive style in favour of a safer but more consistent game.

My own assessment of a batsman depends on how many runs he

gets, not how. Ultimately a batsman's job is to get runs. And usually the more experienced a player gets, the more mature he becomes, the better his shot selection. That's what happened to Sachin. He cut down on the shots that were leading to his downfall, though they entertained the crowd, and he improved the shots that were giving him consistent results. That is why he has been the most consistent batsman I have ever seen.

A few critics might say that in changing his game, he lost the demoralising effect he had on the opposition, but that is a matter of perception. Is it demoralising if you play aggressive shots and risk losing your wicket? Or are percentage cricket and big hundreds more demoralising? I value someone who plays percentage shots, doesn't give the opposition any chance, and plays them out of the game.

Sachin was also a good captain, though the statistics might suggest otherwise. I always tell him that. If he had the support structure available to a captain today – a professional coach, good trainer, physio, fielding coach, logistics manager, administrative manager – he would have done wonders. It was unfortunate that he was captain when the seniors were fading and the juniors were finding their feet. I don't believe in statistics. Thankfully, Sachin didn't take them to heart.

For his team-mates, Sachin was nothing but a morale-booster. Whenever I had any issues with my batting, I would discuss them with him. A lot of cricketers in our time would do that, especially seeking his advice from a technical point of view. He was always there to help us and discuss the game.

I've always respected Sachin the person more than Sachin the cricketer. A lot of credit needs to be given to his parents. In a country like ours, where cricketers are treated like gods, it is very difficult to be grounded. Sachin has strong values instilled in him. He never thinks he is bigger than the game. He respects his fellow cricketers, junior and senior. On flights, whether in India or abroad, everybody wants a piece of Sachin – autograph, photograph. Never have I seen him irritated. That is the hallmark of a true gentleman. Never have I seen him arrogant. Anjali and his brother and his entire family should be applauded.

Sachin used to come across as shy and introverted, but once out of the public view, he is a fun person who enjoys music and meeting friends. During rain breaks, he is the first guy in the dressing room to start playing tennis-ball cricket, or put on different kinds of music. He always made the youngsters in the side feel comfortable. The newcomers would be overawed at first, but he took the initiative to make them feel part of the team.

Having retired a little before Sachin, I must now share with him some of my experiences – somewhat like he did for me by reading the conditions and the match situation when I went out to bat after him! He will enjoy his time with his family. I know how much he respects his family time, especially now that Arjun and Sara have grown up. His family has sacrificed a lot. All our families did. The travel will be cut down, so he will have more time with them now. They have earned it.

VVS Laxman *played 120 of his 134 Tests with Tendulkar, in which the two put on 3523 runs in partnership. Laxman spoke to Sidharth Monga, assistant editor at ESPNcricinfo*

THE LAST ZENITH

SIDHARTH MONGA

Sachin Tendulkar always respected the likes of Mohinder Amarnath and Steve Waugh. He was fascinated even, by their doggedness. A part of him wanted to bat like them. Every now and then he would slip into that mode, and would need a gentle nudge – from people he trusted – to remind him his natural game was to dominate contests, to take the bowlers on, not to survive. At the prime of his powers, this dogged batting was a challenge for Tendulkar, primarily because it didn't come naturally to him. Towards the end of his career, it was an aid when the shots began to go gradually. Arguably the greatest batsman since Don Bradman was now prepared to swallow his ego, to look ugly to get the job done, to take the blows and be the last man standing.

The New Year's Test in Cape Town in 2011 was a fine display of that doggedness, one that matched and completed the red-hot Dale Steyn's irresistible bowling, a contest whose memory still brings a smile to the faces of people who were there on those two hot days –

January 3 and 4 – at Newlands. The usual rush to Newlands train station – it's not advisable to ride the train once it gets dark – to go back to town seemed a little slowed that day; people wanted to savour what they had witnessed.

Capetonians, of course, are no strangers to the joys of Tendulkar. They remember with a certain fondness the sensational counter-attack the 23-year-old launched against South Africa in 1996–97. Back then, Tendulkar was a different batsman, almost unrecognisable from what he is today. Before the start of that match, he asked the logistics manager for some throwdowns. He surprised his team-mates by opening his stance a little and tapping his bat between his feet, as opposed to behind the back foot. They were surprised because he was doing so for the first time, and doing it so close to the start of play.

Out walked Tendulkar, nothing to give away that he was going to change his game, at 25 for 3 – it would soon become 58 for 5 – and blazed away to 169 off 254 balls. In 2011, at the fall of a freakish wicket – the run-out of Rahul Dravid attempting a single when Gautam Gambhir was dropped at gully – the man who walked out at 28 for 2 was a wizened 37-year-old who knew his game inside out, who had eliminated a lot of risk – and with that, some of the thrill – from his batting, who now preferred playing the quicks over the heads of the slips as much as he did back over the bowlers' own, a man who trusted his defence enough to not go looking for that release shot.

In other words, just the man India needed on a brutish pitch with seam, swing and uneven and steep bounce available, against the best fast bowling duo – Steyn and Morne Morkel – in the world. "Quiet please. Maestro @ work. Shachin," read a placard as Tendulkar made his way down the stairs.

In the hand of the maestro was not as much a bat as an object of affection, almost an heirloom. It looked ragged, torn, taped in various places, with lines of wear running through it vertically, wrinkles almost. If you didn't know how much he loved this piece of wood –

he scored more than ten international centuries with it – you would call it ugly. This bat never travelled with his normal kit. Nor was it used in the nets. He had kept it alive by at times applying glue to it. It stayed under his bed as he slept.

Tendulkar would take good care of that bat during this epic innings, keeping it away from the misbehaving ball, leaving it alone 65 times out of the first 225 balls he faced. When he did play at a ball, he did it right under his watchful eye, on most occasions. He went one hour – "one of the best sessions of my life" – stuck at one end, facing the devilish outswing and seam of Steyn, because to take a single would have meant playing away from the body a little. That pushing at the line under his head sometimes gave the impression he had been beaten, but when he did get beaten he was beaten by a long distance, because all he tried to do on most occasions against Steyn was to stand outside the crease, press right forward and play the ball under his head; most times the ball met the middle of the bat or beat him by a long way. He just played the line he wanted to; if the ball moved, he didn't try to follow it.

"I am a batsman who goes by feel," Tendulkar says about the changes he made to his game that day. "If I feel like doing certain things, I just do them. In that particular innings, in the middle of my innings I felt I could stand outside the crease, and I did that. Just to cut the movement and bounce. And I felt comfortable doing that. Against any good, high-class seam or swing bowling, one needs to stay as still as possible and play as late as possible. Whatever the movements are, they need to be precise. Sometimes too many movements can complicate things, sometimes not moving enough can also get you in trouble. Whatever is needed to play the ball, only that much movement is important. That is what I was focusing on."

It was not a perfect innings. He needed some luck. But every time you saw it, you respect the discipline more and wonder how much of it was actually luck. It was definitely no coincidence that two of the most correct batsmen in the match, Tendulkar and Jacques Kallis, were the most successful on the surface. How well Kallis batted, scoring two centuries, one in such pain that it put Mark Boucher in mind of someone trying to cut his own rib. Even Kallis will concede, though, that it was Tendulkar who was facing a far more superior, robust and relentless attack.

There were no standout shots in Tendulkar's innings. Nothing sensational about it, except for the discipline. In the previous Test, he had been dismissed twice driving away from the body. The response wasn't too dissimilar to SCG 2003-04, when he completely put out the cover drive that had been getting him out.

India had come to Cape Town level 1-1, had bowled South Africa out for 362, but were threatening to disintegrate on this tricky surface. With Tendulkar was Gautam Gambhir, gritty but shaken, fighting it out but often getting lured into playing and missing.

Tendulkar himself wasn't the calmest to begin with. The first ball he faced he let through to the keeper. The second he dropped wide of mid-on, and ran straight down the middle of the pitch for the single to take him off the mark. Umpire Simon Taufel had a quiet word with him. Gambhir wasn't quiet at the other end, looking to cut the quicks over the cordon, looking to drive them.

The ball wasn't swinging that much yet. Mark Boucher shouted out, "Let's switch to numbers, boys." Players identify the two sides of the Kookaburra as the "bird" and the "numbers". The bird is the side South Africa like to shine, but 14 overs into the innings that side had been scuffed up, and they now had to change the side they would shine. Not to worry, though. There was enough seam movement off the pitch.

A couple of overs later arrived tea on day two, with India 49 for 2. Tendulkar had clipped a nice boundary off Steyn when he strayed too straight, Gambhir was 22 off 45. Two overs after the break, Tendulkar provided South Africa their first chance, but Ashwell Prince didn't go for a half-chance high to his left at third slip. That's when the drive away from the body was put away, only to make an appearance much later in the innings.

While Lonwabo Tsotsobe was the unfortunate bowler here, Morne Morkel tried to test Tendulkar with the bounce, with a two-thirds third man placed. That fielder had caught Virender Sehwag in the first Test, but Tendulkar would wait for him to leave before trying his ramp over the slips. If anything, Morkel provided Tendulkar the most scoring opportunities – 43 off 48, bowling too full every time he tried the full change-up. The same happened in the 23rd over, when after beating Tendulkar he provided him two half-volleys. Both were driven for fours. The second went off Morkel's hand as he dived in his follow-through, and took Tendulkar to 23 off 33. This scoring rate would slow down drastically as the bowling gradually improved.

Apart from the seam and the swing, the other major challenge was a crack outside the left-hand batsman's off stump. Paul Harris was introduced to see if he could exploit it. At any rate, he would keep things tight in the absence of the injured Kallis. Four years before, India had come 1-1 to Cape Town, but had batted meekly to, among others, "Lord Harris", as Ravi Shastri called him, mocking India's strange tactics. How would Tendulkar face him here in similar circumstances?

To begin with, Tendulkar expected turn, which didn't quite exist. An inside edge ensued first ball, a big lbw appeal soon after. Both times, he had played for the turn. Harris looked annoyed that his appeal had been turned down: replays suggested the ball would have clipped leg. Later in the over, Tendulkar danced down the pitch and drove him between short cover and extra cover. "For f***s sakes," shouted the bowler. "Harris, we have seen your straighter one. Now show some variation," read a placard in the crowd.

That boundary was the end of any contest between Tendulkar and Harris. Tendulkar didn't quite take the spinner on, but his 38 off 93

Harris deliveries were largely without incident. To Gambhir, though, Harris posed threat. Not only because of that crack from where the ball jumped, but with the lip he gave Gambhir. With about 90 minutes left to stumps, Gambhir, who had reached his fifty, had had enough from Harris and Prince, and complained to umpire Ian Gould. As the discussion between the two grew longer, Tendulkar shouted "Gauti, Gauti" from the other end, and got him to split.

"I am not a policeman out here," Gould told Gambhir. "These things do happen." Gunner Gould, who can get worked up easily, is a character. In Centurion, earlier during the series, during Tendulkar's 50th Test century, when Harris asked him why he had turned down yet another optimistic appeal, Gould said something to the effect of "I want to see Sachin bat." Now Gould was watching from the best seat, and Tendulkar would give a great account of himself on the third day.

A man in the crowd wasn't quite pleased with what he was seeing. He streaked onto the ground, and JP Duminy threatened a mock charge at him, sending Harris into raucous laughter. All through the sledging and streaking commotions, Tendulkar focused on facing Steyn, who had come back for one last spell before lunch. He had reached 37 off 66 when the streaker made his appearance. A sense of temporary quiet had begun to take over. Tendulkar could now work Harris for the easy single down the ground, and Gambhir had begun to leave much better. With not much happening, the chatter had begun to die down.

South Africa, though, managed to do what they like to do: dry up the scoring. Only 17 runs came off the 11 overs leading into the final drinks break on a day when play was extended to make up for time lost to rain on the first morning. It was possibly the moisture that allowed all that seam movement. Though loose balls did not come, the Indian pair showed no anxiety. No nightwatchman was padded up. Their aim right now was to bat as long as possible, and then see if a win could be eked out.

As 6pm approached, AB de Villiers dropped Gambhir off Tsotsobe, the partnership reached 100, drawing a faint knock on the bat from Tendulkar in acknowledgement, the shadow of the light tower threatened to swallow the batsman as he took strike, and Robin Jackman on commentary romanticised the cricket specialty that is the drawn-out close of play. Next morning would be much more urgent.

Day three – another hot day – began at 10.07am, with 23 minutes added on to make up for the loss to the rain. A decent Tuesday-morning crowd poured into the trains towards Newlands. Tendulkar was on 49, India 220 behind South Africa, and something beautiful was in store.

Steyn charged in from the Wynberg End, Morkel from Kelvin Grove. Graeme Smith had recovered from a finger injury to move back to slip. The hour that followed, Tendulkar said, was the kind of period you never forget in your life.

And you have to give Steyn credit for that. He swung almost every ball in that five-over spell. Some went like a C, but the really dangerous ones were those that went like a hockey stick – straight, straight, and then curling in the end. And he needed no warming up.

That first over was a glowing endorsement for going to the ground early so you don't miss any action. The first ball was short of a driving length, caught Tendulkar on the back foot, and squared him up as it swung away. The second was fuller, and drew the edge. Steyn was late in appealing, Gould was not convinced, the cordon beside themselves, but many replays later you could see the ball might just have died in front of Boucher. Forget the hindsight. It was proof that Tendulkar didn't always walk. This Test series was much more important than goodwill.

Another outswinger followed. Tendulkar had been shaken. He followed it, got a thick edge through gully to bring up the fifty. To the fourth, Tendulkar pushed inside the line. By now he had started standing outside the crease, and he drove the fifth through cover for four. That, perhaps, was the shot he needed to settle back. It was the last shot he would try in the spell.

Twice in one over Tendulkar had edged, twice he had been beaten, but for no fault of his own. He was playing close to the body, but Steyn had begun to swing and seam it too much. Smith, though, preferred to go with just two slips and a gully, and have that extra man at cover to deny Tendulkar the release shot. Tendulkar didn't need it. He got right behind three outswingers, and left alone three in Steyn's second over of the morning.

Morkel, meanwhile, made Gambhir hop and skip at the other end. This was a completely different mode of attack. There was self-preservation involved here. In doing so, Gambhir gloved one fine of fine leg for four in the fourth over of the day. In the fifth, Tendulkar sought to have nothing to do with Steyn outswingers. Steyn, though, kept getting closer to the stumps. One of the leaves was so uncertain and late that the ball hit the bat even as it withdrew. Four more. Of 14 runs scored in the morning, 10 had been unintentional.

Steyn didn't quite like how Tendulkar had been pushing forward to thwart the swing, and let slip a mean bouncer, which hurried Tendulkar into ducking. He walked right up to the batsman to have a word. Tendulkar wouldn't look at him. You could see Steyn had to call out "Sachin" before he said what he wanted to say. No response from Tendulkar, who walked down the pitch, past Steyn, and did some gardening. The bouncer failed to push him back in the crease: he was right forward to cover the line of the next outswinger.

Steyn began to try harder, and in the fourth over he began to get that exaggerated swing from middle even. Tendulkar, though, refused to look to leg. The bat came down straight, and anything outside off or short enough to carry over the stumps wasn't played at. The smile on Steyn's face grew more wry with every wicketless delivery. This was a spell that deserved wickets, and here was Tendulkar absorbing everything and not even letting him bowl to the other batsman. How long before Steyn tired? How long before Tendulkar tried a release shot?

Around this time there was a fire in one of the kitchens behind the dressing rooms. The billowing smoke sent the players out onto the balcony. As Gambhir finally drove Morkel with conviction for two, Morkel collected the throw in excitement to whip the bails off, only to find Tendulkar had even gone past the stumps behind him. Tendulkar had Steyn to face for possibly one more over, but Steyn was going to give it his all.

The first two balls of that over, Steyn's fifth of the morning, were pretty good outswingers but were defended solidly off the front foot. As he walked back, Steyn smiled the smile of a man who knew he had found his match. The third ball was the best of the morning. It was as if there was extra snap in the wrist, the back spin of the seam harder: that ball almost dipped on Tendulkar, and fell short of his reach, and then moved away to beat the bat. Steyn stared, Tendulkar looked away.

That was Steyn's last over before the new ball, which would be due in 21 overs. The fire behind the dressing rooms went down. Those ten overs featured 53 dots. Tendulkar scored 10 off possibly the most testing 30 deliveries bowled that did not get a wicket. Six of those runs were unintentional. This was not about scoring. This was about outlasting Steyn. He had succeeded.

Tendulkar said later that he didn't target any bowler – on that pitch, he said, you couldn't – but early evidence suggested he saw some release coming when Tsotsobe was introduced. He was mainly interested in playing more shots against the left-arm quick because he didn't pitch the ball up, and the shots he tried off him were mostly cuts and pulls. In the 11th over of the morning, he put behind him two plays and misses, and pulled Tsotsobe away disdainfully for four from outside off, followed by an upper cut for four. Tendulkar was on 67 now, and Gambhir on 79.

With Tsotsobe, it remained a game of cat and mouse for Tendulkar.

While the steep, spongy bounce beat him at times, Tendulkar played at him more often than he did with Steyn. The ramp over the gully and the slips was a shot he often tried with mixed results. Morkel had to be taken off after his sixth over, and Tendulkar got back to milking Harris. The partnership went past 150 with the first single of the day, Gambhir raced towards a hundred but was done in by clever bowling from Harris: a big offbreak from the rough followed up by the straighter one to take the edge.

Tendulkar was on 78 when Gambhir fell, and the new ball was 8.4 overs away. As the new ball, lunch and Tendulkar's century all approached, Smith tightened the field, cut out the boundaries, and asked Tendulkar if he was in a hurry to get to the hundred before the new ball was taken. Tendulkar wasn't, but when he drove Harris hard two balls before the new ball would be due, the ricochet from the bowler's hand into the stumps at the non-striker's end ran VVS Laxman out. The Man of the Match in the previous Test, out. Tendulkar was 94 then, he smiled at Laxman, stuck his tongue out almost in apology, Laxman said something to him as he walked off, and Tendulkar nodded and went back to work.

From a position where India might have entertained thoughts of batting only once, they, at 235 for 4 now, stood a real risk of being run over, given the difficult nature of the pitch and the new ball in the hands of Steyn and Morkel. Before that, though, the lunch break brought an end to what Jackman called one of the best sessions of cricket he had seen.

After lunch, with a two-over old ball Steyn charged in again, outswingers on his mind, the crowd building up to a crescendo as he ran in, and he unleashed hell. Like in the morning session, he didn't need any looseners. He was quick and accurate from ball one. Only, this time he was more audacious, swinging from leg and even outside leg. Poor Cheteshwar Pujara got an unplayable delivery that started swinging from leg and hit his back leg in front of off.

Pujara did most things right with it: he played straight, played right under his head, but fatally a previous shortish delivery had forced him to stay in the crease. The only way to play this would have been to push forward and meet this length ball before it started moving off the pitch. In other words, the Tendulkar way.

The other Tendulkar way was characterised by the judiciousness with which he faced two of South Africa's best quicks. His most profitable shot against Steyn had been the dink into the leg side, but the margins there were fine. Sometimes the difference between defending a straight ball back and turning it to leg would be six inches in its line. He showed similar precision while dealing with Morkel's length. His strike rate against Morkel's awkward length balls was 4.8, but when Morkel overpitched, bowled full or short, Tendulkar struck at 200, 206.7 and 140 respectively. In the second over after lunch, Morkel pitched short. It was a quick and high delivery, and Tendulkar didn't hold back on the hook. He knew if he went hard at it, the top edge would clear everybody. It did, went for six, and brought up his 51st century.

At the other end, though, Steyn looked like taking a wicket with every ball not faced by Tendulkar. MS Dhoni lasted three of them before edging to third slip. It looked like it could end in a hurry.

In came Harbhajan Singh, with no clue how to deal with those late outswingers. One of them completely opened him up, created a woody sound as it passed him, and everybody went up for the catch. Gould, though, kept his finger down, and even nodded when Harbhajan asked if the ball had hit the stump without knocking the bail off. This was a sensational decision. Turned out the stump had dented a little, which could be the possible explanation for the impact not carrying to the bail.

Tendulkar had seen enough. He called Harbhajan over and asked his friend to stop trying to defend like a batsman. "Just hit if you pick the ball early," he told Harbhajan. A couple of those shots came off against Morkel. Tendulkar faced the majority of Steyn's deliveries – whose spell with the new ball read 5-2-3-2 – and somehow saw him off. Morkel even tried blocking him from taking a single – in jest or submission, some might have said – but even that didn't draw a reaction from Tendulkar, who just ran around him.

Steyn and Smith did manage to draw a reaction from him. Gould was at the top of his game again when another outrageous outswinger from Steyn drew a loud appeal for a catch at the wicket. The sound, though, had come from the bat hitting the pad, although the ball was awfully close to it at the time. Tendulkar just shook his head. Smith came in close from slip and said, "Don't shake your head. You have nicked it. Like in the morning." After Tendulkar took a single later, he responded to Steyn's verbals, and Steyn couldn't believe he heard Tendulkar the batsman talk to the opposition in the heat of battle.

The concentration didn't break, though. Harbhajan's adventurous batting brought some scoring and also comic relief. After he hit Steyn for a six down the ground and got two mean bouncers in return, he joked to Tendulkar he shouldn't have done that. "Now he'll hit me."

A mistake finally did Tendulkar in. Close to eight hours since taking guard, having brought India to within 21 of South Africa's total, Tendulkar possibly thought the time had come to be a bit more adventurous. Morkel bowled his length, got the extra bounce. Tendulkar had been defending these back to him without trouble. This time, though, he opened the face, looking for a single, or possibly two. Morkel hit the top of off, the crowd stood as one to salute the maestro, whose reaction while walking back suggested he shouldn't have opened the face.

India eventually led by two on the first innings, Harbhajan used the crack in the pitch to reduce South Africa to effectively 128 for 6, but a mix of gutsy batting from the injured Kallis and Mark Boucher, some tired bowling and defensive captaincy meant India had to bat out a draw on the final day.

Tendulkar's innings – his last in South Africa – deserves the indulgence of being looked at independent of the result. There are various kinds of challenges for a Test batsman. For Tendulkar, it could be the occasion: playing Pakistan, say. It can be the team situation: 30 for 4. This, though, was a pure batting test, of technique and temperament against the conditions and high-quality bowling. Tendulkar dealt with it with the required purity.

Sidharth Monga is an assistant editor at ESPNcricinfo

A SINGULAR IDOL

MIKE MARQUSEE

Of all the emotions evoked by spectator sport, there is one that, for me, supersedes the others. Aware as I have been from an early age that my own sporting prowess was negligible, I have often been touched, when gazing at top-flight competitors, by a sense of awe. There is so much they do with ease that the rest of us can never hope to accomplish even with the most prolonged, dedicated and scientific preparation.

But the great thing here is that this awe does not leave us feeling belittled or inadequate. On the contrary, the wonder and marvel at what one of our fellow human beings can do is life-enhancing: the intricate coordination of mind and matter, strength and speed, the welding together of eyes, feet and hands in the heat of the moment, all driven by a single competitive purpose, yet somehow making a thing of beauty beyond that single purpose. At their best, great

---

This article was first published in *Wisden Asia Cricket* magazine in September 2002

sporting geniuses challenge and extend our notion of what is humanly possible. Normally when this happens outside the sporting realm, it is experienced as disturbing or threatening, but somehow, within that redemptively trivial domain, it is irresistibly seductive.

So thank you, Sachin Tendulkar, for giving me as many of those delicious awe-filled moments as any sporting genius of my time. Tendulkar is one in that narrow stratum of elite sports stars whom people will clamour and even make great sacrifices to watch, regardless of their national identity. If you care for cricket, you must love Sachin (and yes, that feeling can be found across Pakistan as well). In this regard, his peers are few – and mostly found in other sports, and certainly in other lands.

Like Tendulkar, Michael Jordan and Tiger Woods dominate their chosen sports both statistically and stylistically, and like Tendulkar, they are a source of joy to fans of every stripe. From an early age, all three have been compelled to cultivate their extraordinary gifts in the spotlight of a powerful and ubiquitous mass media, in an industry whose commercial, cultural and political importance has swollen to outrageous dimensions in the last two decades. Of course, Don Bradman or George Best had their difficulties with the press, and sport has never been a stranger to big business. But in recent times, economic and technological changes have transformed the scale and nature of these pressures. The social context in which the likes of Tendulkar, Jordan or Woods have explored their inner potentialities has altered profoundly.

To achieve greatness in sport has always required exceptional powers of concentration. That is truer now than ever. Can we be sure that the geniuses of the past would have been able to sustain their best form in the relentless glare of today's global celebrity culture? Or that they would have succeeded in negotiating the numerous pitfalls accompanying a degree of wealth and renown previously undreamed of?

Today Tendulkar, Woods and Jordan are all hugely profitable brand names – and it is not always easy to reconcile the demands of being a walking corporate logo with those of being a fallible, needy, ordinarily inconsistent human being. No doubt, all three have had to pay a high personal price for their exorbitant rewards. In this regard, they serve as apt reflectors of their era – its exaltation of individual success (even in team games), its neurotic fear of personal failure, and its fond embrace of an ethic of single-minded self-improvement. "Just do it" is the message these icons are used to pumping out to the rest of us – the vast majority of whom, I'm afraid, simply cannot do "it".

Compared to the riches reaped by Jordan and Woods, Tendulkar's stash seems modest, though in India, or indeed in global cricket, it represents something of a breakthrough. All three have proved adroit in handling their financial success, cautious and canny in dealing with the powers that be, circumspect, dignified, but also accessible to the media. Significantly, all three are studiously neutral when it comes to political controversy of any kind. None, however, can escape the tangle of contradictory meanings woven around the deities of modern sport.

As an African-American basketball player, Jordan embodies one of the most familiar of sports stereotypes. But as an African-American multimillionaire, Jordan is also one of the least representative of celebrities, as far away from his community of origin as it is possible to get. Yet it is precisely because of his anomalous social status that he has become – in the age of neo-liberal triumphalism – a powerfully symbolic figure. Thanks to his association with multinational footwear giant Nike, Jordan is recognised, even in countries that can barely distinguish basketball from *kabaddi*, as a symbol of individual success in a deregulated, global marketplace.

Woods carries a similar cachet, but with the crucial difference that he does so in a sport in which the great players were previously all white. Busting golf's racial straitjacket has proved a tricky operation. Woods self-consciously defines his ethnicity as a rainbow amalgam of African, Thai, Native American and white. That is undoubtedly an honest self-description from a thoughtful person; but as it happens, it also eases his passage into a particular North American sporting culture where being "black" is decidedly a disadvantage.

African-American sports celebrities have for many generations carried a complex burden of representation – expected to symbolise both the homogenised American mainstream and the distinctive African-American nation within a nation. In earlier eras, individuals as diverse as Joe Louis and Muhammad Ali, Jesse Owens, Jackie Robinson, Wilma Rudolph and Arthur Ashe all found their careers profoundly shaped by American racism and the struggle against it. Thanks not least to their efforts, black sports stars of more recent vintage have reaped hitherto unimaginable rewards for their talents. They have also continued to face the challenges of an enduring racial divide, though in subtler forms than in the past. Jordan and Woods are both global icons, but the connotations of their icons vary both between the USA and the larger world, and within the colour-conscious USA itself.

Some of what makes all three of these living legends distinctive is revealed by a comparison with another contemporary sporting hero, David Beckham, England's innovatively coiffed football captain. Without for a moment underestimating the Indian media's appetite for sensationalism, it can be safely said that Britain's tabloid celebrity culture has a peculiar brutality and coarseness, one mirrored sometimes by its football crowds. Neither Tendulkar, Jordan nor Woods has ever had to endure the kind of mega-decibel sexual and scatological abuse hurled at Beckham by thousands of English football fans. (You have to remember that within the breast of the average English football fan, hatred of Manchester United rivals support for the national team.) Then again, none of the aforementioned triumvirs has married a high-profile pop star or posed as a fashion icon. It's probably unfair on Beckham, but there are times when he does seem an apt symbol of Tony Blair's brain-dead Britain, or at least of its febrile, philistine cult of the rich and famous.

Though he is as much a household name as the others, Beckham does not, and would never claim to, dominate his sport as they have dominated theirs. He has always been more fallible, and therefore perhaps more human and approachable. And while there is no doubt that Jordan, Woods and Tendulkar will be remembered as the defining performers of their eras, it is not at all clear how history will end up viewing Beckham.

Nonetheless, like Jordan and Woods, Beckham is now something of a multinational enterprise, a globally recognised brand name. He endorses products in Singapore, Malaysia and Eastern Europe. In this respect, it is Tendulkar who is the exception. As a saleable icon, he remains confined to his national market and its diasporic extensions. No one in North America, continental Europe or East Asia is going to pay good money to put Tendulkar's name on a pair of trainers or sunglasses. Even within the cricket world, companies sponsor him specifically because they seek access to the South Asian, and in particular the Indian, market.

Of course, in itself that's no mean demographic. But Tendulkar's uniqueness resides in his peculiar importance within that vast market. Jordan, Woods and Beckham may cross more boundaries, but nowhere do their performances carry the weight of expectation that Tendulkar's carry in India (and among the Indian diaspora). Nowhere are they the focus of the kind of fervour that greets Tendulkar when he strides to the crease at Wankhede, Eden Gardens or the Chidambaram stadium. It has been argued that Tendulkar is the beneficiary and victim of a specifically Indian culture of hero worship, but in my view this theory severs Tendulkar from his times, and therefore obscures his significance.

Tendulkar has flourished during a long drought for Indian cricket. In a team that has persistently underachieved, especially away from home, he has had to shoulder an enormous burden. Often it seemed left to Tendulkar alone to salvage national pride. Somehow he has risen above the scandals and the corruption and the incompetence swirling around him. In a demanding context, he has conducted himself with probity and dignity.

It's the image that Jordan and Woods aspire to, and which they work carefully to craft, but one wonders how successful they would have been if they found themselves in Tendulkar's shoes. After all, if Woods or Jordan or Beckham fail, sports fans in the USA, or even in Britain, have a variety of other world-beaters to whom to switch their emotional affiliation. When Tendulkar stumbles, Indian sports fans find the cupboard nearly bare (which is not to deny the excellence of other Indian sports performers, but merely to note the overriding and disproportionate importance of cricket in India in comparison with other sports).

Nevertheless, the intensity of the Tendulkar cult in India is about much more than just cricket. Unwittingly and unwillingly, he has found himself at the epicentre of a rapidly evolving popular culture shaped by the intertwined growth of a consumerist middle class and an increasingly aggressive form of national identity. National aspirations and national frustrations are poured by the million into his every performance. It's a tribute to his strength of personality that he has not burst apart under the pressure.

As the inheritor of the classical tradition of Mumbai batsmanship, Tendulkar has seamlessly blended power and grace, efficiency and elegance, conscientious craftsmanship and quicksilver improvisation. He is the greatest run-maker the one-day format has yet produced, as well as a complete master of the long-established disciplines of Test-match batting. More importantly, he stands at the intersection of the two forms of the game; through him we have seen one enrich and extend the other. He is a modern man playing a modern game in a modern style in the modern world – and that's what makes him of supreme importance to his fellow Indians. He's a home-grown genius excelling in a global game, a world-beater bred in the heart of Mumbai's status-hungry middle class.

During this summer's football World Cup, there was much talk in Britain about the immense burden of expectation that Beckham carried whenever he stepped forward to take a penalty for England. As I tried to point out to football's somewhat parochial devotees, Beckham's World Cup burden was as nothing compared to the weight Tendulkar has carried throughout his career. I also tried to indicate that this weight was more than just a question of numbers. Yes, Tendulkar belongs with the Jordans, the Woodses and the Beckhams as a high-value icon of personal success in a globalised economy. But his specific historical significance resides in his relationship to India and in India's relationship to the world.

In a sense, for non-Indians like myself, the joy of Tendulkar comes unadulterated. The awe he inspires belongs to no culture, carries no nationalist overtones, and is at once both intimately personal and transparently universal.

Mike Marqusee is the author of Anyone But England and War Minus the Shooting, among other books